A Sunset Book

cabins
AND VACATION HOUSES

By the editorial staffs of
Sunset Books & Sunset Magazine

LANE BOOKS · MENLO PARK, CALIF.

ERNEST BRAUN
For details about this cabin, see page 58

Eighth Printing March 1965

All rights reserved throughout the world. This book, or parts thereof, may not be reproduced in any form without permission of the publishers. First edition. Copyright © 1960 by Lane Magazine & Book Company, Menlo Park, California. Library of Congress Card No. 60-5087. Title No. 520. Lithographed in U. S. A.

Table of Contents

Cabin Planning
Introduction: A place for vacations the year around 4
Where can you build a cabin? 6
Cabin planning ideas 11
Designs for cabin living 12
A dozen cabin plans
    No. 1: Storage shelter 16
    No. 2: Shelter for two 16
    No. 3: A big lean-to roof 17
    No. 4: Double-decker 17
    No. 5: Big-little cabin 18
    No. 6: Cabin for four 18
    No. 7: Five-room cabin 19
    No. 8: Accommodations for eleven 19
    No. 9: Three-room cabin 20
    No. 10: Expandable cabin 20
    No. 11: Four-room cabin 21
    No. 12: Four-room log cabin 21

Cabin Construction
Building practices and specifications 22
How four families built their own cabins
    One big open room 30
    Split-level plan to fit a sloping site 31
    An expandable cabin "core" 32
    Pivoting walls and a big deck 33
Advice from families who have built cabins 34
Snow trapdoor 35
Pre-cuts and pre-fabs
    The "pre-built" idea ... and a case history 36
    Case history: Built on a two-week vacation 38
    Manufacturers: A browser's guide 39
    Pre-cut A-frame cabin 42
Working with the A-frame 43
This A-frame is a double-decker 44
Low-cost leisure—with plenty of room 46
Owner-built in timber and river stone 48
How difficult is stone masonry? 49
With this camp cabin you add a part each year 50

Cabins for Mountains, Lakes, Snow
Glass walls in a mountain cabin? 54
Mountain cabin by a rushing creek 56
Lake cabin with a "floating roof" 58
A-frame ski cabin 60
Rough-timbered, roomy 62
Cabin with a view 63
"Mountain lookout" with a folded roof 64
It's shaped like a piece of pie 66
This cabin sleeps 16 67
Triangular frame cabin 68
Summer comfort on a mountain lake 69
360 square feet of weekend living space 70
Cabin with a built-in terrace 71
Octagonal room captures the view 71
They added a deck to their pre-cut cabin 72

Beach Cabins
Glass walls and a wide deck 74
It "floats" above the sand 75
"Glass house" 76
Log cabin on an island 76
Sun and weather controls 77
This beach house lets its owners relax 77
Ideas for making beach living enjoyable 78
All-weather beach house 80
Built where the weather is whimsical 82
The deck is bigger than the cabin 84
Designed for beach living 85
Beach house now—garage later 86
Built to take coastal weather 87
Ocean cabin at the bottom of a steep bluff 88
"A no-housework summer house" 90
How to build piers and floats 92
This simple boat slip might be all you need 93

Desert Cabins
Planning ideas and building suggestions 94
Building with concrete masonry 94
You build one stage at a time 95
A wooden "tent" for the desert 98

Arranging the Interior
Ideas for furniture 100
Beds and bunks 101
Dining arrangements 105
Convenience in the kitchen 107
Storage facilities 109
Interior finishes 112

Improving the Site
Building your own stretch of road 113
Water: First consideration when you select a site 117
How to develop a spring 120
Septic tank and filter systems 122

Cabin Care
Fire precautions 124
Your own fire hose 125
Tips on closing a cabin 126
Financing and insurance 128

What is a cabin's greatest appeal?

A place for vacations ... the year around

There was a time, not so long ago, when mention of the word "cabin" brought to mind the image of a crude hut in the wilderness. It was a word with a ring of the past to it (pioneers, Indians, Abraham Lincoln). There was a certain dream quality; it meant many things to many people. One thing about cabin life was generally agreed: the wistful philosophy of "It must be wonderful, but I'll probably never get the chance."

All this is changing, swiftly and dramatically. In the years since World War II, and particularly since about 1952, the idea of the "vacation cabin" has caught on and spread rapidly. Many of today's owner-built and pre-cut or pre-fab cabins are within reach of the average family's budget. Modern automobiles and highway networks make it possible for a man to come home from work on Friday, pack up the wife and children, and have supper at the cabin that same night. This means that on any weekend of the year—fall, winter, spring, or summer—a family with a cabin has the opportunity for a two-day vacation.

These frequent escapes from the pressures and the habit-patterns of everyday life can open up a wonderful new way of life for the city dweller. In his second home, he may find the time and the state of mind to indulge his "second self." No more jangling phone, no more factory smoke. Less housework for the women, and a welcome break in routine for the small fry. The pace slows down to an early morning stroll by the ocean, a chance encounter with a chipmunk on a mountain trail, a family wienie roast by the fireplace.

A good part of the pleasure in working out a cabin plan is in looking over the ideas that other people have developed. Often, the cabin planner can get more help from skimming through a scrapbook of cabin pictures than he can from studying a ready-made, detailed construction plan. For the benefit of the cabin planner and the cabin remodeler, we have gathered into this book a varied collection of ideas. Some are from the pages of *Sunset Magazine*, others are from a predecessor to this book —*Sunset Ideas for Cabins and Beach Houses*—and many were gathered especially for this work.

The cabins in this book cover a wide variety. Geographically, they represent the forests of the Northwest and California, the lakes and streams of the High Sierra, the sandy beaches of Southern California, the bluffs of Oregon, and the foothills along the inland valleys. Structurally, they range from simple storage lockers just large enough to hold a family's camping gear, to many-roomed beach and woodland houses that could easily be transplanted to a city site. Architecturally they range in style from Lincolnesque log cabins, through simple framed buildings, to structures so bold and fresh in design that they actually help to set the pace for some of tomorrow's residential architecture.

A rapid scanning of these pages brings out one fact: the one-time distinction between *cabin* and *house* is slowly melting away. Many of the newer cabins are being built with the

DESIGN: ELDRIDGE T. SPENCER & WM. CLEMENT AMBROSE; PHOTO: ANSEL ADAMS

generous window areas and imaginative use of structure that characterizes today's domestic architecture; and, in turn, many city houses are being built with the simple framing, natural materials, and open floor plan of the typical vacation cabin. A well-planned cabin—whether drawn up for beach, mountain or desert use—is designed to function unobtrusively. It is a simple machine for living that provides shelter, warmth, shade, and facilities for cooking, eating, bathing, and sleeping. No frills are needed. The nice refinements of the city house are usually out of place—either inappropriate to the majestic natural surroundings or simply in the way of a crowd, too busy having a good time to notice or appreciate fancy trimmings.

WESTERN WAYS

The site for this cabin in Gallatin National Forest, Montana, was carefully chosen for its view of the surrounding mountains

Where can you build a cabin?

The first practical question you have to answer after you decide to build a cabin or beach house is: "Where?"

Of course, you may have a site all staked out — especially if you have considered building a vacation house for some time and know the general vacation areas within reasonable distance of where you live.

If you don't have an area picked, then your selection will probably be made by a gradual process of elimination, arriving eventually at the most desirable single region. This process is complicated by the diversity of areas within driving distance of most Western residential locales.

You probably have some degree of choice among high mountain, foothill, lake, beach or desert sites. Which you choose will probably be dictated by your interests and those of your family.

HOW FAR WILL YOU GO?

One good way to begin to localize the area in which you will seek a site is to decide just how many hours' driving you are willing to invest in reaching your leisure retreat. If you plan to go there weekends throughout much of the year, distance as measured in travel time from your home is of great importance.

When you decide the number of hours you are willing to drive, multiply by your average driving speed on local roads. Use this radius to mark on a map the various available potential vacation areas. You will probably come up with a half-dozen or so possible areas from which to make a final selection.

WHICH AREA IS BEST?

To make a choice, you need basic information about each area. Answering these questions may help:

1. How do your family's recreational interests and needs match up with those available in each area? What about hunting, fishing, swimming, skiing, boating, and so forth?

2. What is the climate like? Check maximum rainfall, snow, temperatures throughout the year. At the beach, how many sunny days are there each month? How long is the use-season for each area?

3. Is the area as accessible or remote as you desire? What kinds of roads reach it, and who maintains them? If you are interested in winter sports, are the roads kept open through the snow season?

4. What are the basic features of each area—topography, flora and fauna?

5. What about building costs? Is the area a popular or fashionable—and hence, expensive—one? Would it be prohibitive to bring building materials into the area? What materials might be available on the site?

SOURCES OF LOCAL INFORMATION

You can answer a lot of these questions by writing to local information sources. Check with forestry or park officials. Write to the editor of the local newspaper, the nearest town or county chamber of commerce, local real estate agents. Talk to friends who may have lived in or visited any of the areas which you have not seen. Get weather digests from the Department of Agriculture.

Of course, the best way to get detailed information is to visit the area in question for a long enough period to explore it thoroughly and discuss it with local people. Some correspondence plus a weekend trip or two will probably serve to trim possibilities down to one or two areas.

ARE BUILDING SITES AVAILABLE?

When you have thus narrowed the field, you will be ready to start thinking about and looking for actual cabin sites. Again, nothing will substitute entirely for actual on-the-spot investigation. However, if you are unable to make the necessary trip now, you can put your leisure time to good and profitable use, gathering information that's sure to be to your advantage when you do visit the area. Check in with the local newspaper editor, chamber of commerce and real estate man for a preview of availabilities. The local bank might also help you. In addition to local contacts, work through basic sources of cabin sites (beach sites are almost entirely privately owned, so you will probably have to locate one through a real estate agent).

NATIONAL FORESTS

In National Forests, sites are available—but competition for them is keen. Until the Government's Outdoor Recreation Resources Review survey is complete (it is still in progress as we go to press), many Forests will not have lots available. You can't buy a National Forest cabin plot, but you can occupy one and build a cabin on it by getting a Special Use Permit, costing $30 to $95 annually.

The Forest Service opens tracts each year in most Western National Forests. Tracts include anywhere from several to a hundred or more lots, each of which averages about one-third acre, depending on topography and cover.

There are so many National Forests in the West—18 in California, 13 in Oregon, and 7 in Washington, for instance—that a wide diversity of climate and topography is available. There has, however, been an important change in the type of site made available for cabins within each forest: Areas like stream sides and lake shores, formerly assigned as cabin plots, are now being retained for use by the general public. However, sites are usually within easy reach of waterways or lakes.

If you are interested in obtaining a Special Use Permit, write or call on the Forest Supervisor or nearest Forest Ranger of the particular National Forest that you are considering. Ask him what areas, if any, are open. If he has a forest officer available, he will arrange for him to visit the property with you. A personal visit is desirable but not absolutely necessary before applying for a permit. If you need general information on the National Forests, or if you wish to obtain the address of the Forest Supervisor in a particular forest, you can write or visit the nearest Regional Forester. Western offices are located in San Francisco, California; Portland, Oregon; Missoula, Montana; Denver, Colorado; Albuquerque, New Mexico; Ogden, Utah; and Juneau, Alaska.

Application for permit may be made in writing to the Forest Supervisor, or Forest Ranger, specifying the location of the property, the use to be made of it and the estimated cost of the improvements you intend to make.

Permits are no longer granted on a "first come-first served" basis. Where there is a waiting list for cabin sites, a drawing system is usually used to choose applicants to whom permits will be granted. When you are granted a permit, you will be asked to choose the specific lot you want.

The Forest Service issues two kinds of Special Use Permits in about equal volume: *Annual* Special Use Permits, which are automatically renewed each year upon payment of fees; and *term* permits, which are issued for periods from 20 to 30 years. Term permits are issued when a substantial investment, possibly including financing, is to be made.

Regardless of the type of permit issued, the Forest Service exacts certain requirements of tenants in National Forests. Basically, these include:

1. Plans for your cabin must be submitted for approval *before* a use permit is issued.

2. Cabins and sanitary facilities must be

JOHN ROBINSON

Cabin built on small island in Upper Echo Lake, California, can be reached only by boat. Ideal boating, swimming, fishing

MAX HEINEGG

Stanchly-built cabin, fashioned of site-quarried granite, rests on a huge boulder in a bend of the Yuba River in California

Snow cabin *at Squaw Valley, California, is handy to winter sports. Low bench around deck, instead of railing, permits unhindered view from within. Architect: Henrik Bull*

built within the specifications of a basic Forest Service code (discussed in some detail on page 22).

3. Permanent construction must be completed by the end of the second season after the permit is issued.

4. Cabins must be occupied at least 15 days each year by the permittee or his family. You can rent—with the approval of the Forest Supervisor. But you will be held responsible for any infractions of your permit by your tenant.

5. You must agree to abide by any rules and regulations agreed upon by a majority of permit holders in your immediate area if they have organized a cooperative public service group or association. If a majority of members decides to undertake cooperative construction of a boat dock, road, or "services or utilities of general character and benefit which promote the protection and improvement of the Forest Service lands," all permittees are subject to assessment for the project regardless of whether the individual assents to the project or is a member of the association.

6. You may sell your cabin and improvements at any time, but the transaction must be approved by the Forest Service. Before selling, the owner must inform the Forest Service that he intends to sell by turning in a "Transfer Form," available from the service's offices in the forest. If the cabin or improvements are not up to current standards, the Supervisor may make the sale conditional upon improvements to be made within a specified period by the new owner. The new owner will receive a new permit rather than that of the previous owner in all cases—in order that the conditions of the permit can be brought up to date.

DELINQUENT TAX LANDS

One very promising lead for unimproved cabin or beach sites is the county assessor or tax collector. Tax delinquent lands are sold several times each year at open auction. You can get information on delinquent lands from the assessor or tax collector at the county seat; information on sales is ordinarily issued in bulletin form and published in a local newspaper by the tax collector two or three weeks before the sale. You can request a list of tax sale lands from the county tax collector. These lists generally show only the legal description of land; you can check geographic locations on maps at the county assessor's or tax collector's office. Some real estate offices in the immediate area may also have maps containing both legal and geographic information.

It is necessary to be present at the auction in order to bid on tax delinquent land.

SMALL TRACT ACT

Few have heard of the relatively unpublicized Small Tract Act, passed by Congress in 1938. Administered by the U. S. Bureau of Land Management, it allows citizens to lease or purchase certain lands (up to five acres) from the Federal Government for residence, recreation, business, or community purposes. These lands are not free; they may cost anywhere from a few hundred dollars on up to several thousand, depending upon the desirability of the tracts.

There are approximately 168 million acres of vacant public land in the continental United States (1958). Of this, more than 99 per cent is located in the western states, with their generous proportion of desert and foothill country. Nevada alone has nearly 46 million acres. (Not included in these figures is Alaska; although it has an impressive total of 270 million acres of vacant public lands, most are unsurveyed and practically inaccessible.)

If you are interested in obtaining small tract land, you should:

1. Ascertain from the county clerk or county assessor the legal description (section, township, and range) of the land whose availability you wish to investigate. Send this information to the nearest land office and request that they inform you of the status of the tract; or visit the land office, look over and make notes of available lands from their complete records. You may wish to enlist the service of a professional land locator, who, for a moderate fee, will inform you of what public lands are open for filing.

2. Go out and select a tract from those available. Fill out an application form (available from the land office) and file it at the land office. The bureau will not accept it unless you certify that you have personally inspected the desired tract, or land within one mile of that tract.

3. If the land you have selected has been classified for small tract lease with option to purchase, you will be allowed to lease it as soon as your application is processed. If the land has not been examined previous to your filing and so is not classified,

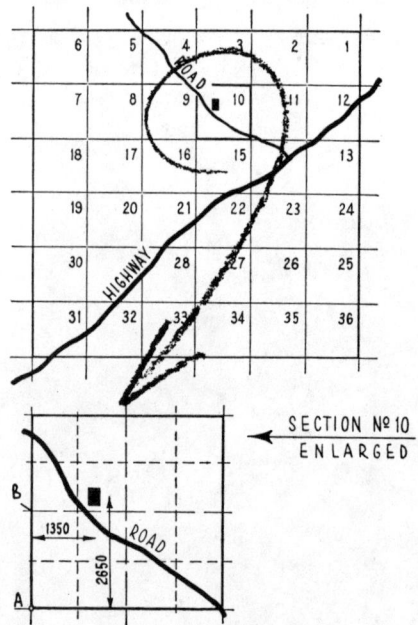

A township *contains 36 numbered sections, each 1 mile square, 640 acres. At each corner is a section marker—brass cup 3 inches in diameter. Data on each marker establishes exact point on section map. Solid portion in sketch above, 1,350 feet east and 2,650 feet north of the southwest corner of section 10, is described as lying in the southwest ¼ of the southeast ¼ of the northwest ¼ of section 10 in township 6 south, range 20 east*

CHAS. R. PEARSON

Perched boldly *on tip of an island, this Northwest beach house by architect Lionel H. Pries has a sod roof to take rough weather*

you may have to wait a considerable time for classification.

Your application should be accompanied by a $10 service fee and $15 toward the advance rental charge (advance rental for business sites is $100).

4. You ordinarily have three years in which to build a cabin and make "suitable improvements." You can apply to purchase the land at any time after you have completed suitable improvements.

5. When your cabin meets the bureau's requirements, you will be allowed to buy the property at the price set when your application was approved.

If you do not wish to go through the complexities of the "search out and apply" procedure, check with the land office to see when and if any public auctions or public drawings are scheduled. Classified land is often thrown open to public bidding when original lessees fail to make required improvements or fail to purchase before expiration of lease.

For more complete information, contact the manager of the nearest branch office of the Bureau of Land Management (U.S. Department of the Interior). Offices are located in Los Angeles and Sacramento, California; Portland, Oregon; Spokane, Washington; Phoenix, Arizona; Santa Fe, New Mexico; Reno, Nevada; Salt Lake City, Utah; Denver, Colorado; Boise, Idaho; Billings, Montana; Cheyenne, Wyoming; and Juneau, Alaska.

LUMBER AND LOGGING COMPANIES

Policies on sale or lease of logged-over lands vary widely from company to company. There is an increasing trend among these concerns toward retention of all lands as tree farming areas.

You can get specific information directly from lumber companies; or the local editor, chamber of commerce, and real estate agent may be able to furnish basic information on lumber company lands in their area.

RAILROAD LANDS

The vast area of land granted to Western railroads in the early days still includes many desirable cabin sites on land not used for railroad rights of way. Unfortunately, however, most of this land has been withdrawn from sale.

STATE AND NATIONAL PARKS

As you may know, cabin sites are not sold or leased in National Parks.

State parks and forests are also generally closed to residential building of any sort.

REAL ESTATE BROKERS

If you are planning a beach house, you will almost certainly find and buy your site through a real estate broker, since by far the greatest portion of Pacific Coast beach property is privately owned.

PINPOINTING THE SITE

Just about when you have decided to sink or swim with a lake frontage site, Junior is likely to remind you that it sure would be nice to have a real trout stream at the door, as on that lot at Bear Mountain.

Or, the site that you really prefer on the basis of its other merits may be disqualified completely because you discover that you would have to lug bottled gas one hundred yards uphill to provide fuel for heat and cooking.

Ordinarily, one best way to get off the horns of this dilemma is to check the sites from which you are to choose on the basis of the various specific factors which might influence your choice.

Here are eleven phases of selection which may guide you in comparing various properties:

1. Orientation: How is the lot situated in regard to sun? Is it in the path of, or sheltered from prevailing weather? What about view? Can a cabin be placed to take advantage of morning sun and afternoon shade? How private will it be? Does orientation allow for later expansion of the house? An ideal site would be oriented to get morning sun, afternoon shade, and be out of heaviest winds.

2. Utilities: Water is of foremost importance: stream water is often unsafe; springs are satisfactory if not contaminated from above by waste or sewage; a dug or drilled well is perhaps best. Check available water by having it tested. Ordinarily, county or state health departments provide this service without charge. Get a sterilized bottle from the local health officer, fill it and mail to the place designated. What are sanitation alternatives? Are there local ordinances or laws governing septic tank or other sanitary installations? What fuel is to be used? Is wood available on the site? Is delivery available "to the door," or will you have to transport fuel? If electricity is available, what will be the installation cost?

3. Weather: In the mountains or at the beach, weather varies over a very short distance. Two sites in the same general area may have widely different "microclimates." Mountain and sea winds generally blow up-canyon and away from water during summer days, down-canyon and toward water at night. Avoid choosing a natural wind gap as a building site —you can spot such a gap because trees grow lop-sided, with heavier growth on the side away from the wind. If mosquitoes are a constant problem, you may want a site where wind will tend to blow them away. Don't choose a location that is downwind from a swampy or brushy place where mosquitoes and insects breed.

Remember that cold air tends to settle in pockets. Mountain meadows are often excessively cold at night unless they are fairly open to circulating air. Also, check winter weather which might affect your choice: Is winter snow excessive? What is the annual rainfall? How much fog is there during months when you plan to use the house?

4. Topography: What effect will contour and soil condition have on building and living? How about drainage? Is there a danger of flooding, from watershed, stream or tides? Is the site in the path of a wet weather stream or drainage ditch? Are snow or landslides possible? Are overhanging rocks or earthen banks a possible threat? If gardening is to be done, what is the soil condition? Will future construction in the immediate area cause drainage or other problems? Would the property tend to collect drifting snow in winter? What kind of support will soil afford to structure?

5. Accessibility: Is the site up- or downhill from closest access road? It is ordinarily much easier to transport building materials and cabin supplies down rather than uphill to a site. Can access road and parking area be constructed and maintained? How would supplies be transported to the house? What escape routes are available in case of forest fires? Do you have to cross through private property? If fire protection is available, can it be brought to the site? If cabin is to be used in winter, what is distance from an all-weather road? Can you keep your own access road open in winter? Keep in mind that roads and trails may be excellent in good weather, but impassable when it rains or during winter. Has relative accessibility of sites possible effect on resale value?

6. Construction Costs: Check distance at which building materials are obtainable, cost of transportation. Are native materials available on the site? How far will it be necessary to transport building craftsmen? How much clearing of vegetation and trees will be necessary? Will excavation be essential? Cost? What road and bridge construction will be required—and what cost is involved? Will special material construction be necessary to allow for special conditions like building on a steep hillside, heavy reinforcement for snow load at high altitude, or necessity of a sea wall at a beach site?

What are local building and code restrictions? Is financing available? Locally or where you live?

7. Maintenance Costs: What are fares, insurance rates? What about present or future assessments for roads or utilities? What will maintenance costs be for private roads, trails, bridge? How will purely local factors affect upkeep: corrosive effect of sea air on paint and some metals; heavy snow load, etc.? What will be costs of opening and closing the cabin each year? Cost of private police protection? (See chapter at end of this book on cabin insurance.)

8. Vegetation: How do present trees affect shade and wind? What trees and other vegetation will have to be removed? Does the plant life of the area conflict with family allergies? What about poison oak, ragweed, other polliniferous plants? If you plan to keep horses or pack animals, what is availability and cost of grazing and feed?

9. Fauna: What about the wild animal life you may want to hunt or protect: deer, rabbits, squirrels, waterfowl, shellfish and fish?

What are local rodents and animal pests: deer, bear, rats, porcupines, mice, snakes, etc.? Are there local insect pests? Check on relative problems with mosquitoes, yellowjackets, ant infestation.

10. Recreational Facilities: What are local conditions and/or facilities for dancing, swimming, surfing, boating, hunting, fishing, hiking, community sports, mining? Are pack and riding animals available? How far will you have to drive to see a movie?

11. Legal Responsibilities: Sometimes the purchase or acquisition of rural real estate involves the buyer (or seller) in a tangle of legal complications involving water or mineral rights, easements. If the lot that interests you is located on a stream, has a spring that residents have been using for years, or has an informal road across it that cabin owners have been using for some time to gain access to their cabins, you would be prudent to check your legal obligations before you acquire the site. This is preferable to discovering afterward that you may not have exclusive right to your own spring water, cannot dam the stream for a swimming pool, or must maintain a road or bridge for the benefit of your neighbors.

ROBERT C. CLEVELAND

Beach house located on a bluff has wide-ranging view, accessibility to the surf below

Cabin planning ideas

On lakeside or seashore, opening rooms to the water is desirable at times, but wind and sun must be under control always. Here, garage doors, similar to those in the cabin below, and vertical screen give this protection

THE DIFFERENCE between an inexpensive cabin and a house in the mountains is one of a degree of smoothness, a degree of comfort, of luxury.

Comfort compared with *no protection* can be found in any place that is dry and warm. To a camper caught in a storm, a trapper's cabin with a dirt floor and a fire is luxurious. Comfort compared with a highly mechanized town house seldom is found, except in another town house, whether built on a lake or a seashore.

A dish washing machine is more expensive in the mountains than in town. A bed that folds into a wall may save space without saving money. A table that disappears may be more efficient but it often costs more than an ordinary one.

Rough, unfinished walls, plank floors, exposed roof, shelves instead of cabinets—any avoidance of finish or polish —spell out the important difference in cost between house and cabin.

The plan idea that most often distinguishes the cabin from the house is the *open* plan as compared with the *partitioned* plan. All of the activities—sleeping, eating, cooking—take place in one room.

There are two ways to approach planning of a one-room space:

One is to keep all of the various elements lined up along the walls of the room, allowing the center of the room to be used for the activities important at the moment. Such a room can be switched from a dining to a living room by sliding the dining table against the wall and by turning the furniture toward the fireplace.

The other approach to the plan, and probably the most successful, is to control space by limiting areas. Let's examine a few examples of each:

In Plan No. 1, there are no divisions of activities. It's a kitchen-bedroom-living-dining room, with accent on the kitchen. Looked at without thought of cabin, it's a perfect barbecue shelter. Because many cabin locations have native stone available, we have indicated a counter height stone wall on two sides of the cabin. Low wall construction is not beyond the capabilities of the non-professional.

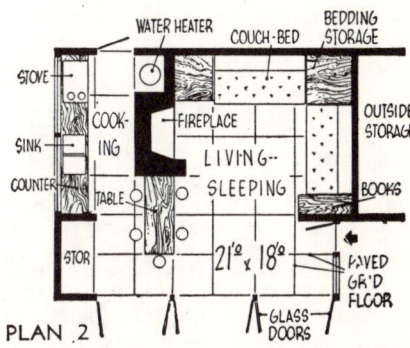

PLAN 2

In Plan No. 2, the kitchen area is controlled. The fireplace becomes the partition between the cooking and the living-sleeping unit.

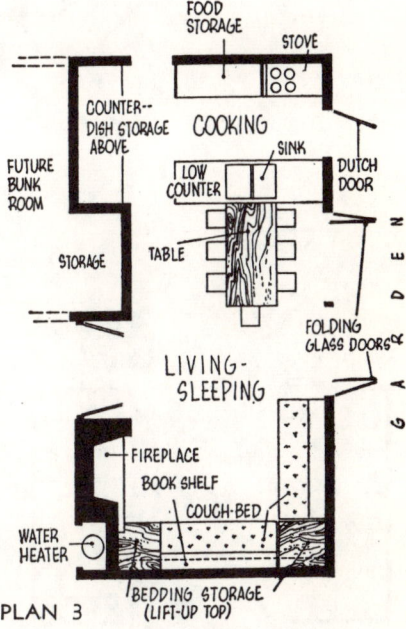

PLAN 3

Plan No. 3 separates kitchen from the other functions with a low counter. A dashboard between dining table and sink is called for. To homebuilders, this arrangement has possibilities as a kitchen-living room. It provides for direct and wide access to a terrace or dining patio.

One way to use stone when available on the site. This cabin would make a barbecue-shelter-guest house in a large garden

PLAN 1

11

Designs for cabin living

THE IDEAL CABIN should give these values:

- A complete change in environment
- A structure that is in tune with its surroundings
- An invitation to simpler living
- A cost which totals less than that of a house

In the old days, the cabin delivered most of these values — naturally. Most often built from materials close at hand by old-timers schooled in the tradition of the area, they were simple, inexpensive structures, native to the place.

As costs rose and as native materials were used up, the natural structures became more expensive than a conventional town house of comparable size. The result, in most cases, has been the building of small homes rather than cabins.

Looking over the Western vacation spots, we found exceptions to the general rule. If we combined the thinking that went into a dozen of the most interesting examples of beach, lake, and snow-country cabins we have seen, the end results would be the cabins we have pictured on these pages, as worked out by Designer Gordon Drake.

Costs? If you give a cabin all the conveniences enjoyed in a house, you'll have a near-house cost. If the minimum protection of roof, walls, and fireplace heat is satisfactory, these basic structures are economical. All three aim directly at the essentials of cabin living.

Beach cabin

Features

- Screen against afternoon sun and wind
- On the beach side, sliding doors with narrow windows
- Brick and concrete floor throughout
- A passageway through the entire cabin, for going in and out without disturbing main living area
- Fenced-in area at rear for children to play under supervision
- A change of pace, sheltered retreat when wind and glare are oppressive outside

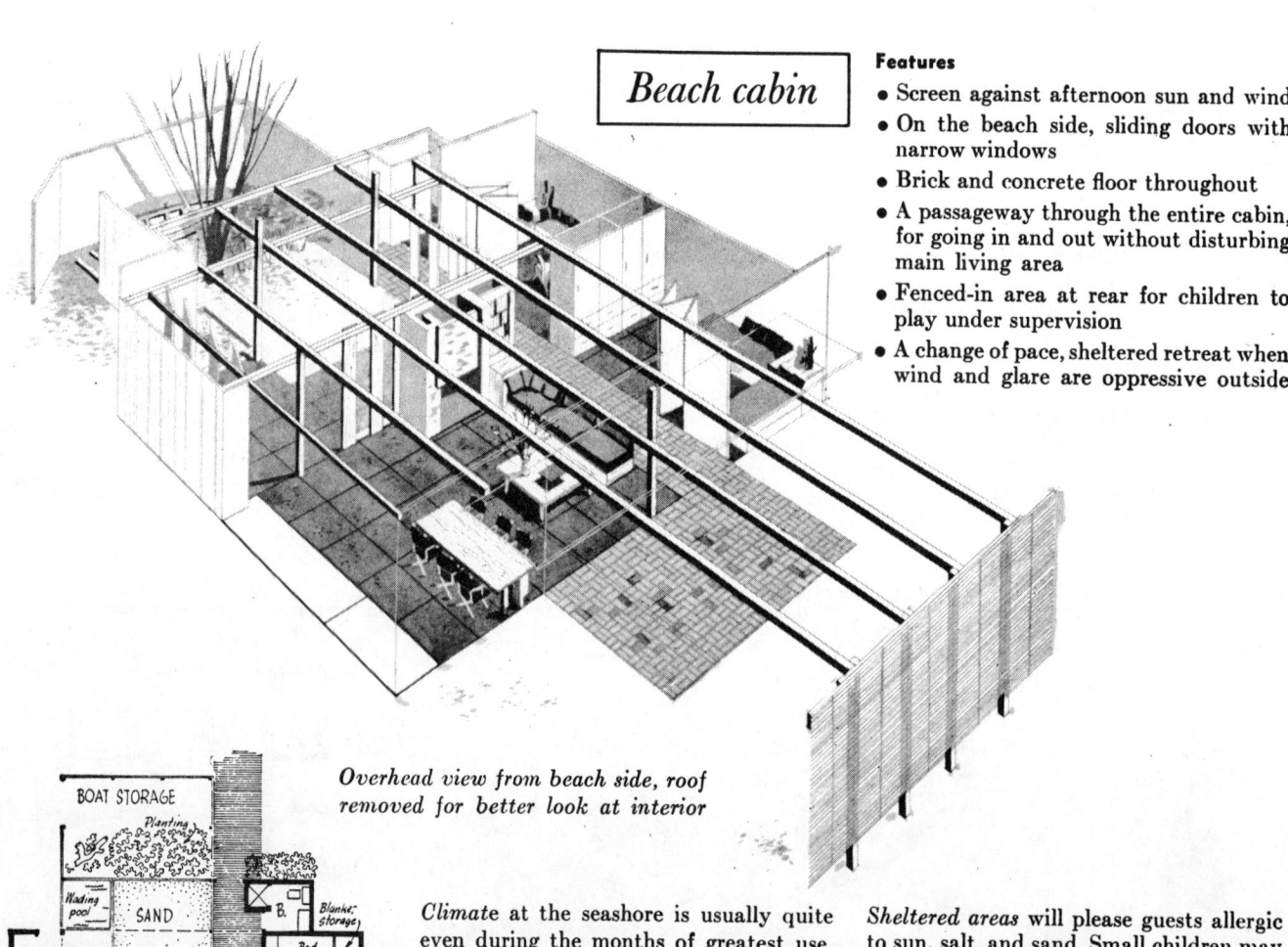

Overhead view from beach side, roof removed for better look at interior

Climate at the seashore is usually quite even during the months of greatest use, May to September. Sea and sun are the major attractions, but they also cause major problems. Glare from the ocean side is especially bad from about 2 to 4:30 P.M. An offshore wind usually blows up at about the same time.

Two controls are provided: a wind screen set out from the house toward the ocean (possible coverings may be bamboo, glass, plastic, canvas); and sliding doors made from surplus garage doors with long vertical panels of window. You can open up the whole side of the cabin. Or you can close the doors against glare and wind without making the interior too dark.

Sheltered areas will please guests allergic to sun, salt, and sand. Small children may play in perfect safety, under supervision, inside the rear fence.

Tracking in of sand is no real problem because walks are brick laid in sand. And all bedroom, dressing, and bath facilities may be reached conveniently by using the through passageway.

You can lock up the whole cabin securely during the off-months. Leave the boat in the back yard and lock the fence gates.

Construction can begin with the bath, and one bedroom, then the other bedroom, and the cooking-dining-living area. Foundations in sand should be shielded so that winds won't expose and undermine them.

Lake or river cabin

As seen from water: deck and main living area at left, sleeping platform—one possible arrangement—at right

Usable both summer and winter, the cabin has two main sections: a large, all-year room; and an expandable area that can be covered with canvas for summer sleeping; conversion into bedrooms optional.

Construction would disturb the site as little as possible. There would be little or no excavation. You would build a deck out from the hillside and put a roof over it, using post-and-beam support rather than studding. A porch at one end and a sleeping platform on the other would hug the hillside.

Step by step, you could start with bathroom and storage areas, adding progressively the large pavilion roof, walls and windows, and the sleeping platform.

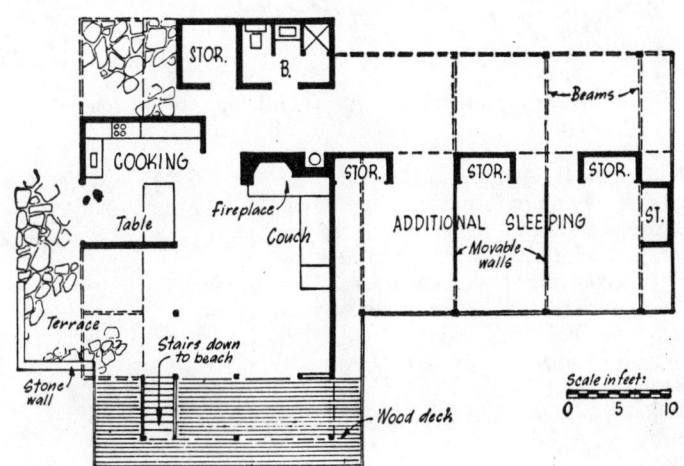

Looking toward the water across terrace adjacent to kitchen and living room

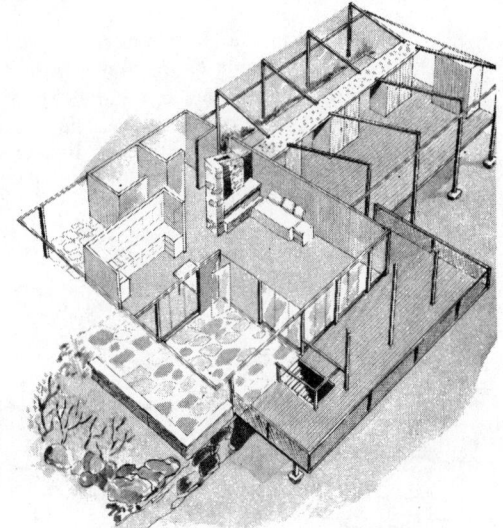

Overhead view, with roof removed

Features
- A large roof shelter, spreading like a circus tent over main living area
- Sleeping wing which can be anything from tent platform to fully-finished bedrooms with a balcony facing the water
- A roomy deck outside main living area
- Terrace at the side, tying into the hill, a logical place for outdoor cooking

13

Snow cabin

Mountain cabin in summer, with end wall and roof section removed so that you can peek into the main living area

Winter snow conditions most strictly dictate the design of this cabin, even though it also is planned for summer use. In winter, you enter via a ski ramp at the second story, eight feet above ground level. Windows at either end of the cabin begin at this level. The tepee roof is not only steep enough to shed snow, it is also extremely strong bracing for the entire house.

Sleeping area for children is on the second-story loft, where beds are backed up by a storage wall or other barrier at least three or four feet high. Adult sleeping is provided in the two rooms on the main floor at either side of the stairway.

In summer doors at upper and lower levels can be left open. And on the upper level, shutters are put down on top of a trellis framework to create additional deck space. (NOTE: If this cabin were to be built in an area with extreme snowfall, the flat roofs would have to be substantially built and supported to withstand snow load.)

In winter, still usable when snow is banked up to its second story

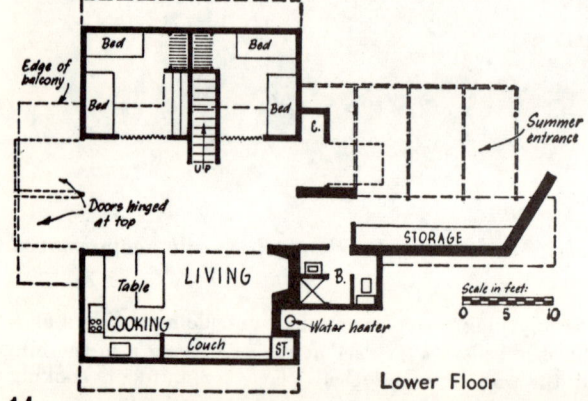

Lower Floor

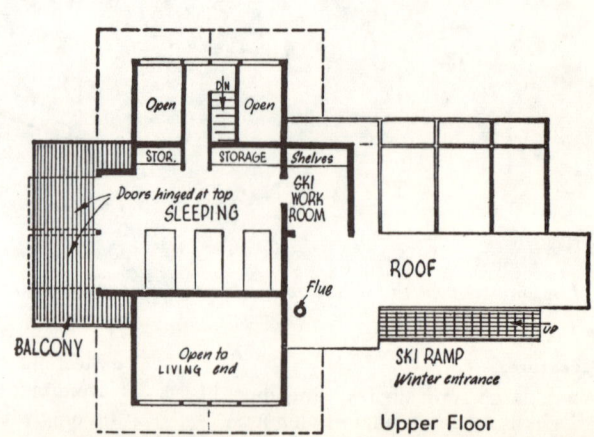

Upper Floor

Opposite living space, cutaway shows bedrooms on main floor, sleeping loft for children, more space on balcony

Features

- Teepee roof sheds snow, adds strength to house structure.
- Ground-level entrance for summer through doors that can be thrown open for more light and outdoor feeling
- Second floor is suspended like a diaphragm. Both ends left open to let light from windows down to main floor.
- Upper floor accommodates children's sleeping as well as skiers' equipment
- Entrance above snow-level via ramp to the second floor.
- All windows are above the second floor level. Protected by overhang, they can be shuttered if necessary

Summer entrance and sheltered area next to cabin. Main winter entrance is through ski work room directly above

A dozen cabin plans

Many potential cabin builders find they can develop their dream cabin quite easily from a sketch plan and a drawing of the cabin that matches it. On the following pages are 12 such plans, basically little more than cabin ideas that do not pretend to be complete plans that you can follow to the last nail. Some are merely architects' suggestions, but most of the plans are based on actual cabins. However, no construction details beyond those shown are obtainable.

No. 1: Storage shelter

You start with a storage wall of waterproof plywood, set on redwood blocks so that it will be kept clear of the ground. For bracing against strong winds, cleat it to a pipe set several feet into the ground, or make it fast to a sturdy tree. Set the roof at an angle so that water will run off.

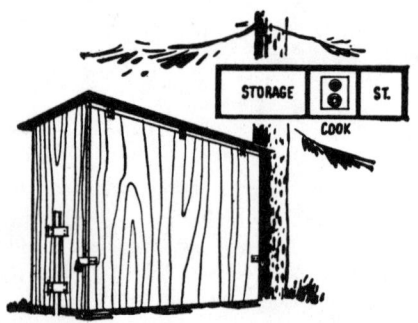

Inside, divide the storage wall into compartments for cots, tarps, cooking utensils, shovel, axe, lanterns. Line one compartment with fireproof materials to hold a small stove for cooking. With ¼-inch mesh hardware cloth, rat proof all or parts of the interior.

Fit poles to hold up the door into holes or grooves. Or cleat them on. To make sure they don't topple over, sink them a foot or two into the ground.

The roof should also slant to allow rain to run off. The overhang of the main roof will prevent any leakage around the hinged joint. A drainage ditch around the structure is sometimes advisable.

This box can be padlocked at both ends when not in use. It can be expanded by adding one or more of the following:

Use hinges on the door at the top so that it will swing open to form the roof of a small sheltered room. You can use tarps or other material and the whole enclosure would be suitable for both cooking and eating as well as sleeping.
Base of concrete, wood, or firm ground.
Cave wall, completely sheltered, with a hearth and fireplace for snugness on cool evenings and on rainy days. A metal hood over a stone hearth would be quite satisfactory. If the cave wall is placed adjoining other solid walls, it needs a window or other opening to let in daylight for cooking and other activities.

Cover, set at a slight angle for water runoff. This could be canvas, burlap, logs, logs or saplings plastered with mud, thatch, or the more solid materials used in conventional house construction.

The storage wall in this combination is an expanded version of the one above, with built-in bunks added.

When these elements are put together, there is a further open area in the middle. The open sides could be screened for additional protection. Plumbing and further construction could increase the livability. The nucleus of a cabin is here.

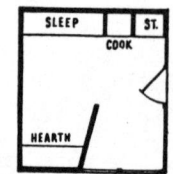

Weatherproof shelter, or the fundamentals of a permanent cabin

No. 2: Shelter for two

This little log and stone shelter should appeal to the man who likes to go back to his favorite trout stream or hunting country each year, yet who doesn't want to go to the trouble and expense of a permanent cabin. Two men can build the whole thing in a few days, using materials that can be picked up right on the spot.

Since a hunting lodge is often used in cold weather, it would be wise to have the floor raised off the earth a few inches, either with an all-around stone foundation as shown here, or with a series of flat boulders. The latter, however, do not keep out much of the cold.

No. 3: A big lean-to roof

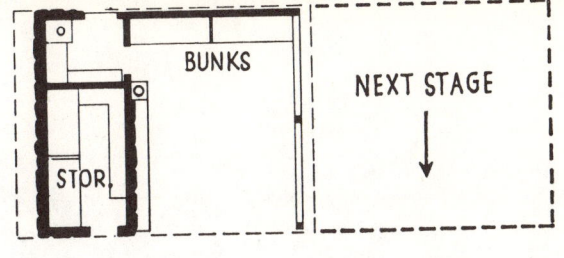

This cabin begins as a simple lean-to cooking and storage unit, with or without plumbing. Roof extension is canvas the first year, solid roof later. Plan could be considered complete now

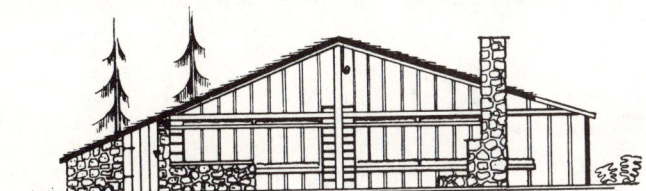

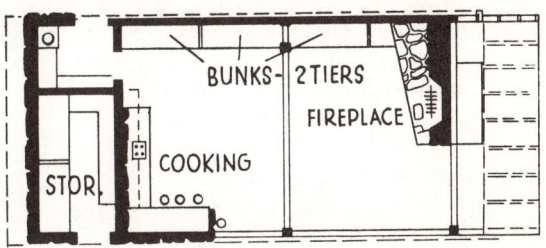

Next step: frame second half of the roof, cover with canvas. Last, roof permanently, close in sides. Siding could be lumber, plywood, hardboard, glass. The fireplace is a cabin luxury. Highly suitable alternate is an old-fashioned pot-bellied stove

The important thing about any cabin building which is scheduled to go on from season to season is that you start with the final plan on paper—so you know just where you're going.

Try to work in big units: for example, a whole section of floor, a complete cooking center, all the framing.

Avoid temporary construction — and the inevitable discouraging task of ripping out later.

No. 4: Double-decker

Here's a little cabin that will fit into almost any sort of sloping site. Shown here, it's a mountain cabin with masonry foundations that form the walls of a garage for two cars. However, with only a few minor changes, the same plan could be used for a beach house, and the garage could be transformed into a boat house.

Construction details are simple. The foundations, stairway and retaining walls are built of stone or concrete. The upper structure is wood frame, covered outside with milled siding, inside with wallboard or plywood panels.

If the cabin is to be built in snow country, such a flat roof would have to be supported with unusually strong beams. The simplest covering would be composition roofing. To provide a serviceable walking surface, a wood floor raised on slats should go over this built-up roofing. Another excellent—and cheap—roofing for a deck that will have considerable foot traffic is made by applying canvas over matched roof boarding, just like the deck of a boat. If kept painted, this type of roofing is entirely satisfactory.

This is essentially a one-room structure, but it includes in a compact space all the conveniences of a much larger house. At one end of the living area is a small but complete kitchen, screened by a cupboard. On the reverse side of this cupboard is a hinged table that swings down at meal times.

Sleeping quarters include two double-deck bunks against one wall, with closet room at one end and the bathroom at the other. This entire area can be screened off with sliding curtains hung from a ceiling track. There is also room for a couch or day bed on one side of the fireplace. Wood storage is outside, but the small closet by the fireplace could be used for this.

Another interesting feature is the barbecue on the roof deck. It is built into the chimney.

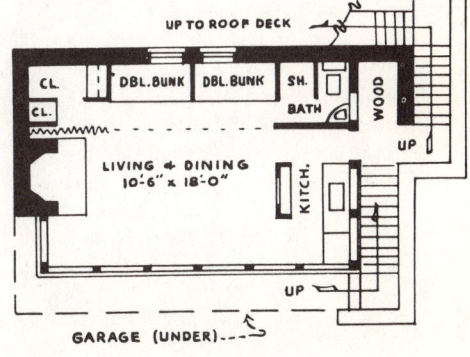

No. 5: Big-little cabin

Some people would be cramped for space in a ten-room house, while others live with perfect freedom in a pup-tent. It's all a matter of adapting oneself to the situation.

Here, for example, is a cabin that might be too small for two persons, while as a matter of fact it will sleep six without crowding at all. That's not just a theory, because a similar cabin has been used for several years up in the Mt. Rainier country with great success.

As illustrated this cabin has an exterior of wide planks and a roof of shakes. It would make an ideal log cabin, or take any one of a number of finishes. If any kind of siding is used, a beautiful effect could be obtained by use of a silver-gray stain that would make the cabin look as if it had stood through many winters. If shakes or shingles are used for roofing, you can include about 10 per cent of dark-stained ones with the lighter colors, to give a dappled look like sunshine through trees.

The secret of this little cabin lies in the use of three folding double beds instead

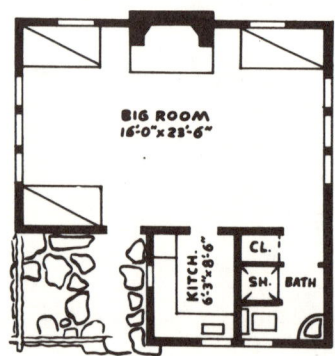

of the regular kind of bunks. They are hinged at one end and can be put up out of the way, concealed behind curtains or cupboard doors. Built-in double-deck bunks are, of course, a fine addition to any cabin, but they do cut down the space even in a 23-foot living room.

The little flagstone entry insures against mud puddles at the front door.

The kitchen is particularly well arranged, with lots of work table space and room for storage shelves above. The bath, although not large, contains all the comforts of home.

No. 6: Cabin for four

For the amateur builder who wants to try his hand at a cabin, this attractive design presents a minimum of construction problems and calls for only a very modest outlay for materials. At the same time, if the work is well done, this cabin can be made as smart and attractive as one costing twice as much.

The most satisfactory, as well as the easiest way to build this cabin, would be with a frame of redwood timbers covered with half-round imitation log siding. Another finish that is not difficult to work out is with a combination of vertical and horizontal board and batten, running the boards vertically for the walls and horizontally at the gable ends.

Since this is first of all a rustic cabin, it should by all means have a roof of shakes. The manner in which these are laid is responsible for lending interest and charm to an otherwise rather plain roof-line.

The front porch may be either flatstones or heavy planks, although the latter would, of course, call for a foundation. The two seats make an inviting place to rest, but as will be seen from an inspection of the floor plan, they serve for more than ordinary seats. They have corresponding seats inside the living room, and

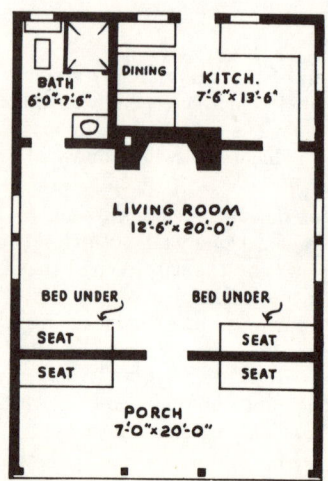

beneath them are concealed two roll-away double beds. Such construction for the beds is a great advantage in a small cabin, since they can be pulled out or put away as needed. This leaves the whole living room, which is 12½ by 20 feet, for any style of decoration you like.

The fireplace parallels the 20-foot dimension of the room and may therefore be fairly large. A general rule is to make it one-third as wide as the longest dimension of the room.

The kitchen is very conveniently arranged. It has three windows, affording ample light. A dinette, which could be made with a drop table and folding seats if necessary, occupies one side of the room. The stove can be placed so that the flue can go up the fireplace chimney.

This plan was furnished through the courtesy of the California Redwood Association.

No. 7: Five-room cabin

Four walls, a roof and a floor will make a cabin after a fashion. But a glance at the illustration above will show what a little thought, care, and imagination on the part of a good architect will do to those same four walls.

This simple, inexpensive country cottage, sleeping four comfortably, has all the little touches that distinguish a house of real charm. Because of its simplicity, this cabin is adaptable to almost any site. The original was designed by Angelo Hewetson, San Francisco architect, to fit between four huge redwood trees, and to be in keeping with the natural beauty of the location.

The exterior is of heavy sawed siding, although board and batten would also be effective. The roof, stained a rich brown, is of shingles laid irregularly. The siding is stained pearl gray, for a weathered effect, with trim to match, and the doors are painted a soft rose. Inside, this cabin is equally charming. The living room is broad and comfortable, and features a massive fireplace. A "waterback" may be installed in the back of the fireplace, connected with a storage boiler to furnish hot water whenever the fireplace is in use. At other times a water heater, burning liquid gas or oil, would heat the same tank.

Walls and ceilings in the living room and alcoves are sheathed in knotty pine boards of random widths from 4 to 10 inches, and the doors are all of planks of similar material. All is stained driftwood gray with a touch of rose for warmth. The kitchen and bath are in cream with soft green trim.

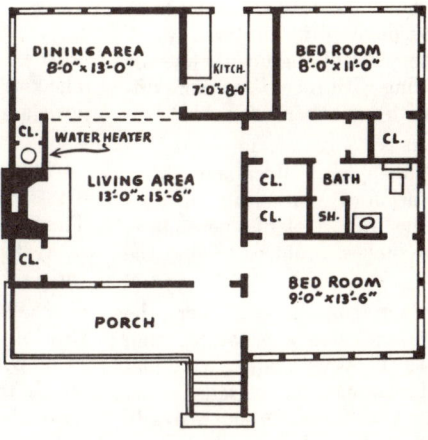

No. 8: Accommodations for eleven

Just at a glance, would you think it possible for eleven persons to be acommodated in the cabin illustrated here? It is only 20 by 28 feet in inside area, yet such a feat is possible by intelligent use of every bit of floor space. The real secret lies in utilization of the loft formed by the high roof. This is transformed into a balcony-bedroom, with space enough for two double beds and a single cot. Curtains or screens give the necessary privacy. That takes care of five persons.

Downstairs, the living room is furnished with a long refectory table and benches, several easy chairs and a day bed that opens into a double bed at night. That's two more. Then, in the alcove off the living room, are two double-deck bunks—and there's the total of eleven!

As in the case of most of these cabins, this one is adaptable to a number of exterior treatments. Real logs or frame construction with siding and boards and batten are indicated in the drawing. The porches provide two more suitable rooms, where meals may be served in good weather.

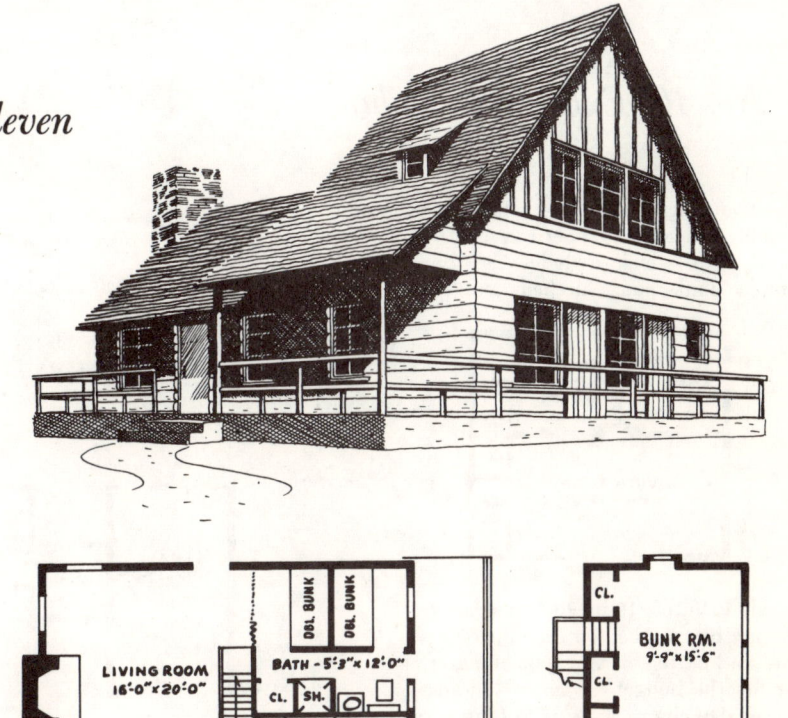

No. 9: Three-room cabin

One of the principal drawbacks to a real log cabin is the amount of work involved, as well as the expense. On the other hand, the cabin shown here is an example of what can be done with "imitation logs" that give the effect of real ones, while the task of building with them is no more difficult than with any other finished lumber.

If this cabin is to be left unpainted, it could be stained with silver stain. This gives the illusion of weathering and does away with the "raw" look of a new house. The roof, of shakes, could be treated the same way.

To avoid cluttering up the living room, the designer has provided a separate room for the bunks. This one holds two double-deckers and a large clothes closet. A short hall connects with the bathroom. A really novel feature is the pair of small windows which light the "upper" and "lower" of each set of bunks.

The kitchen is well lighted with three windows and a door, and has ample space for roomy cupboards and a work table. The stove can be placed so that the flue connects with the fireplace chimney.

The living room is large enough to hold a fairly large fireplace. It has windows on three sides, in addition to a pair of French doors opening on a rustic terrace.

One of the advantages of this kind of cabin over a real log one is the ease with which the interior can be finished. Perhaps the most suitable finish would be natural-color oiled plywood panels. Knotty pine or redwood paneling would also be attractive.

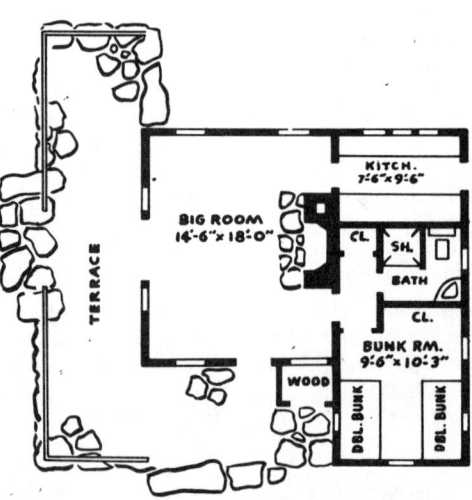

No. 10: Expandable cabin

This cabin can be built in several phases. In its first stage, the owner can erect the central core, which includes the living room, a bunk-room, kitchen, and bath.

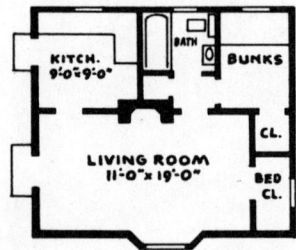

This all fits into a 19 by 20-foot structure, and may be sheathed on the outside with board and batten, or any type of material that fits the budget. A feature adding a great deal of charm is the pair of casement windows at the front.

This much of the house could be built the first year, with perhaps a temporary shelter for the car at the rear. The following season, or as soon as needed, two bedrooms could be added on one side, converting to closets the space formerly taken by bunks.

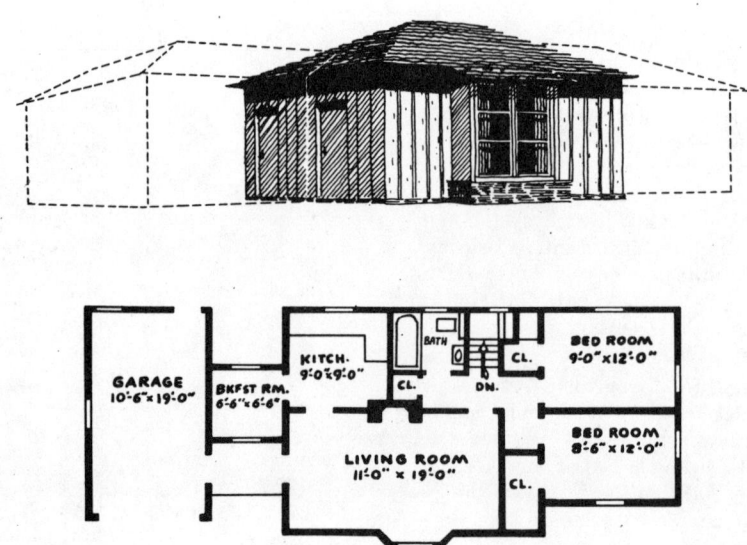

On the opposite side of the house, a garage or another bedroom may be constructed, either attached directly to the house or, as shown here, with a small porch and a breakfast room in between.

This plan was designed by Howard H. Riley, Seattle architect, and was furnished through the courtesy of the West Coast Lumbermen's Association.

No. 11: Four-room cabin

The sketch shows a cabin with an exterior finish of redwood boards and battens, combined with a small amount of stone for added interest, but the same plan would be adaptable to almost any treatment—logs, for example, laid up in stockade fashion, or milled redwood siding or even an all-over covering of hand-split shakes. The roof could be of shakes, stained brown or just left to the weather.

A stone terrace and a landing stage for boats are shown in the illustration, but these features are, of course, optional.

Inside you'll find a 12½ by 18½-foot living room, dominated by a fireplace that takes up most of one wall, but well lighted by windows and doors at each end. The fireplace chimney, incidentally, also serves the kitchen stove.

The two bunk rooms offer ample quarters for four persons even if twin beds are used, but to conserve space double-deck bunks might be preferable. There's plenty of closet space, too—one of them even has a window in it.

There are a number of other points of convenience about this cabin that may not meet the eye at first glance. Note the kitchen has its door opening onto the terrace, making meals outside much simpler to serve. The bathroom is far more convenient than some found in urban homes; just to keep the whole family happy, the shower has been placed in a separate enclosure from the main bathroom.

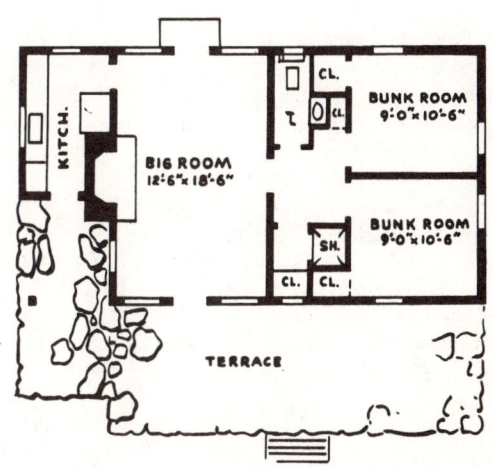

No. 12: Four-room log cabin

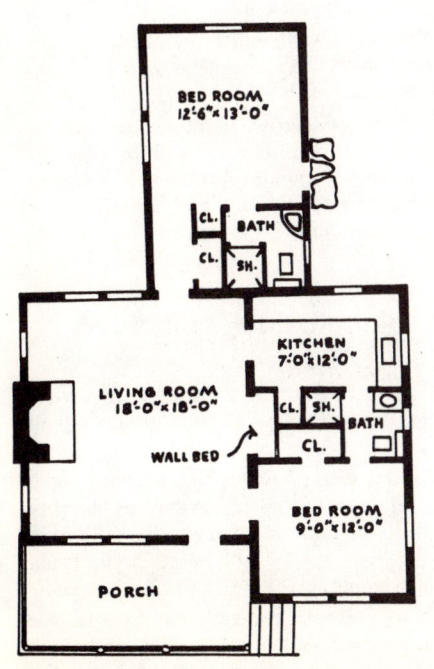

For anyone who wants to satisfy that inner urge to live in a real log cabin, no better guide could be followed than the plans shown here. A glance at the illustration really doesn't give an idea of the roominess and comfort of the place that is apparent from a study of the floor plan. However, this cabin would be quite a task for an amateur builder to undertake.

The original of this cabin was built in the Santa Cruz Mountains. The rustic idea is carried out in every detail, with real logs, a rough stone fireplace and rugged rafters, but inside are all the conveniences of a modern residence. A pergola of rustic poles shades the front entrance.

Because of the size of the cabin it is unnecessary to crowd the living room with beds. There is one, but it folds up and is concealed in a closet. There are two comfortable bedrooms, each with private bath. One of the baths also opens into the kitchen.

Light is an important factor in a log cabin; so much care should go into planning the color scheme. If the cabin is of peeled logs a handsome interior finish can be given with a couple of coats of clear varnish. This brings out the whiteness of the logs and makes them easy to keep clean.

The bedrooms, for contrast, might be done in greenish blue and the kitchen in gray or tan.

Building practices and specifications

1. General specifications

The Forest Service long ago found it necessary to establish a general code governing all cabin construction in the National Forests. The basic objective set forth in designing National Forest developments was ". . . to have them perform their intended function and at the same time harmonize as much as possible with the natural environment."

You will probably apply the same general principles to any cabin or beach house you build, regardless of whether it is located in a National Forest.

Though your personal interpretation of what constitutes "harmony" with the natural environment may differ somewhat from Forest Service standards, you may profit from a quick perusal of the service's instructions to Special Use Permit holders.

FOREST SERVICE STANDARDS

Building Design: Generally, cabins fit the ground more readily when horizontal lines predominate and building outlines are low and sprawling.

Wall and Roof Materials: Cabins are fundamentally rustic vacation homes and should present that effect when completed. Rough wood and stone are considered the best basic materials. They harmonize easily with surroundings, have a long life with minimum maintenance. Smooth-surfaced and thin materials, on the other hand, look manufactured and lack the strong, rugged appearance necessary in most mountain sites. Approved materials are: peeled logs, hewn logs, log siding, rough sawn lumber, wood shingles, shakes, shingle-tile, composition shingles, and stone. Concrete, masonry blocks, and brick may be used in portions of the exterior in combination with more natural and rustic materials, providing over-all design is rustic. Smooth or finished lumber may be used for trim and minor areas of the exterior when the basic exterior material is of rougher or more natural stuffs.

Sheet metal, stucco, cobblestones, flexible paper, or felt materials, composition wall materials, and mechanically-laid masonry are classified "undesirable" because of unnatural color, texture, or unsatisfactory performance against the rigors of mountain winters.

Roofs, too, are required to be of rough-textured materials. Exceptions are when a flat or low-pitched roof is used, little of which is visible from the surrounding ground. Built-up tar and gravel, painted sheet metal and other similar materials may then be used.

Design Details: Foundation should be as low as possible consistent with good construction. Use of masonry, concrete or concrete blocks is approved. Pier construction must include siding or heavy latticework which extends to ground level to enclose the underpinning.

Windows and doors should be of uniform size and shape. Top or head-level should be at uniform height above the floor. Window area must assure adequate indoor light.

Chimneys and fireplaces are required to be of safe, substantial construction with a solid masonry or concrete foundation. Flue lining is necessary.

Exterior Color: Colors generally found in the soil or the bark and foliage of trees are recommended: subdued red, gray, gray-green, or warm brown. Stain or paint may be used, or exterior walls and roof can be left to weather naturally.

Doors and trim may be painted lighter or darker shades of basic colors. Bright colors may be used for small exterior areas, including doors.

Administration of Standards: Approval of plans and specifications is up to the individual Forest Supervisor. He may allow for architecture, materials and colors which are not generally approved. For example, sheet metal may be approved in a high fire hazard area and in heavy snow country to reduce snow damage.

When otherwise inappropriate materials are allowed, they must be painted an appropriate color.

2. Snow-load specifications

Cabins built at relatively high altitudes must be constructed and stressed to withstand heavy snow loads of up to 10 feet or more.

Here, verbatim, are U. S. Forest Service "Specifications for Buildings in Regions of Deep Snow":

"The following minimum requirements are recommended for one-story structures:

"In post and girder construction, supporting posts should be 4 by 4 inches spaced not more than 7 feet apart in any direction and should rest on concrete or stone blocks 12 inches square. Girders should be 4 by 6 inches. Continuous footings are recommended for outside walls. Floor joists should be not less than 2 by 6 inches spaced not more than 2 feet on centers. All the above requirements also apply to open porches.

"Studding in outside walls having vertical siding should be 2 by 4 inches spaced 4 feet apart. One 2 by 4 (girt) must be placed around the building, horizontally, half way between the 2 by 4-inch floor plate and the two 2 by 4-inch ceiling plates. There should then be continuous 2 by 4-inch diagonal bracing running at 45° in each direction between top and bottom plates.

"Where horizontal siding is used, studs should be 2 by 4-inch not more than 2 feet on centers, with top and bottom plates. Diagonally brace between studs at all wall corners.

"Headers over all openings should be *doubled* and proper beams or bridging should be installed on openings over 3 feet wide.

"All roof rafters must be trussed with ceiling joist. Provide vertical bracing at center and diagonal bracing from center at joist to midpoint of each rafter. This bracing must be well spiked. The connections between rafters and ceiling joist must be well spiked or bolted for spans under 12 feet and must be bolted with not less than 2 bolts per joint for spans 12 to 16 feet and with 3 bolts or more for spans 16 to 20 feet, or equivalent connectors shall be used.

"Rafters should be not less than 2 by 6 inches and be spaced not more than 16 inches on center.

"Ceiling joist should be 2 by 6 inches spaced same as rafters.

"Trussed rafters and ceiling joists shall be well spiked to wall plates.

"Joints of low pitched roofs must be made stronger than those of steep pitched roofs for the same snow load.

"Foundations should be of stone or concrete. Wood should not be used for foundation material.

"NOTE: Collapse of most structures is due to lack of diagonal wall bracing, inadequate foundations, lack of trussing joints and rafters, and *skimping on nails or bolts.*"

3. Foundations and floors

FOUNDATIONS

You run smack into a contradiction when you start planning a foundation for your cabin or beach house.

First, it seems obvious that such an unfinished, sometimes-lived-in house shouldn't need the same kind of sturdy underpinning that you would insist on for your own home.

Then, you start thinking about the rugged or precipitous site, the rough and often unstable ground that your cabin may sit

JOHN ROBINSON

Rough sawn lumber was used as sheathing for lakeside cabin. Lumber lapped, one board over other, bottom to top. Angle of boards is controlled by wood bar nailed to the sill at bottom

JOHN ROBINSON

Log siding was used in this Lake Tahoe cabin. It was applied with mitered corner joints. Deck is made of unfinished 2 by 6 planks. Shingles set in pleasingly uneven "sawtooth" lines

JOHN ROBINSON

Imagination, rough materials make this lake cabin harmonious, friendly. Exterior is red-painted board and batten, white trim

P. A. DEARBORN

Unpainted cedar shingles accent strong horizontal line of beach house, match sand color, give better insulation than wall board

JOHN ROBINSON

Rough, unfinished pine siding, lapped and mitered, and shake roof. Mitered corners help make a lap-board cabin weathertight

CHARLES R. PEARSON

Informal house on lake shore made of logs that grew on site. Logs peeled, jointed, fitted together have weathered to soft gray

on, the unmerciful season-by-season beating it will have to take from the weather —and you're ready to double and redouble your original foundation requirements.

After you have thought further and investigated or examined the various most-used foundations and compared their values with your actual requirements, you'll probably come up with some sort of compromise between these two extreme viewpoints.

Here is a short introduction to foundations, their basic characteristics, advantages and disadvantages.

1. Posts: Wood posts are often used to support smaller structures—but they are not generally recommended by building experts. Cedar, locust, redwood and cypress heartwood can be used without special protection. These woods have tight grain and high resin content—are resistant to decay and insect attack. Woods impregnated with pentachlorophenol or zinc naphthenate also resist exposure well.

Posts should be a foot or so in diameter, long enough to extend below the frost line, or, better yet, down to solid rock or dense gravel. A large flat stone is generally placed at the bottom of the hole dug for each post.

Posts are the least dense of all basic foundation materials. They disintegrate more quickly than denser materials, are susceptible to rot, insects and other ills. If you have to buy posts, cost may be as high as if you use concrete piers.

2. Stone: Two large, rather flat boulders laid one on the other make a common and often serviceable support. Two stones are used because the joint between them stops the rise of moisture and the top stone remains dry. Stones should not be cemented or mortared together.

Care should be taken to choose rocks which fit firmly and evenly together to prevent slipping or shifting under the building's weight.

Boulders are best used where the cabin site is more or less solid rock. Otherwise, it is necessary to dig down to solid rock or firm gravel and use concrete piers up to grade level.

3. Concrete Piers: Perhaps the commonest cabin foundation is made of a series of concrete piers. Piers can be cast at the cabin site using wood, metal, or building paper forms. Or, if civilization is close at hand, you can buy and haul in pre-cast piers. Pre-cast piers are inexpensive and adequate. They can save you a great deal of time and trouble if transporting them is no problem.

BUILDING-PAPER PIER FORMS

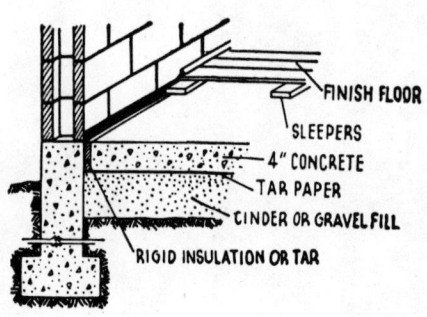

STONE PIERS...

If you object to the traditional pier shape, you can cast tapered circular piers. Integral burnt umber dye can be used (4 pounds per 100 pounds of cement) to dye the concrete dark brown to harmonize with wood or log construction.

In cold weather country, piers should extend below the frost line. Regardless of location, they should extend down to solid support.

Piers allow excellent ventilation under a cabin, but they won't keep rodents out. Properly installed, they will provide sturdy, long-lasting support for any but the largest cabin.

4. Continuous Concrete: Continuous concrete is the most satisfactory and permanent foundation. Weight is evenly distributed and even support for the whole structure is assured.

The rule of thumb requirement for concrete foundations is that they be based on footings which are at least twice as wide as the finished wall. In marshy or unstable soil, an even wider footing may be necessary. Foundation wall width varies according to the weight to be supported. It is a good idea to make walls at least 2 inches thicker than the logs or timbers that are to be supported.

Cost of a concrete foundation is determined by availability on the site of usable sand and gravel, transportation costs, type and size of construction, topography and soil characteristics of the site. Cost is generally lower if pre-mixed concrete can be hauled a short distance to the site.

FLOORS

The problem of whether to have concrete slab or wood flooring can cause the prospective beach or mountain cabin owner a lot of soul-searching and vacillation.

The site and other construction materials to be used may actually make your choice for you. A concrete slab is easy to pour if your site is fairly level and close to roads, or, better yet, close to a pre-mixed concrete plant. It is the best surface on which to lay flagstone, brick, linoleum, or tile floors.

Abundant sand and gravel on the site makes concrete mixing relatively easy. A slab is rodent-free. It helps keep the house close to the ground—makes for low, pleasant building lines and ease in landscaping. A slab also is easier to clean than a wood floor.

If the site is well drained you need not use a waterproof membrane in slab construction. Unless soil is rocky, a foot of crushed rock or gravel under the slab will help keep it dry.

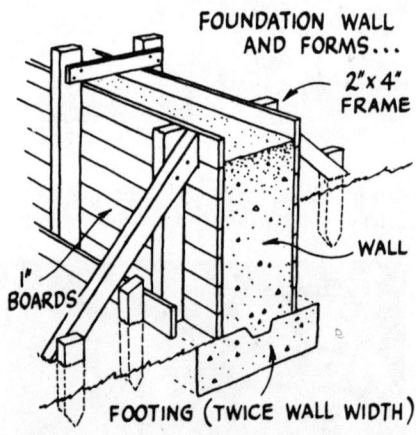

Site and other problems may eliminate a slab. Cost of transporting cement to a remote site may be prohibitive. Excavation necessary for slab installation may come too high — or be impossible. Absence of usable sand and gravel often eliminates use of a slab in isolated areas. Sea beach sand and gravel cannot be used because their high salt content interferes with proper bonding.

Steep slopes and rocky or adobe soils are against slab construction. Where the ground freezes, slabs tend to buckle and disintegrate under the constant and extreme expansion and contraction caused by temperature changes. Unstable soils and adobe may have almost as disastrous an effect on a slab.

Wood floors generally are more aesthetically complementary to log or rough-textured construction.

In cabin areas, there are often saw mills where rough lumber and delivery service are available at low cost.

Given weathertight construction, wood floors are ordinarily warmer to the touch than is concrete. Wood is a less effective heat conductor than concrete—hence less heat is lost.

Wood floors can be made of almost any rough or finished lumber, depending on availability and the degree of finish desired. Tongue and groove 2 by 6 boards make a very weathertight floor. They are particularly effective where no subflooring is to be put down.

If your cabin or beach house site permits use of either a wood or concrete floor and you have not yet made up your mind, it might be a good idea to talk to people who have places near your site. Though your problem may be a somewhat special one, the experience of others under roughly similar conditions may help guide you to a practical decision.

If standard materials don't answer your floor problems, or if you are of an experimental turn of mind, you may want to investigate materials which are not ordinarily used for floors: asphalt, asphalt-cement compound, concrete or light aggregate bricks, exterior grade plywood, compressed sawdust, panels, wood blocks or earth packed hard and stabilized with an asphalt compound.

4. Frame and log construction

Perhaps the greatest single advantage of frame construction is its inherent versatility. You can make of it what you will—from simplest fishing shack to luxurious beach house.

The essential details of each building might even be the same.

There is a vast assortment of wood building materials, many and adaptable construction methods to choose from.

Which you choose will no doubt depend on several factors: Availability, distance from the site, transportation and building costs, available site materials, site topography, climate, available foundation materials, and your own likes and dislikes will probably influence your choice.

Here, quickly, are standard materials and building techniques:

1. Unfinished Lumber: Rough sawn lumber is easy for the amateur to work with. Applied board-and-batten or lapped, it makes handsome and serviceable walls. Board and batten construction is probably the easiest method for the amateur carpenter. In lightweight structures, elaborate wall framing is unnecessary because the vertical boards and battens form a relatively strong bearing wall.

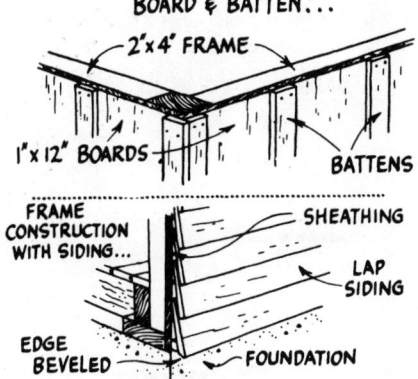

Rough sawn broad boards or planks are used. Between each pair of boards runs a strip of batten which may be nailed flat over the seam, or you can get specially milled battens that have a groove into which the wide boards fit.

Rough boards can be lapped horizontally, shingle-fashion, to create a rugged, durable wall. To strengthen this type of construction, apply sheathing over the frame before lap-siding is applied.

Regardless of how they are applied, unfinished boards are one of the most attractive and serviceable of wall finishing materials.

If your building site is in the mountains or along the wooded portion of the Pacific Coast, you may be able to buy rough lumber directly from a mill. Some mills will even haul lumber to the site. Of course, lumber purchased at the mill is less costly than it would be from a lumber yard.

2. Milled Sidings: Around 200 different sizes and styles of wood siding are milled. If there is a well-stocked lumber yard near your site, you will find that it has dozens of types of sidings that might be used.

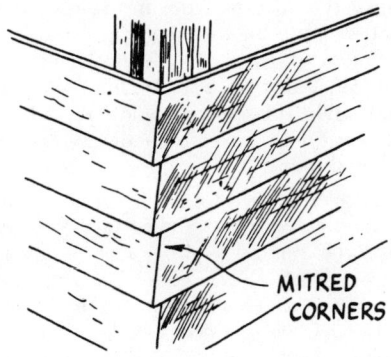

The basic problem in using milled siding is one of fitting it to a somewhat rugged mountain or seashore environment. On the other hand, if you are building at a large beach or mountain colony, finished lumber may be perfectly acceptable. Cabin plans must be submitted to the Forest Supervisor for approval before starting to build.

3. Specialty Sidings: You can buy from many lumber dealers rounded siding that gives the effect of smoothly finished half-logs, or timbers which have a chipped finish that simulates hewn timbers. Widths are generally from 5½ to 8 inches; thickness varies from 1 to 3 inches. Both shiplap and tongue and groove jointed types are milled. Some yards stock special end pieces which can be attached to give the effect of projecting log ends.

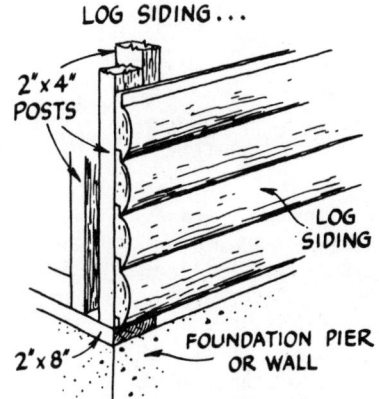

These materials have something of the "feel" of logs or hewn timbers, yet they can be put up in the same manner as finished siding. Where logs are scarce or expensive, these sidings may be less expensive than the real thing.

4. Crib Construction: Crib construction utilizes 2 by 4's or 2 by 6's, laid face to face with each "course" nailed securely to the member below. Corners are ordinarily cross-lapped as illustrated.

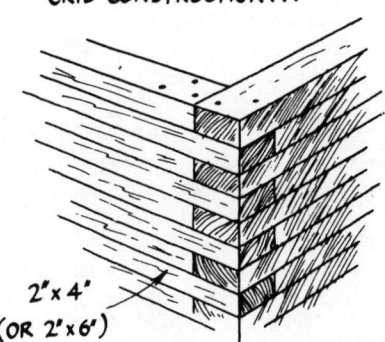

The resulting wall is strong and fire-resistant. Crib construction is used by industrial concerns for fire walls.

This type of wall also eliminates most vertical framing—and the inside surface can be used as the finished inside wall.

Mill ends and other odd lengths of relatively low-grade, low-cost lumber can be used.

5. Shingles and Shakes: Western cedar, redwood and cypress shingles and shakes can be used for siding on beach or mountain cabins. Composition shingles designed for use as siding may also be used for beach house walls.

SHINGLE OR SHAKE WALL...

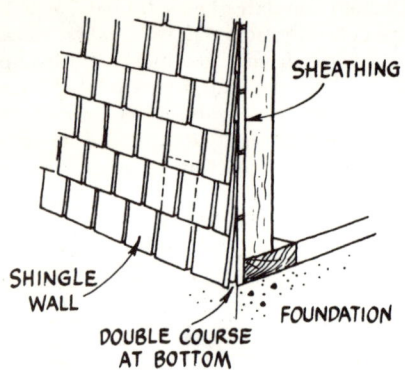

Both shingles and shakes are easy to apply, long lasting, easily stained, and are almost universally obtainable. Shingled walls, when laid properly, give more insulation than board siding.

When used on side walls, shingles or shakes can have more area exposed to the weather than when they are used as roofing: on a roof, 16-inch shingles are usually laid 5 inches to the weather—on walls 6 or 6½ inches can be exposed.

6. Stucco: Stucco is often used for beach house outside walls. It may also be used for cabin construction at lower levels and in the desert.

At high altitudes where foliage is heavy, stucco is less desirable both aesthetically and practically. It tends to disintegrate when exposed to long, cold winters and heavy snow.

Providing skilled labor is obtainable or if you are able to do the work yourself, the cost of stucco is about the same as siding where both are available. Its use for cabin walls in National Forests is usually prohibited.

7. Plywood: If you have to haul building materials over a considerable distance, to a remote cabin or beach site, plywood may be the most practical siding to use. It is light, strong, easily worked. *Exterior grade* plywood holds up fairly well when exposed to the weather. It should be thoroughly primed, sealed, and painted — including *all* edges.

8. Logs: Most people who think of building a mountain cabin think first of building a log cabin. The cozy log cabin in the woods has a strong romantic historical appeal.

Actually, there are a good many complications to log cabin building.

If you have to buy logs and hire men to erect your cabin, a log structure will probably cost more than an equivalent cabin made of lumber. Skilled help is hard to find. Even the customary tools are often unavailable.

There are two styles of log construction—the traditional kind with the logs laid horizontally, and stockade construction in which logs or half-logs are placed upright. Stockade construction is the easier

STANDARD LOG CONSTRUCTION...

method: Skilled axe work is not required to notch log ends, and smaller logs can be used, since they are merely spiked to the horizontal members of a timber frame.

STOCKADE CONSTRUCTION...

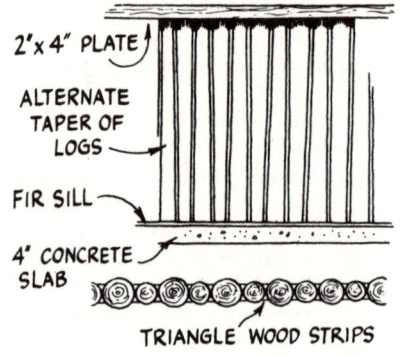

If logs are not available on the site, you can buy them from a lumber company, from a public utility company's supply of power-line poles, or you may be able to cut your own on a nearby National Forest, for a nominal stumpage fee. You may also be able to buy and cut logs on nearby private land for a stumpage fee.

If you plan to build your own log cabin and have no experience in log construction, it would be wise to get and read one or more of the available books on the subject. When you start to build, the help and advice of someone who has had experience with log construction would be of great value.

9. Prefabricated Cabins: You can buy prefabricated cabins and cottages of various types and sizes—from a simple quonset hut to a five-room house. Prefabricated structures are either fabricated in sections with windows and doors already hung on frames—or they come with materials cut and marked so elaborately that little more than a hammer and wrench is needed to put the structure together.

Costs depend on size and finish, and the distance over which materials or sections must be transported.

A prefabricated house would be of special value on a site which is being leased. Should the lease be terminated, the house could be dismounted and moved.

10. Roofs: Beach house roofs can be of practically any material — except those which do not hold up well when exposed to salt air. Metal roofing materials should probably be avoided unless they are specially treated to resist sea air. If summer heat is a problem, a reflective roof will help keep temperatures down. Crushed dolomite over built-up tar and gravel, or roofing canvas painted a light color are two roofs which will reflect a good deal of heat.

The restriction on cabin roofs is mainly an aesthetic one. Materials like wood shakes and shingles are most attractive in a forest setting. Composition shingles and composition roll roofing in appropriate colors fit satisfactorily into the landscape.

Sheet metal, metal shingles, built-up tar and gravel and bright-colored composition roll and shingle roofing are less aesthetically desirable for roofing except on a flat or shed roof where they are more or less concealed.

At high altitudes where there is heavy snowfall, however, a metal roof of shingles or flat or corrugated sheets often justifies sacrificing aesthetic standards for extra strength and durability.

5. Masonry and earth construction

Masonry — like any other basic building method—has its proponents and detractors.

It has distinct advantages:

No great skill is needed to erect a rough masonry mountain or beach cabin. Once it is erected, there is practically no upkeep. It is impervious to termites, rats, mice, and other pests. Weather — even high mountain cold and snow — is no match for good masonry construction.

Site materials can often be used for adobe or stone construction. Masonry cabins of native materials fit the site harmoniously. If you do your own masonry work, using site materials, cost is relatively low.

Fire risk is low in a masonry structure, and fire insurance rates are lower than for frame construction.

Detractors of masonry construction point out that building is slow if you do the work yourself; it is hard work, includes a lot of heavy lifting.

Most masonry construction requires heavier foundations and footings than are needed for frame construction. Erecting a masonry house at an isolated site may pose problems of transportation for steel reinforcement, concrete and other materials. And, an unsightly masonry house tends to become a more or less permanent

Above. Sturdy peeled log cabin on stone and mortar foundation. Log joists, rafters used. Low-pitched roof safe for light snows

Right above. Unusually straight, even logs used here. Note precise job of cupping and fitting at corners. Shake roof and field stone chimneys accentuate traditional mountain cabin style

Right center. Side view of cabin above right shows peeled log porch frame. Posts, headers, rafters are straight logs, vary in size. Because of tight construction, little chinking is necessary

Right below. Site materials decided construction of cabin near Kirkland, Wash. Small, second-growth trees used vertically stockade style for main bearing walls. Interior wall detail below

Below. Inside of cabin below right. Trees cut late fall to retain bark. Interior surface of logs rubbed with steel wool to remove loose bark, treated with linseed oil. Chinking is wet newspapers, then cedar strips forced between the logs inside and out. Unlike the horizontal type of construction, vertical placement has structural weakness because no lateral bracing

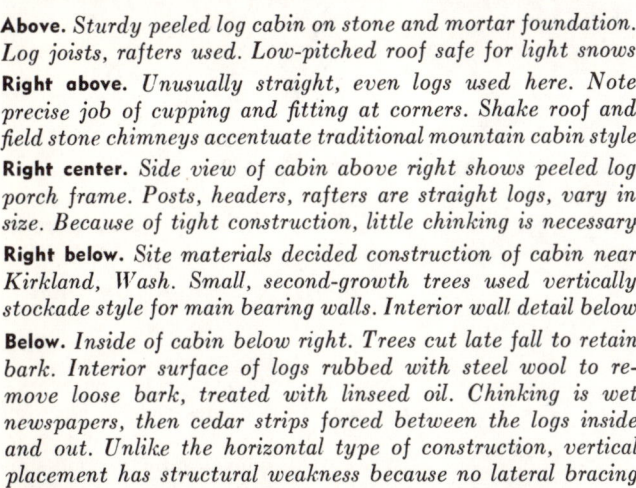

CHARLES R. PEARSON

Combination boat house and beach cabin just above water level on a Washington lake is made of native field stone. A heavy concrete foundation and retaining wall which supports the masonry doubles as a low breakwater when storms push waves up almost to the level of the house

PHILIP FEIN

Mountain cabin utilizes local materials and rough textures to harmonize with its rustic surroundings. Rugged stone walls and massive chimney are key features of construction. Stone was picked up in local area. Redwood shake roof, board and batten walls integrate easily with stone

monument to its builder's mistakes. Earthquakes may require special reinforcement of masonry construction in some areas.

Here is general information on some of the basic masonry methods and materials which may help you in deciding whether to build with masonry and which type of material might best suit your purposes.

1. Stone: Bearing walls of stone require a full concrete or rock foundation. Walls will, of course, be extra heavy, so footings as well as foundation walls should be proportionately wider and thicker than for log or frame structures.

Stone walls should ordinarily be at least 1½ feet thick at the bottom (remember this when you build the foundation), and taper to 8 inches or so at the top.

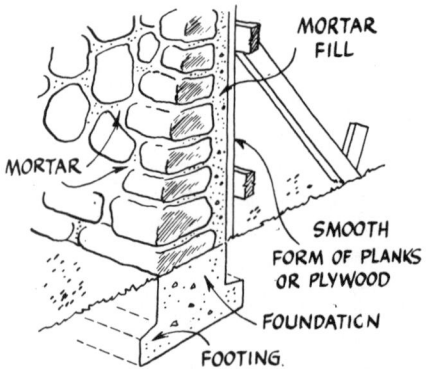

STONE WALL CONSTRUCTION...

There are two basic types of stone work— *rubble* (uncut stones) and *ashlar* (cut stones). Most stone cabins and beach houses are of rubble. Ordinarily, cut stone would be too costly to buy and transport to a cabin. *Uncut* stones laid so the finished wall has strength and a pattern that

is pleasing to the eye make a handsome structure—one that blends well into almost any environment.

In choosing stones, or checking to see that an adequate supply is available, keep in mind the scale of the finished house and choose sizes accordingly. A good rule to remember is that the face area of the larger stones laid should not be more than five or six times the face area of the smallest stones. Large stones, of course, can be broken to size while the work is going on.

There are various techniques that vary the construction of stone structures. One that might be helpful where stone is scarce and concrete is readily available is the Flagg masonry wall which utilizes a facing of natural stone backed by concrete. The Flagg wall requires full forms on both sides of the wall.

2. Concrete or Light Aggregate Blocks: Blocks or bricks of concrete or light aggregate are basically a much more satisfactory material for a masonry vacation structure than poured concrete. Pouring calls for more machinery, special techniques, and additional materials.

Ordinary concrete blocks are dense and heavy; others, in which porous, lightweight minerals take the place of the usual sand, are often light enough for a large block to be lifted easily with one hand. Weight and density vary with the ingredients. Light aggregate blocks are better insulators than those of regular concrete.

CONCRETE BLOCK WALL CONSTRUCTION...

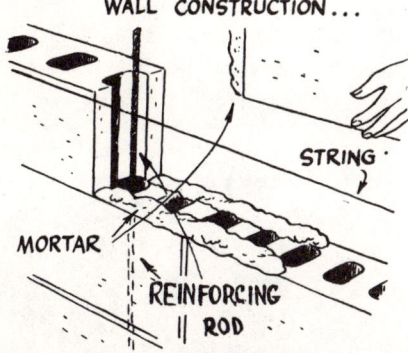

All good blocks — light or heavy, dense or porous — many times exceed building requirements. Blocks come in many sizes (the commonest is 8 by 8 by 16 inches), and in units of special shape for corners, ends, partitions, door jambs, joists, window sashes and the like.

Again, a heavy foundation—in this case, footing — is necessary. Most normal requirements are met by footings as deep as the foundation is wide and about 8 inches wider than the wall. Unstable soil, shifting or marsh ground require the advice of an engineer. Local building codes may, of course, require longitudinal reinforcing with steel or set other special conditions.

Concrete blocks are a sound basic building material. They are fairly easy for the amateur mason to handle.

If you are interested—but object to concrete's color—remember that blocks are available in various colors; and that you can paint concrete any color you wish.

Block construction is relatively low in cost if you don't have to pay freight or drayage charges over a long distance. Availability may be limited in many of the more isolated cabin areas.

3. Adobe: If the site of your future cabin is within easy delivery range of an adobe brick manufacturer, you may wish to look into the possibility of building with this material. Adobe bricks (also called blocks) are several times the size of standard clay bricks—typical size of those used for walls is 4 by 8 by 16 inches. This means you can get your walls up in a hurry, with one important *if:* The heavy blocks (about 30 pounds) should be delivered as close as possible to where you'll be working—within a few feet or a few yards.

For names of adobe brick manufacturers who might be in your vicinity, see the yellow pages of the telephone book, under "Adobe Brick" or a similar heading. You can obtain a list of California adobe manufacturers and also the names of some architects specializing in adobe by writing to the American Bitumuls and Asphalt Co., 320 Market Street, San Francisco, California.

If you are thinking of making the bricks yourself, you should be forewarned: It is slow, exacting, painstaking work; unless you have considerable talent (and patience) it's best not to try it on your own. If you decide to try, here are some things about adobe that you should know:

With the exception ironically of "adobe" soil which cracks when it is baked, adobe bricks can be made of almost any soil without intricate machinery or expensive ingredients. Bricks are often "baked" on the site by merely laying them out in the sun. Principal ingredients are soil, water, and a stabilizing waterproofing agent, usually an emulsified asphalt. Ingredients can be mixed by hand or with a simple, homemade, mud-mixing machine, or a plaster or dough mixer.

Simple molds are used to form the bricks. Thirty to ninety days' curing is required, depending on weather. Cured bricks can be left in the open. Water and weather won't damage them.

For this reason, adobe is especially appealing to the amateur builder. He can set his own speed, and abandon and resume construction from time to time or year to year without harm to partially-completed walls.

Another advantage is that adobe is a site material. If your soil is satisfactory for adobe bricks (companies which manufacture asphalt stabilizer will ordinarily laboratory-test it for you), you can actually manufacture your own building material, and then construct a house of it.

Adobe homes are easily heated and hold their warmth in winter. They are cool in hot weather.

Cost varies greatly. A contractor-built adobe may cost a little more than a frame structure. If you do your own work, discounting the cost of your labor, adobe can be a relatively inexpensive building material and method.

Adobe has some basic structural limitations. Critical formulas govern wall height in proportion to wall thickness; length of single, unsupported walls; percentage of single walls which may be used for windows and other openings; and spacing of open spans in the wall.

These limitations may be eliminated by design or engineering in some cases, but they should be carefully checked before actual building plans are begun.

It is a good idea to do some reading up on the subject if you plan to work with adobe. Your local library may have references. There is a chapter on adobe blocks in the *Sunset* book, *How to Build Walls, Walks, and Patio Floors.*

4. Rammed Earth: Perhaps the simplest, most rudimentary, and inexpensive stuff of which to build a cabin is rammed earth. Like adobe, rammed earth is basically a site material. Only requirement is that the earth on your property dry from mud into firm-textured dirt.

The wall-building process is simple. First, heavy, reinforced plank forms are erected. Forms are usually sectional, their two sides held together by long steel bolts.

RAMMED EARTH WALL FORMS...

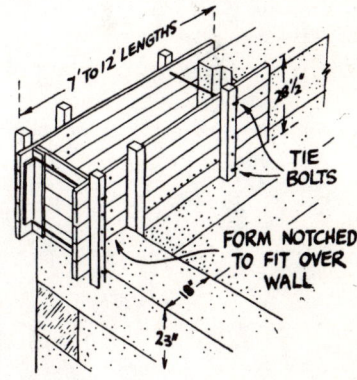

Straw or some other binding material is added to a quantity of loose, firmly mulched earth. Water is added and the resulting mass is mixed by hand, or with a mixer such as suggested for adobe, until it becomes plastic yet very stiff.

When the right consistency is reached, the mixture is dumped into the forms and tamped solidly into place. Tamping compresses the materials into a firm, dense mass.

Forms are removed when they are filled with the compacted earth and the earth is allowed to dry and set, becoming so hard and durable that normal wear and tear ordinarily have little effect on it.

How four families built their own cabins

Most of the families we know have, at one time or another, talked about the idea of building themselves a little cabin in the mountains, at the beach, or in the desert.

For many families, enjoyable stages of dreaming are as far as it goes. But not for all. A truly astonishing number of families believe in the dream, and go ahead. In a wonderful variety of ways, they manage to build themselves cabins with little or no professional help, and often on remarkably modest budgets. To us, it is a revelation to see how much and how well these people have done with so little building experience.

On these pages are the case histories of how four families got the cabin they wanted without going broke in the process.

OWNER-BUILT CABIN NO. 1: *It is one big open room*

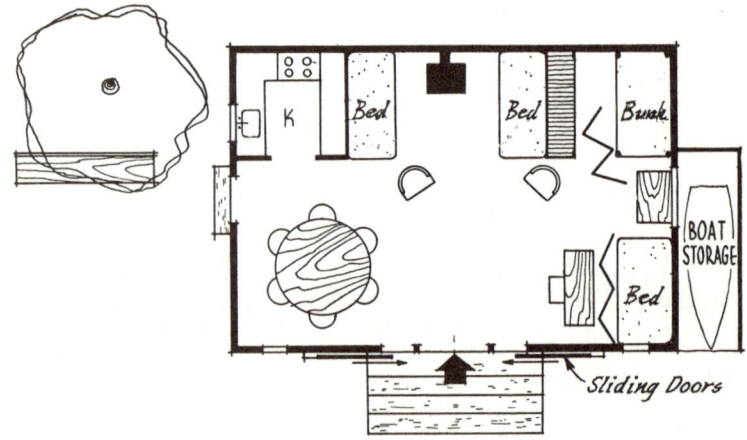

The materials for this owner-constructed lakeshore cabin cost less than $1,000.

Only a short way downhill from their home, it provides them and their children some priceless summer fun. Set on a post and pier foundation, the 20-by-30-foot cabin is built of ¾-inch cedar boards and battens with a shingle roof. Sliding front walls are on roller skate wheels on a track at floor level outside the cabin.

Plan shows partitions are arranged for privacy. Living area center. Kitchen-dining on one side, sleeping on other

ART HUPY

One-room interior divided with folding screens and two 6-foot partitions. One is a wardrobe, one a kitchen cupboard. Beds on left wall and far end. Kitchen on left

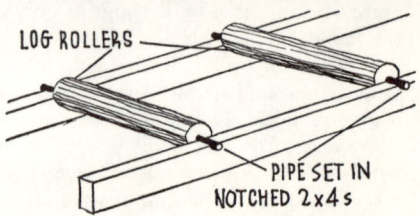

Boat shelter at end of cabin. The rollers make it easy to move the boat in and out

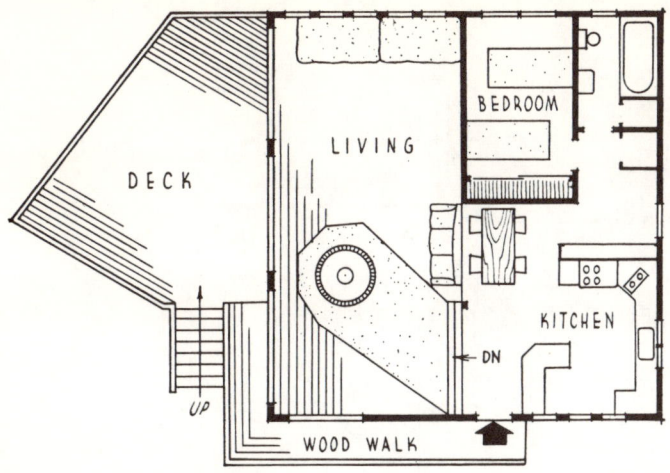

OWNER-BUILT
CABIN NO. 2:

A split-level plan to fit a sloping site

From the lake *side showing the deck. The latticed extension of the roof overhang helps shade windows. Foundation and framing are built to support a bedroom story on back half of cabin*

Designing and building this cabin on the Oregon coast was a labor of love, and the cabin shows it. After the plans had been very carefully worked out, the owner and one carpenter spent two weeks and a few extra weekends putting up the basic structure. Once this was done, the owner and his family began to put on all the finishing touches in their spare time. The cabin is only 45 minutes from their home, and they use it on weekends as often as they can.

Fireplace *of expanded shale blocks. Galvanized hood drops down for starting fire and to contain coals at night. Rail is copper pipe. The double beds against far wall sleep four extra people*

From the dining *area looking toward the deck and lake. Kitchen counter in foreground. Windows have bamboo screens above center, draperies below center which give privacy and cut glare*

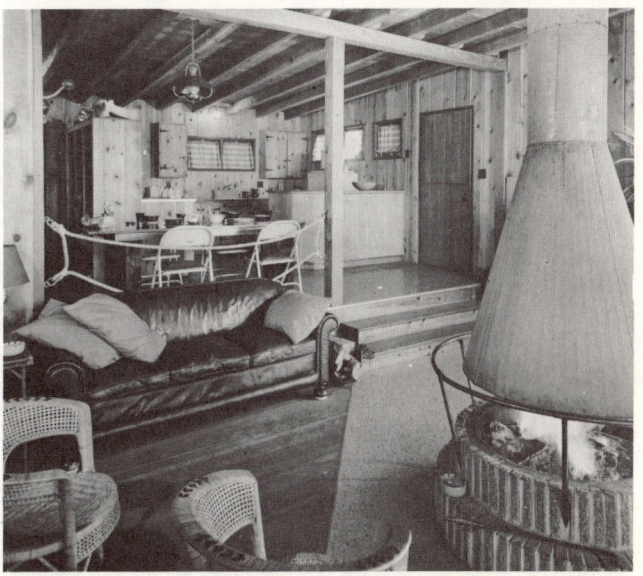

Living area *is on a lower level to fit slope of site. Dining area behind couch, kitchen beyond. Main entry is Dutch door right of kitchen. Linoleum on traffic lane around circular fireplace*

OWNER-BUILT CABIN NO. 3:

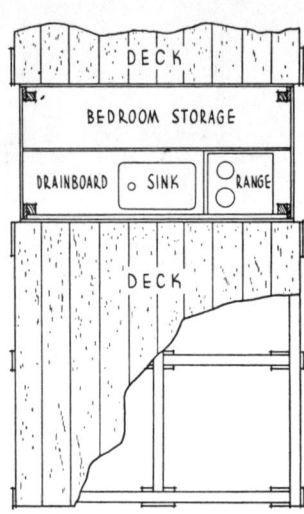

An expandable cabin "core"

After 30 years of more conventional camping, the owners of the structure you see here decided they needed a permanent camp where they could "settle down" for weekends and vacations. The sketch above shows how the cabin will look when finished. They prefabricated it in their basement during the winter. With the help of their two sons, they took it to the site—next to a mountain river, about 80 miles from their home. Cost of the entire project: about $350.

At 10:45 a.m., July 4, 1956, the owners were just getting started with the cabin's simple wood foundations. A tent (not in picture) was used as a "construction camp"

3:30 p.m. July 4. Walls and ceiling are in place, and the combination folding wall and deck is hinged to the bottom of the frame which sits level on concrete blocks

5:00 p.m., July 5. The kitchen and pantry is equipped, stocked, and ready for service. Corrugated plastic overhead is attached to top of frame with piano hinges

Plastic panel is folded down while the roof work is being finished. Roof framing was all pre-cut and ready to put in place; this made quick work of an awkward task

Here's the cabin in action. Roof over the "front porch" is supported by two aluminum poles. Bedroom addition will be identical but on the other side of the frame

Locking up until the next weekend. Foundation for hinged floor is made of 6 by 6 cedar timbers. Saplings were leaned against frame for winter snow protection

OWNER-BUILT CABIN NO. 4:

Pivoting walls... a big deck

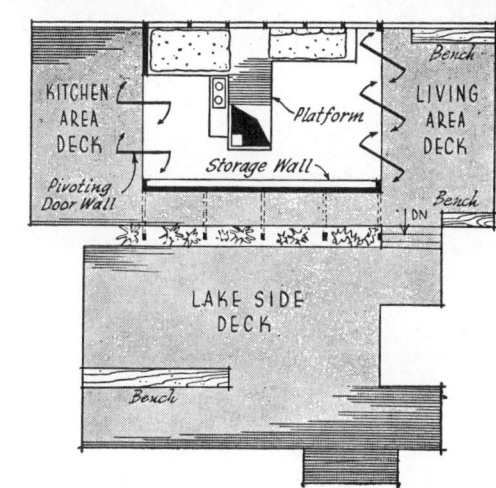

The way this cabin works is best shown in the plan on the right. Basically it is a box with end walls made of pivoting panels which open to the generous decks on three sides. On the edge of a lake, the cabin was designed by the original owner, who proceeded to build it with his wife's help. Access is by boat. The materials—which cost approximately $1,200—were all floated in.

Above *you see the cabin with the end panels closed. The panels have a hollow core and are faced with hardboard.*

On the right *you see the cabin with panels open at each end. This is the "living" end, "kitchen" is on the other side of the fireplace. The deck and cabin floor are of two by fours on edge. Roof is corrugated steel. Note the storage along the wall above the stools on the left*

TOM BURNS, JR.

Raised T-shaped platform *has fireplace in center and beds on each side. Canvas behind fireplace drops down to separate the two areas. There's an upper bunk above the bed on the far side*

From the kitchen side. *The present owners plan to add dishwashing facilities on the deck, and install a large window in the wall on the right. Kitchen storage in right foreground*

OWNER-BUILT CABINS...

Advice from families who have built a cabin "on their own"...

As a family project, *building a cabin is one of the best. There is always some kind of useful work for everyone involved*

The people we've talked to who have built their own cabins are all enthusiasts for the idea. They have found it a wonderfully rewarding experience as a family project, especially when there were children old enough to take part.

They all agree that it is something that "anyone" can do if he puts his mind to it, doesn't get in a rush, and will take it one step at a time. They point out that the labor on a cabin is 40 to 50 per cent of the cost.

CHOOSING A CABIN SITE

Here is cabin builders' advice: Don't build a cabin too far from home or you may find you won't get as much use out of it as you would like. How far is "too far" is something only you can decide, but you should give it careful thought before you decide on a location.

Know the local climate, and the specific microclimate of your cabin site. If possible, observe the site for a year and see how the climate changes with the seasons. Camp on the site if you can before you buy it—and certainly before you build.

Know for sure that you have a good supply of pure water nearby. If there is any question about the purity of the water, check with your county health officer. He can test it for you, or tell you where to have it tested.

If the spot you like is on a bluff, slope, or the edge of a lake or river, make sure there's no problem of slippage, or flooding.

Be sure of legal access. It is not safe to assume you have legal access to your site unless it is on a dedicated public right of way. Back country surveys may be inaccurate and real estate salespeople may not know the exact lines. It is a good idea to measure off your site from the nearest accurate markers and to confirm your findings and also check any easements with county records.

PLANNING THE CABIN

Be sure you know the seasonal pattern of sunlight, and also the prevailing winds before you decide just where to place your cabin. You usually want to capture the sun in the woods, and protect yourself from the sun at the beach and desert.

Consider future improvements and expansion. If you don't plan to have electricity, water, or indoor plumbing at first, keep in mind the fact that you very likely will want these facilities later on.

Cabin owners are especially outspoken on the subject of planning:

" . . . Design your cabin to be complete without paint or extra maintenance. It should be a place that will weather gracefully. If it gets too fancy and takes too much work to keep up you'll never know you left home."

" . . . A deck is wonderful for outdoor living, no dust or mud underfoot."

" . . . Careful planning is in a way more important in a little cabin than a big house; there is less margin for error."

" . . . You often have guests, and because facilities are limited we found a compartmented bath a good idea."

" . . . If it is a cabin you may lend to others, make it as foolproof as you can. Be sure to observe all the recommendations for fire prevention."

" . . . For a cabin in snow country, an upstairs entry is a good idea for use when drifts are deep."

" . . . By all means check with neighbors and local residents to find out about local building practice."

" . . . The smartest things we did in planning were to camp on the site before we located the cabin, and to make a model of the cabin and all the equipment and furniture that was to go in it. We found mistakes which, without the model, would have been built into the cabin."

BEWARE OF DRAINAGE

Before you build be sure you know how the water runs off your land. The best cabin sites are often in locations with extremes of weather. If you find it necessary to cut and fill, be sure you know what the action of the water will be. You may have to dig ditches to divert runoff.

ORDERING MATERIALS

A builder we talked to recommends that you make up a complete list of all the materials you will need for the entire job and send it out to lumber dealers for bids. Mail the list several weeks before you start to build and be sure to indicate the cabin location so the yard can figure delivery costs. If there are lumber dealers close by, be sure to get local bids.

WHAT FOUNDATION?

In some areas the county will have a building code which you must observe when you build a cabin. The code may specify, among other things, a certain kind of foundation.

If your cabin is to go on a fill, let the fill settle for at least one year before you start to build.

A continuous concrete foundation is usually best if your budget permits. Such a foundation is strong and permanent; there's practically no deterioration and it is termite, rot, and rodent proof. It distributes the load of the house evenly around the base. Unfortunately it is also the most expensive and difficult to install.

Budget and convenience are the reasons why pre-cast concrete piers are used most for cabin foundations. If you decide to use piers, the best method is to dig down to a solid base and pour the hole full of concrete to make a foundation for the pier block. You can also use log rounds. They should be at least 12 inches in diameter, treated with wood preservative. If you don't use either, the posts should rest on a large flat rock set well in firm soil below the frost line.

Two flat stones can sometimes be used as piers if the subsoil is stable. Pick two stones that fit together so well that there's no need to cement them. Water may rise in the bottom stone, but will not pass the open joint to the top stone.

If you can get ready-mix concrete without too long a haul, you may want to build your cabin on a concrete slab. We've talked to a number of satisfied people who have. They say the slab gives them a warmer cabin—no drafts of cold air under the floor. Also, as one cabin owner put it "... Skunks can't exhale under the cabin if it is on a slab."

GET IT STARTED RIGHT

There's a temptation to try to rush a cabin building job as you see the summer weekends slipping by with so much left to do. Yet experience proves that it pays to take it slow. Get the corners square to start with, keep the horizontal lines level. Keep the vertical lines plumb.

WHAT ABOUT THE ROOF?

Because of their more rustic look, wood or composition shingles, or shakes, are required by the Forest Service on the roofs of most cabins built within National Forests. Sheet metal, asphalt, and gravel roofs are usually allowed only where they can't be seen.

If you are concerned about the time it takes to shingle a roof, one cabin owner-builder offers this experience: "I put ¾ inch sheathing over the roof beams—the roof is a half pitch—and stapled heavy roofing paper over this. The roof worked fine. Three years later when I got around to putting on the shakes, I put furring strips parallel to the ridge 9 inches apart, and nailed the shakes to them. This made an air space under the shakes and it seems to be a very efficient roof."

WHAT ABOUT HEAT?

A fireplace is the classic heat source for a cabin. If it is your only source of heat, you may want to install a circulating type fireplace with a prefabricated metal fire box. It can be set in the wall just like a regular fireplace, but it has vents that take in cool air and circulate warm air back into the room.

In cabins where weather is cold, you may want an oil-fired heater, or an LP gas furnace. If there's a road to the cabin, you can usually get a truck to replenish your supply when necessary.

You'll make the most of the heat you have in a winter cabin if the cabin is insulated and weatherstripped.

If you don't plan to put in a fireplace when you build, it is a simple matter, and not too expensive, to frame in for one in case you want to add it later.

Popular hood-type *fireplace has 12 square feet of reflecting surface. Versatile and economical. Design is by Wendell Lovett*

Electric auxiliary heat makes good sense in a cabin, but it does have one drawback in remote areas; service isn't always too dependable. It is not unusual for storms to blow trees down on the wires and cut off the power.

There's a lesson in one cabin owner's experience with an oil system: "... We put the oil line from the 100-gallon drum to the cabin right on the ground. Cold weather cracked the pipe and we lost 80 gallons of oil. When we replaced the pipe we buried it under ground. I'd also recommend getting the best valves and fittings you can buy."

CABIN PLUMBING

Where winter weather is cold, bury all the pipes below the frost line, and wrap them with insulation where they leave the ground.

One builder reports that he prefers copper pipe to the galvanized variety: "Fast and easy; no elbows to put in, no threads to cut. You can bend it the way you want it and sweat the joints together with solder and a blowtorch."

When plumbing is first installed, it is a good idea to have pipes arranged in such a way that they can all be drained at once—at the lowest point. This idea is particularly useful in cold-winter regions.

STORAGE IS IMPORTANT

Most families find they need more storage space than they first anticipate. One good idea is to leave a wall that can be expanded later on for added storage if you need it.

In a winter cabin, there's need for a place to store window shutters, skis, firewood, and a place to dry wet clothes. In a summer cabin you may need a place for window screens, fishing equipment, maybe a place for a boat and an outboard motor. When you close a cabin for the season, you may want to plan ways to use the interior living space as between-seasons storage space.

TOOLS FOR CABIN BUILDING

You will need the standard hand tools, of course, but most amateur builders feel that some power tools are worth the investment—assuming you have electricity available. A hand-held circular saw is a wonderful help. It cuts quickly and accurately, and has become one of the carpenter's basic tools. If you have a power table saw, or combination power tool, you might want to take it to the job.

We know of two families with adjoining sites who went together and bought a portable concrete mixer. They used it originally for foundations (one family built on a slab), and have used it since for terraces and retaining walls.

If you have much tree cutting or bucking to do, you may want a chain saw. An 18 or 20-inch, one-man saw, which is large enough for most uses, costs around $200. As you clear your land, you can stockpile wood for future fireplace use. Most cabin owners we've talked to say a live fire in the evening is indispensable to the good cabin life. And it's all the better if the wood is your own.

Snow trapdoor

Here's a suggestion for mountain cabin owners who may not be around during winter to shovel snow away from large glass areas.

Hinged trap doors (far one is shown closed) in the deck of this mountain cabin fold back against the door frames. Snow slides off the roof, through the deck, and down to the ground below.

Designers were George W. Roach, Jr., and architect Henry C. Burge.

The "pre-built" idea... and a case history

Of all the ways to get your dreamed-of vacation cabin actually built, once you know what you want and where you want it, buying a pre-cut or pre-fab cabin is usually the quickest.

Most prospective cabin owners already know that they can save substantially on cost by doing most of the work. Mass production of materials brings cabin prices down even further, and—most important to the amateur builder—many construction problems are pre-solved in the process.

If you don't want to do the whole job, you can have cabins of this type partially built. Most manufacturers will send out their own builders (you pay by the hour, or by the job) or will recommend contractors who will do as much of the work as you want. Some companies will supervise your work (for a small cost included in the cabin price) or will recommend someone who will do this. Some professional help is usually needed for wiring and plumbing.

Most of the smaller cabins are set on concrete piers for which construction instructions (but not materials) are furnished. A few models require a more extensive and more substantial foundation.

Unless you are equipped to carry several tons of materials from the end of the road, your cabin site should be accessible to a truck of at least 1½-ton capacity.

Most manufacturers make free delivery only within a few miles of the mill where the wood is cut to size. A few firms, however, deliver free within a radius of 50, 75, or even 150 miles. Beyond the zone of free delivery, you pay standard truck freight rates. Here are examples of approximate charges for shipping materials for a 300-square-foot cabin (about 7,000 pounds): Seattle-Tacoma area to Snoqualmie Pass or Hood Canal, $40; Seattle-Tacoma to San Francisco, $350; San Francisco Bay Area to Lake Tahoe, $120; Los Angeles area to Palm Springs, $80. For a browsers' guide to some representative styles and models of pre-built cabins, see page 39.

AN OWNER-BUILT CASE HISTORY

The owners of the cabin shown on these two pages believes the "pre-built" was their best buy, even though they had neither the time nor the inclination to do all the work themselves. For manpower, they relied on the help of friends plus some paid professional help (see below left, this page).

As usual, there were unexpected problems:

The bulldozer, clearing for the access road, uncovered an abundant spring and the resulting stream of water had to be channeled around the house site. The truck delivering the cabin accidentally backed off the steep access road and half the cabin landed in the blackberry bushes (unharmed, fortunately). The portable gas generator brought along to run a power saw broke down.

Nevertheless, problems surmounted and job done, the owners still consider this their best possible bargain in a cabin.

DARROW M. WATT

Immediate occupancy was a "must" for the owners, who wanted to live in the cabin while finishing it. Note unpainted sections of roof overhang, and the unfinished porch paneling (behind car)

Wednesday... to Sunday

The sequence of 11 photographs, starting at right, shows the construction of the cabin over a time span of five days.

The manufacturer (Vacation-Land Homes) agreed to supply help in the actual construction (at the standard wage rate) for as many days as might be needed. When the cabin was finished, including painting and cleaning up, the owners figured they and their friends had provided a little more than half of all the labor.

The cabin is 32 by 24 feet (including an 8 by 24-foot covered porch). The cabin shell, including interior partitions—but not interior finishing materials, plumbing, or wiring—cost approximately $2,500, delivered. The owner hired about $250 worth of expert help to put up the cabin shell. He did the wiring himself because he'd had experience in this field; the plumbing was installed by a contractor.

1. *Setting foundation piers on pier footings. Contractor had laid out the exact position the week before; owner dug holes (saving $30). Contractor's price for piers was only $20 more than if owner had made them. Each weighs 25 pounds*

2. *Each pier footing is about 5 inches deep. Concrete is mixed and poured, then piers are laid on top when concrete is partially set up. Note the string in lower right corner; this outlines the house walls; outside piers must be in alignment*

3. Site is uneven. To get right height for posts that support the 4 by 6-inch floor joists, the builder extended leveled board from highest pier (on which no post will rest) measured the distance from it down to piers, and cut posts to fit

4. Looking down on building site with all but the last row of the floor joists in place. This is the second day of construction; truck is backed up to the site with a load of sub-floor boards. Note the drainage ditch carrying water around site

5. Trimming the 2 by 6-inch tongue and groove subfloor (generator for power saw wasn't working yet) on morning of third day. The truck in the background is loaded up with half the cabin walls. The rest are in bushes up hill to the left

6. Two men can put up the 300-pound sections of wall—but four make it easier. Walls are very wobbly until the corner sections are attached. Whole building isn't considered very stable until the gable ends and supporting beams are up

7. Sections must fit snugly together. They're nailed together down their length, and the plates overlap at top and bottom. Here you see how the pre-built panels are constructed. Grooved, exterior fir plywood is used on outside of frames

8. Two wall sections forming corner are stable enough to stand alone while other walls are added. Building paper overlaps around corner. Note the pre-cut window openings; whole aluminum sash already filled with glass will be added

9. Three "slave laborers" and two "foremen" get a roof beam in place (there are two more men at the other end of the beam). This is one of the two main roof beams running through the house, here being fitted into a slot in the gable end

10. With roof beams in place, rafters, supporting cross beams are added. Then roof "sheeted" with plywood panels. Later, these were covered by composition shingles. Underside of the plywood panels is textured—forms the ceiling of the cabin

11. This photograph, taken at same time as one at left, shows sloping site, covered porch, interior partitions, method of roof construction. This was the fifth day—by dark the roof panels were on, and windows and doors were in place

Owner-built pre-fab:

They put it together on their vacation

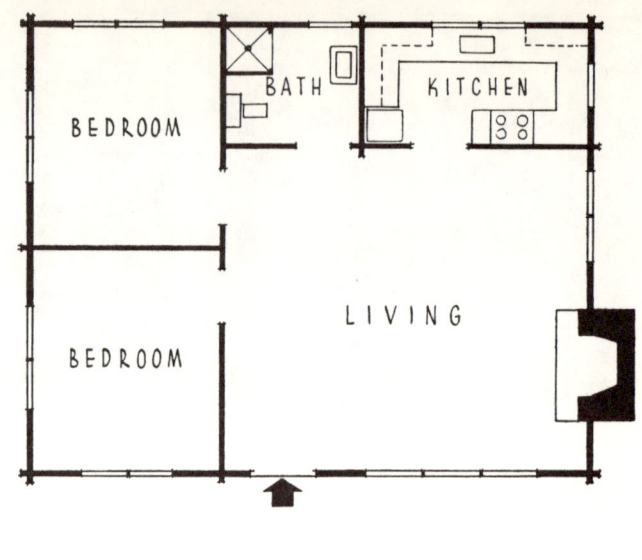

On-the-site camping by the owners, plus the help of friends, got the results you see here during a two-week vacation. It cost $1,850 FOB Kennydale, Washington (in 1955). Trucking the pre-fabricated materials to its site near La Honda (30 miles south of San Francisco) cost $400. The owners experienced no trouble putting the cabin together, despite their unfamiliarity with such projects. They spend about every third weekend at the cabin with their children, and find that they use the cabin the year around. It's only an hour from their home.

Truck had to unload the pieces about a half mile from the cabin site. It took 15 loads with a pickup truck to move it into place. All pieces were in the shipment and they all fit together well

Foundation is ready-made concrete piers set on concrete poured in holes dug down to a solid base. Notice the detail of the overlapping corner pieces. Dog proved to be a good tool carrier

The final stage—as the roof sheathing goes on. On left you can see part of the permanent camp used while cabin was under construction. Pipes are on outside of single wall construction

Finished cabin—except that a fireplace has been added to the end wall on the right. The owners cut the trees to make the clearing. Weed killer used to keep stumps flush with the ground

Pre-cuts and pre-fabs...a browser's guide

A **potpourri** of what manufacturers have to offer in the way of pre-cuts and pre-fabs is shown on these pages. If you are in the "just dreaming" stage of cabin ownership, sit down in your living room some quiet evening and give this section a real going-over (perhaps your spouse will want to look over your shoulder).

The wide and varied selection may surprise you; it would, indeed, were you to see illustrations of all the many other models these manufacturers carry. (Most will send you literature if you request it.) While we have made no reference to price, because of the fluctuating nature of economic conditions, you can get a very rough idea in most instances by figuring $5 per square foot. Some models are considerably less than this; others are more.

The listing on these pages is only a sampling. Look under "Buildings—Pre-Cut and Prefabricated" in the yellow pages of your telephone book to get a complete list of companies in your area.

"PRE-CUT" OR "PRE-FAB"?

There's not much difference between these two types. *Pre-cut* cabins have all the wood cut to size and assembled in a deliverable package. *Pre-fab* cabins also have the wood (or steel) cut to size, and in addition, some or all of the walls are partially assembled at the factory. Pre-fab cabin doors and windows are usually pre-hung, and the panels often weigh as much as 200 pounds, requiring two-man installation.

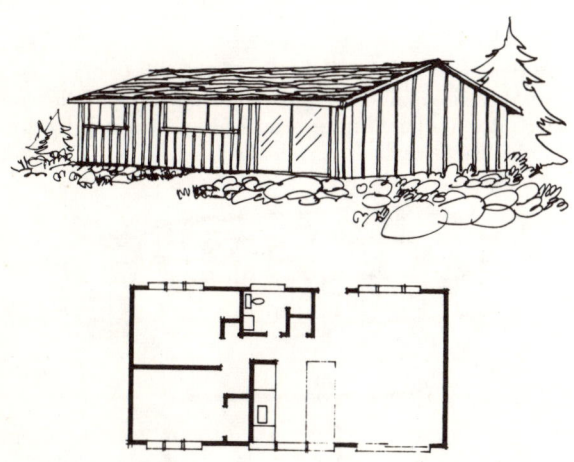

THE BREAKERS　　　　　　　　543 sq. ft.
Loxide Packaged Homes, 9004 South 19th Street, Tacoma, Wash. Twelve models. Vertical red cedar planks form exterior wall. Conventional or exposed-beam ceilings. Extras: deck materials, bunks, cabinets, cedar shakes.

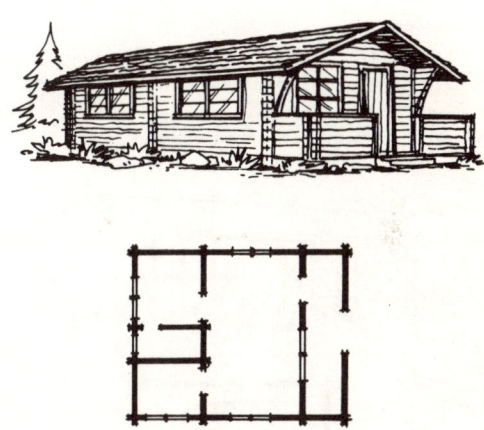

MODEL #336　　　　　　　　336 sq. ft.
Pan-Abode, Box 249, Kennydale, Wash. One-room cabins to large year-round homes. Solid-wall construction. Cedar logs laid horizontally, joined with tongue and groove. Material for porch and interior partitions included.

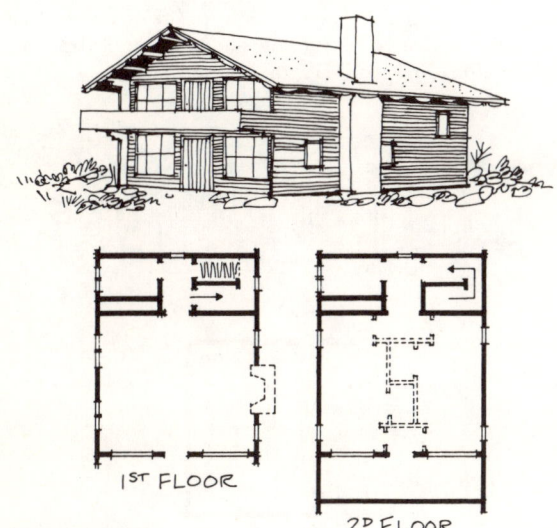

MODEL #500　　　　　　　　500 sq. ft.
Solid Cedar Homes, 2116 Taylor Way, Tacoma, Wash. Many models. Custom construction also. Double tongue and groove cedar wall timbers and ceiling boards kiln dried. Corners, partitions tied together by patented dove-tail joint.

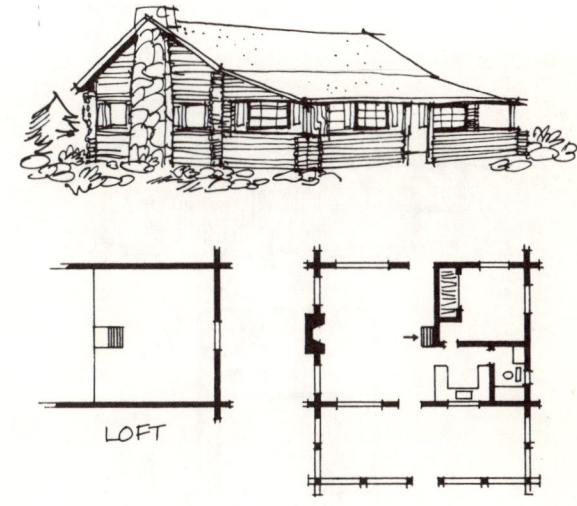

PLAN #112-L　　　　　　　　600 sq. ft.
Air-Lock Log Company, Box 1073, Prescott, Ariz. Fifty-four models. Also custom construction to any plan or design. Pre-cut logs for walls, gables, beams, rafters. Logs treated for protection against moisture and termites.

Pre-cuts and pre-fabs . . .

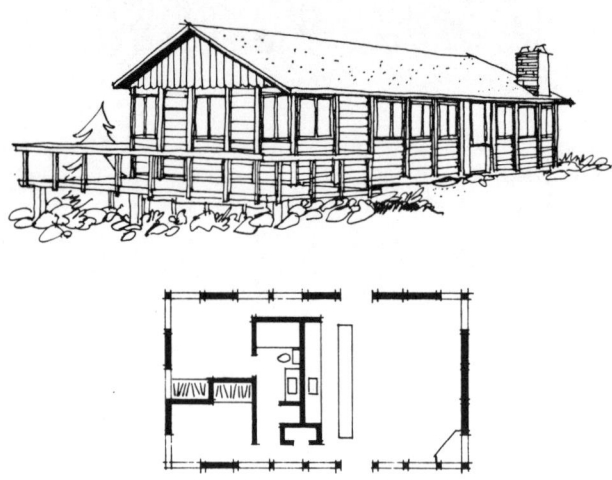

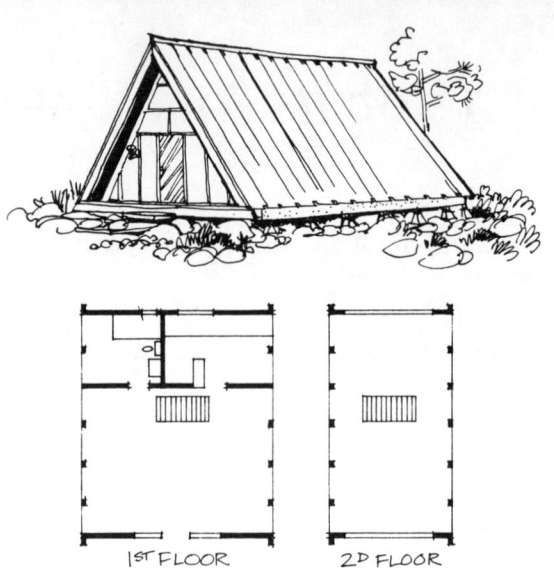

Timberlodge — 720 sq. ft.
J. F. Pritchard and Co. of California, 4625 Roanoke Pkwy., Kansas City, Mo. Redwood log cabins. Three basic module sections allow custom planning. Walls, doors, redwood or aluminum windows, roof sheathing, and rafters supplied.

Holiday Frame — 688 sq. ft.
Pierson Homes, 4100 Broadway, Eureka, Calif. Completely pre-cut, pre-drilled cabin shell. Redwood frame, foundation posts. Interior kit, plumbing kit, or electrical kit optional. Cabin will withstand heavy winds or snow loads.

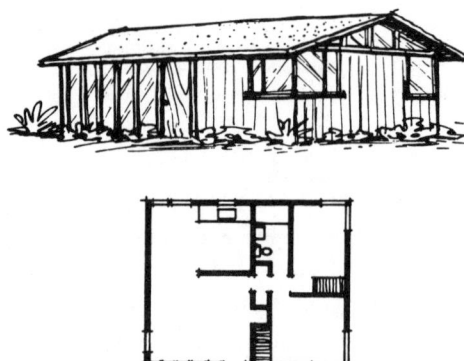

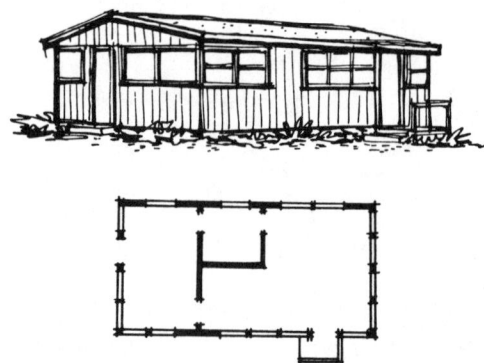

The Napa — 850 sq. ft.
ABC Package Homes, 2616 Springs Road, Vallejo, Calif. Forty models, from 375 square feet. Includes pre-fab walls; interior, exterior materials except rough plumbing, wiring, floors, painting, hot coat roof. Free delivery to 100 miles.

Model #412 — 412 sq. ft.
J-M Construction Co., Box 1340, San Mateo, Calif. Twenty expandable models. Redwood panels on fir frames. Includes engineering advice, construction supervision. Extras: wiring, plumbing kits. Free delivery to 100 miles.

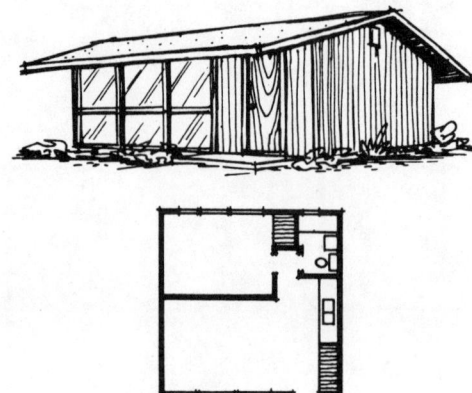

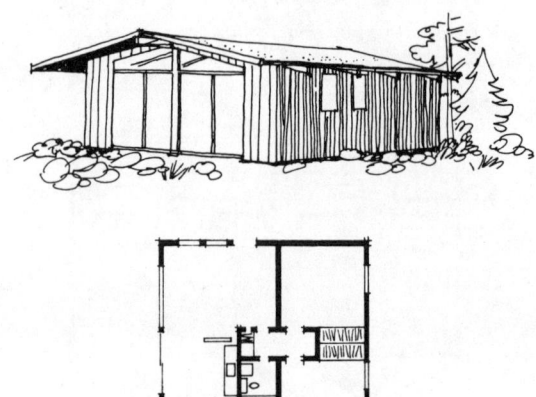

Leisure Time Cottage — 414 sq. ft.
Loctwall Corporation, 16530 Highway 99, Lynnwood, Wash. Twenty-nine models, 400 to 3,200 square feet. Varied floor plans permit buyer to custom design. Cabins supplied as economy package, or plumbing, wiring, heating included.

Prefabricated Model — 700 sq. ft.
Economy Certified Homes, Box 1518, Studio City, Calif. Many models. Fully-equipped, finished homes. Sliding glass doors, beam ceilings, and full bath. All plumbing, wiring, and kitchen cabinets included.

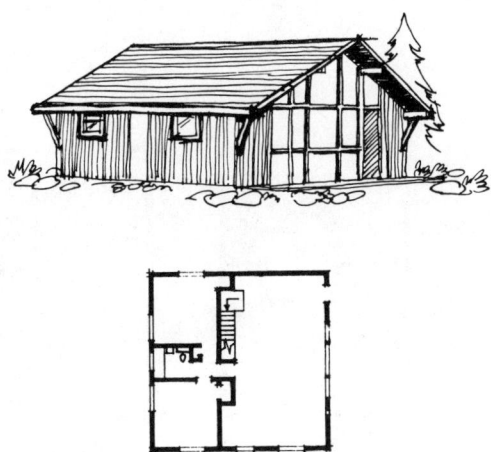

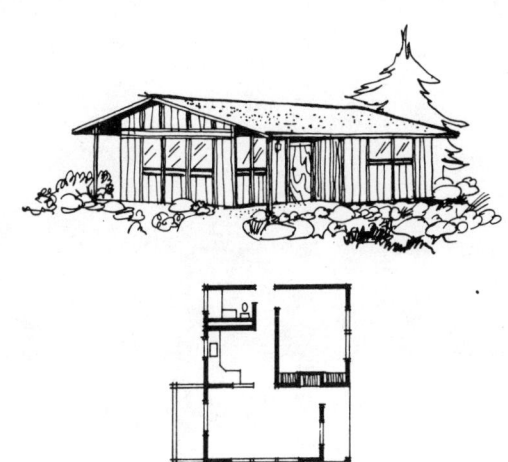

The Tahoe — 765 sq. ft.
Lindal Homes, Box 647, Burbank, Calif. Thirty-two models, from 270 to 1,900 square feet. Solid timber floors, walls, partitions, and roofs. Natural cedar finish inside and out. Experienced help available for construction.

Paradise — 672 sq. ft.
Rockport Redwood Homes, Box 97, Cloverdale, Calif. Nine models, from 240 to 1,296 square feet. Pre-cut interlocking components. Redwood tongue and groove floor decking, floor girders, roof sheathing. Roof beams of Douglas Fir.

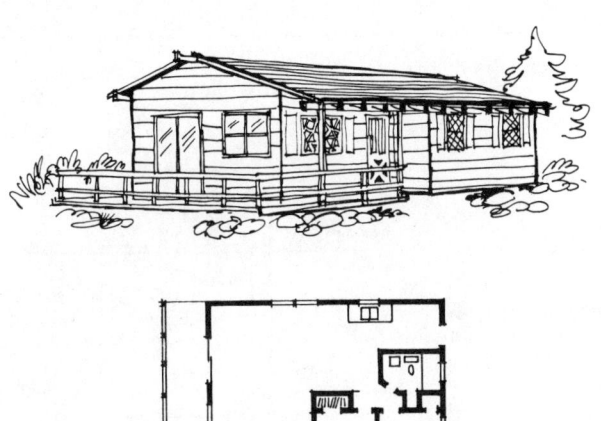

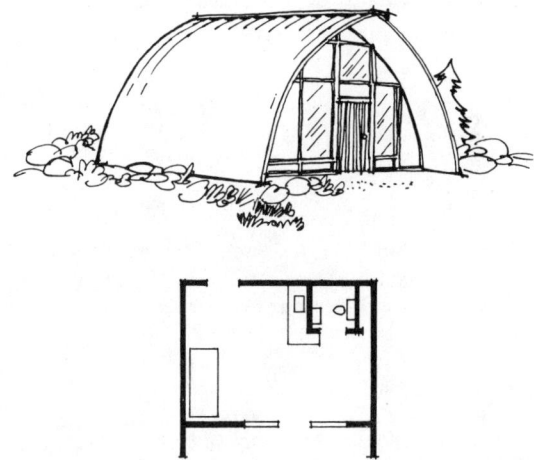

The Alpine — 912 sq. ft.
Jim Walter Homes Corporation, Box 9128, Tampa, Fla. (Offices in California and Nevada.) Five models, with custom construction. Cedar shingle roofing, cedar siding. Floor is combination sub-flooring and underlayment.

The Highland — Square footage optional
Behlen Manufacturing Company, Box 569, Columbus, Nebraska. Packaged system of fluted steel panels which bolt together. Requires no framework. Available in 19-foot widths, any desired length. Factory-insulated with polyurethane foam.

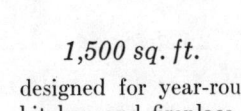

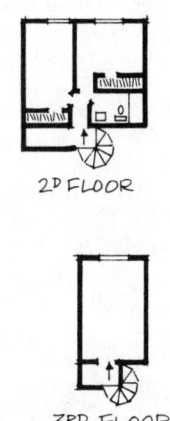

The Sequoia — 1,500 sq. ft.
The Inter-Mountain Company, Box 247, Auburn, Calif. Six models, 764 to 1,500 square feet. All models fully insulated, designed for year-round living. Each plan includes spacious kitchen and fireplace central to living area.

Pre-cuts and pre-fabs...

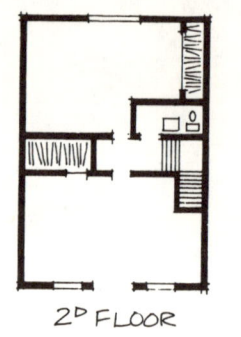
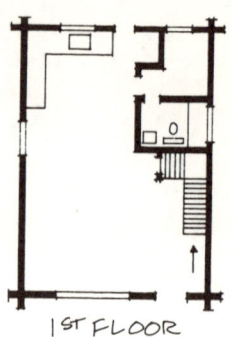

Chalet

Red-E-Cut Log Industries, 327-22nd Street, Oakland, Calif. Twenty-nine models, from cabins to permanent residences.

1,144 sq. ft.

Will pre-cut to plan. Interlocking fir logs have high insulation value. Roof will withstand heavy snow loads.

Pre-cut A-frame cabin

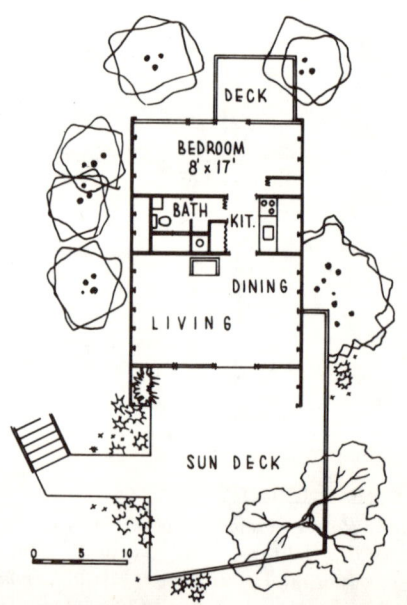

This packaged cabin was designed by Campbell & Wong & Associates, San Francisco architectural firm, to fill the need for a leisure house that could be quickly, easily, and inexpensively assembled. All the necessary structural parts may be taken to the site, ready to erect. The designers have found, by actual test, that the house can be put together in 4 to 7 days by two persons. Only tools required are a hammer, wrench, and a 12-foot ladder.

The cabin is designed in a basic unit (floor plan shows it full sized) that can be expanded by adding 4-foot sections. The basic unit is 18 feet wide and 24 feet in length from the rear wall to the front deck. The cabin is fashioned of a series of 11 equilateral triangles of 2 by 6-inch timbers. These members are fastened at the base with bolts; at the top, they are butted against a 1 by 10-inch ridge rafter that runs the full length of the house. Exterior panels are waterproof marine plywood, secured by 2 by 3-inch battens. The interior flooring of ¾-inch plywood and the deck covering of spaced 2 by 6's are applied to 2 by 6-inch floor joists. The plans show a plywood rear wall, doors, interior partitions, framing for glass.

The basic plan provides room for a living-sleeping-dining area, a galley-size kitchen, a closet, and a bath with linen storage. A sleeping balcony uses space above the kitchen and bath. By expanding the basic leisure house with 4-foot sections, a larger bath or kitchen may be provided. Addition of three 4-foot sections gives ample space for a two-bedroom house or a unit with living room, bath, kitchen, and bedroom plus a sleeping balcony.

Depending on local regulations, foundations may be simple concrete piers, continuous concrete footing, or any other suitable type.

Plans, available for $15 per set, may be obtained by writing to the architects.

MORLEY BAER

Triangular cabin *fits unobtrusively into woodland setting. Note generous use of glass, in the front and also in the roof sections; roof overhang serves as a weather shield*

Working with the A-frame

It's self-bracing, simple construction with minimum joinery. It has disadvantages—but you can minimize most of them

The triangular framework, the shape of the simple tent, was one of the first that man used for shelter. It still makes a good deal of sense. It is a self-bracing form that requires minimum joinery, and lends itself to one-man construction.

There are several examples of A-frames in this book. On the facing page is a pre-cut. Turn the page for a two-story version with excellent do-it-yourself possibilities. There is a magnificent ski cabin on page 60, a rough hewn one-roomer on page 68. The "Desert Cabins" section has other adaptations.

Although the A-frame is probably best suited to a cabin, it works just as well for a garden shelter costing $500 or less and has occasionally been adapted for a full sized house. In its simplest form, both sides and the floor are equal size, and joined at three 60° angles. The equal size simplifies your job of ordering construction materials. An equilateral triangle makes a good compromise between longer sides (extreme roof height) and shorter sides (reduced headroom).

In many ways the A-frame is ideally suited to do-it-yourself construction. Let's look at some of the particulars.

ADVANTAGES OF THE A-FRAME

Simple, easy construction is one of the big advantages.

The framework, the inside skin, and the outside skin are the three basic elements of a building. In an A-frame building, all the framing units can be built on the ground. When they are raised in place and the outside skin (sheathing) is put on, the structural job is done. The sheathing is both roof and wall, and often—as in the cover cabin—serves as the inside finish as well.

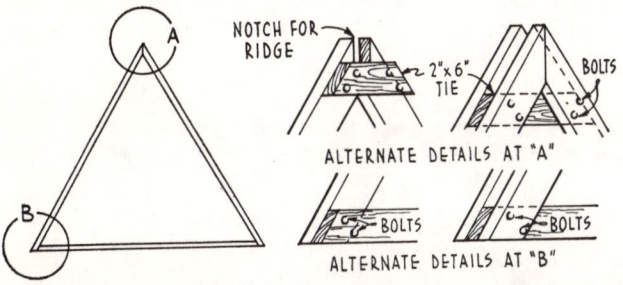

Two ways to join corners of A-frame. One has a single member and ridge pole, the other, double side members, single at bottom

It is especially valuable for a small building. The high roof peak gives a welcome sense of space. When the basic triangle has 16-foot sides, for instance, the roof peak is about 14 feet high. The room seems larger than the usual rectangular box enclosing the same cubic feet of space with an 8-foot ceiling. It is easy to add a deck to an A-frame. This is especially

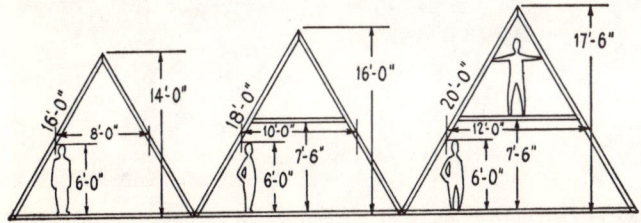

For an idea of the headroom you have in A-frame cabins of different sizes, here are three with figures sketched in to scale

valuable on a steep slope or wherever the surrounding area is not suitable for lounging out-of-doors.

DISADVANTAGES OF THE A-FRAME

One big problem with a triangular framework is the "lost" space in the corners. Furniture and storage units should be placed in corners, and traffic paths kept toward the center. Page 60 shows efficient handling of kitchen-dining area. Ductwork, pipe, and wiring should be in corners.

When the cabin is large enough, you can use part of the top of the triangle for a balcony. Sketches below show two other ways to modify the A-frame to gain more useful space.

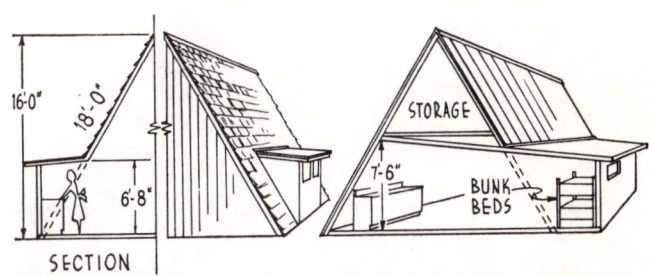

Dormers added to A-frame for more usable floor space. Desert house on right shows how members carry through the opening

For most people the unconventional look of a house or cabin with a triangular frame limits its use to the mountains, beach, or desert where the tent shape is in familiar surroundings. One subdivision builder in California, however, uses an A-frame for one room of a house that is otherwise flat-roofed.

When you cut a window or door opening into the sloping roof, you have to take special pains to prevent leaks. Some flashing details are shown below.

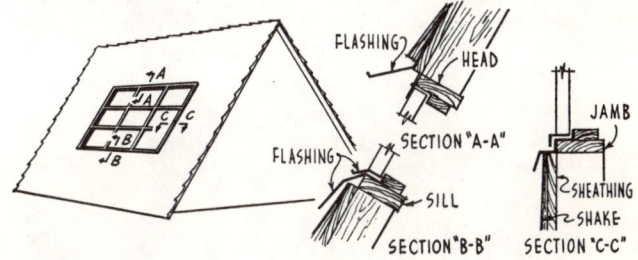

Section drawings of flashing details for waterproofing a window

Doors cut into the slope of the roof have to swing out—against gravity—and are hard to handle. You can solve this problem with a dormer, but the joint between the dormer and the roof must be flashed and sealed very carefully or it may leak. Doors and windows on the vertical end walls are easiest to install, but you usually need some windows on the slope to balance the light from the ends.

A fireplace can be a problem, too. Often the most convenient place for it is at the side of the room under the sloping roof, as in the cabin on page 60. However, this requires a tall outside flue that may be difficult to support. A hood-type fireplace (see pages 35 and 45) can be a good answer. Easiest way to handle the problem is to put the fireplace against a vertical wall, and carry the flue out the peak of the roof.

This A-frame is a double-decker

Front view. *Stairway, with hand rail for safety, leads from lower to upper deck. If this were a mountain cabin in deep snow, doors to second floor could become primary winter entry*

Simplicity and strength combine with ample space and a sweeping view in this two-story A-frame shelter, on Puget Sound near Tacoma, Washington.

The interior (700 square feet) is roomy enough to make this a vacation cabin for weekend fun and entertaining. Decks on both levels nearly double the usable floor space, and generous use of glass both upstairs and down permits an overall effect of spaciousness. Kitchen, bath, living room, and a small corner for bed space are on the first floor; there are two dormitory-type bedrooms upstairs, plus a closet nearly 8 feet wide.

Dr. David Hellyer, who designed the cabin, had economy in mind as well as ease of construction when he limited the foundation to just nine concrete piers. The cabin's shape is formed by two frames consisting of heavy end beams joined at the top by conventional notching and slipping together of 4 by 6's, followed by spiking. Much of the construction work can be done by owners with some basic building knowledge and aptitude, but professional help is advisable in the early stages as well as with wiring and the installation of plumbing and fixtures.

Although designed primarily for vacations and weekends, there is easily enough floor space to qualify this cabin for year-around use. Also, because of its design and its rigid construction, this cabin withstands snow and would make a good mountain shelter. Complete working drawings are available by sending 25 cents to the Douglas Fir Plywood Association, Tacoma 2, Washington.

Siding *on ends of cabin is vertically grooved, ⅝-inch fir plywood panels, unsanded for rustic effect. Crossed beams, top windows can be likened to Indian tepee's poles and vent flaps*

Looking out *into Pickering Passage. Deck extends nearly 9 feet past doorway, gives eyes an easy transition to distant view. Lumber for the 16-foot-wide deck is 2 by 6's, spaced ½-inch*

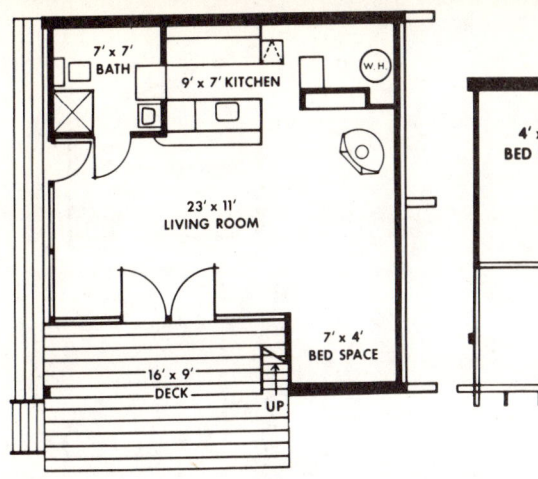
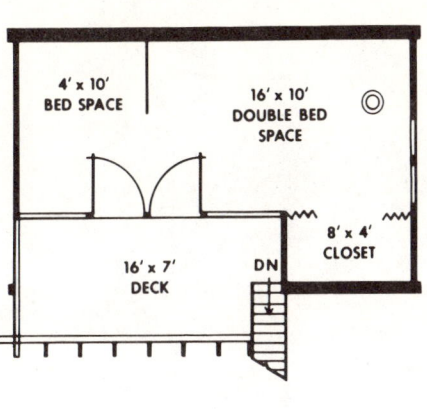
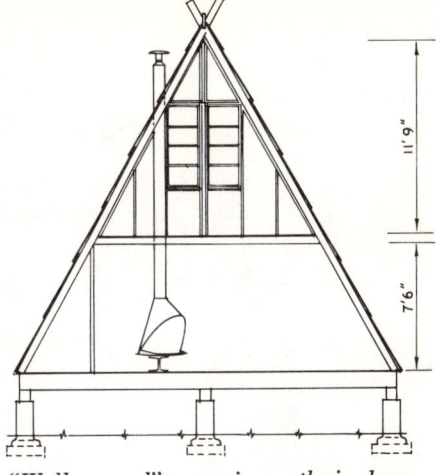

First floor. *Note single-door side entry from narrow deck along left side of cabin*

Second floor. *Deck has ¾-inch plywood panels; weatherproofing agent was applied*

"Walk-around" space is mostly in downstairs area, because of roof's 60° pitch

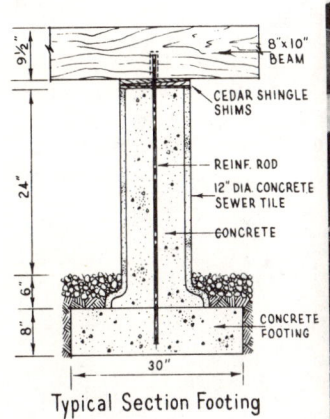

Foundation *has nine concrete piers in rows of three, spaced 12 feet apart. Each row supports an 8 by 10-inch floor beam 28 feet long. It is wise to get professional help for locating the foundation as well as placing it*

Sub-flooring *for first floor consists of ¾-inch fir plywood over 2-by-12 floor joists and 2-by-4 blocking. The second floor joists are all 3 by 8's*

Rear view *shows roof of ⅜-inch exterior type fir plywood panels lapped like giant shingles. After non-drying mastic is applied to joints, they are covered with battens (not shown)*

Hub of activity *on rainy days is metal fireplace, with gravel "beach" contained by aluminum garden edging. Kitchen has counter, string-pull trap door to garbage can beneath cabin*

Cabin's peaked roof has look of hat at a rakish angle. Two-way fireplace can be added on this side (see plan); this would enhance the interior and also provide a handsome brick barbecue for the "outdoor dining room"

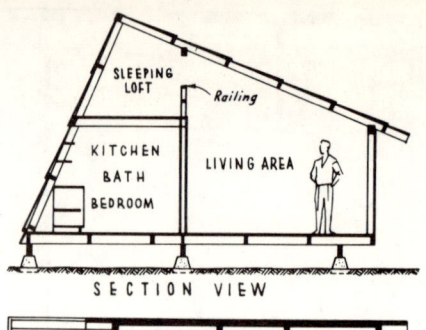
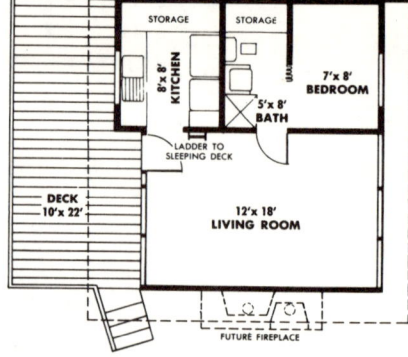

Floor plan can be switched around easily, to suit owner's needs. Bedroom could be used for study, hobby room, workshop

Low-cost leisure... with plenty of room

How many times have you read something like this about a house or cabin: "Bigger than it seems" or "Glass makes it seem larger" or "There's more here than meets the eye"?

It wouldn't be right if we said these things about this Gig Harbor, Washington, cabin and then let it go at that. Because this cabin doesn't merely *seem* spacious; it really *is* spacious—in its fashion.

Architect Walter D. Widmeyer designed this cabin interior for 400 square feet, counting the open half-attic. Outside, the deck adds another 220 square feet across the entire front of the cabin. The 12 by 18-foot living room is bigger than those in many of today's tract homes. The bedroom is ample by cabin standards, and it adjoins the bathroom (via a folding door) to make a suite. The kitchen has walking and turn-around space and plenty of room for opening refrigerator and oven doors. The attic loft serves as an extra sleeping area; some or all of this deck can also be put to good use for storage. One other important space factor: The roof's pitch means there's plenty of overhead room within.

The relatively simple design lends itself quite well to do-it-yourself construction, although amateurs with no previous experience would be better off to hire professional help and stick to the role of "assistant."

The structure rests on a concrete block foundation. Floor joists supporting the plywood floor panels are 2 by 8's; the decking and the wall studs are 2 by 4's; roof joists are 2 by 6's. Wall siding and roof are 3/8-inch fir plywood panels; roof panels are lapped like shingles. Siding is nailed directly to the studs. Joints of the plywood panels which form the roof and siding are covered with battens, sealed with non-hardening mastic for protection against water.

There are many possibilities for future expansion, to front or rear or both. This might include a dining room, another bedroom, bigger living room, or even another deck (in back).

For complete working drawings, send 25 cents to the Douglas Fir Plywood Association, Tacoma, 2, Washington.

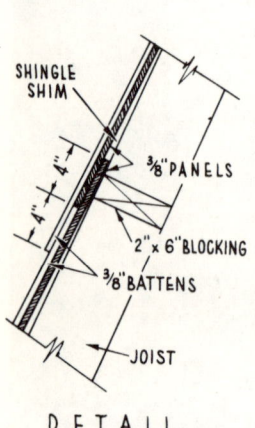

Plywood battens, 3/8-inch by 3 inch, are nailed over joints between panels. Non-drying mastic is first applied to joints and battens' undersides. In detail drawing, note how panel overlaps panel 4 inches, then is overlapped 4 inches by batten

Top left. *Sub-flooring of ¾-inch fir plywood is nailed to floor joists. Structure could also rest on pre-cast concrete piers*

Top right. *Steep pitched roof adapts to heavy snow, resists wind. Roof joists covered with exterior type fir plywood sheathing*

Right. *Successive panels are lapped over lower sections. Simplicity of design provides chance for some off-site fabrication*

Bathroom *has stall shower, no tub. Paneling is a high density overlaid fir plywood, a relatively new plywood panel with a hard surface*

Extra-large windows *brighten the cabin's interior. Kitchen also has window, so that lady of the house can look out to deck and the view beyond. Air from ventilating louvers can be controlled by half-doors. Ladder leads to the sleeping loft*

Interior of the cabin has soft warm colors. Beams and ceiling are weathered old logs and unfinished boards. Walls, built-ins are waxed clear western red cedar; fireplace mantel, plant container, old bear trap used as ornament over mantel are iron. Radio speaker is covered with burlap. Seat covers made of bright orange denim

Windows project from the face of the cabin's stone wall. Cabin is on a rock promontory. View in three directions

Owner-built in timber and river stone

Few pre-cut materials went into the cabin which Architect Alan Liddle of Tacoma designed and built near Mount Rainier.

From a deserted sawmill, he stripped off weather-silvered boards to use on the cabin ceiling. He took rough logs for the beams and split his cedar shakes from other logs on the land. He made the walls of stones from the nearby Nisqually River. For his story on building with stone, see the facing page.

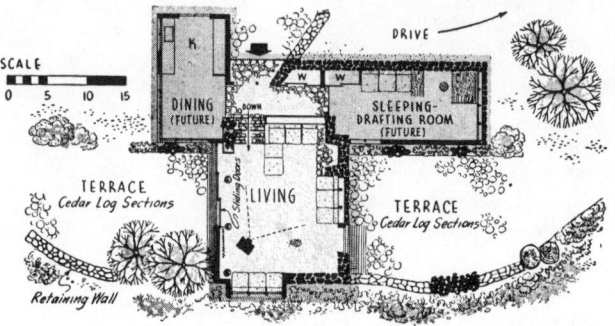

The long window seat can be used for sleeping. Big, square seat shown at right can be moved. Floor is black asphalt tile. High windows, upper left, light seating area around fireplace

Camera location shows angle of interior photograph, upper left

How difficult is stone masonry?

"Building with stone is one of the most satisfying experiences I know," says Architect Alan Liddle, designer and builder of the cabin shown here and on the facing page. "Although I worked most of one entire summer, building the fireplace and entry for my weekend place, it was the pleasantest summer I've ever spent."

There was no trouble finding materials near the building site in Nisqually Valley in Mt. Rainier National Park. The sand and a few of the stones came from nearby Nisqually River. Most of the stone, however, was gathered along the logging roads which had been blasted through rock. Liddle chose only those stones which were the size needed for the wall, using a stone hammer merely for trimming.

WATER SUPPLY

As there was no water on the site, he had to haul that, too. He bought a 60-gallon galvanized can at a surplus store, set it on a bank several feet higher than the mortar box, then ran a garden hose from the can to the mortar box. This siphon system provided the necessary pressure. A cut-off nozzle on the end of the hose made it possible to use the hose full volume for mixing mortar or cut down to a fine spray for wetting the masonry as it set. Five-gallon "jeep" cans, which fit easily into a car, were used to carry water to the big 60-gallon tank.

This was the mortar mix:
- 5 parts river sand
- 1 part Portland cement
- 1/5 part slaked lime (quicklime mixed with water)

MORTAR BOX

For actual mixing, Liddle built a three by eight-foot mortar box of shiplap and divided it in the middle. Mortar was mixed in one end; the lime was slaked in the other. If he were doing the job again, however, he would buy hydrated lime.

"One part" equaled the contents of a 10-quart water bucket. A batch of mortar could be mixed and entirely used up within 2½ hours. With a hoe he mixed the sand, cement, and lime dry; then, continuing to mix, slowly added water. The mortar had reached the proper consistency when it no longer stuck to the hoe. The unused mortar was kept in the shade so that it would not dry out.

Stones were segregated into three piles: (1) Fairly rectangular pieces of a pleasing color, with a flat side which could be exposed on the surface of the wall; (2) pieces of the same size as those in the first pile, but not so attractive; (3) small chips, preferably with sharp edges, to be used to chink between the larger stones in the middle of the wall.

The stones had to be clean to insure a good bond with mortar. If the stone had been lying in the sun, it was immersed in cold water just before it was laid up, to keep the mortar from drying too fast.

Liddle used a five-inch trowel, even though it didn't hold as much mortar as a larger one would, because it allowed more flexibility of hand movements. In preparing a bed for the stone, he found that it paid to be lavish with mortar.

He set each stone in the mortar with care, then gently worked the stone back and forth until it was aligned with the others. New work had to be wet occasionally and protected from the sun to keep it from drying too fast.

The next day he scraped off the excess mortar and raked the joints one-half inch in order to accentuate the stone. After the wall had been brushed with a stiff fiber brush, it was clean except for stains which could be scrubbed off later with a 10 per cent solution of muriatic acid. Exterior walls were left untouched.

VARIETY VS. UNITY

To build a wall which would be esthetically pleasing, each stone was set with its length in a horizontal position, using stones with long, thin proportions. It was necessary to use several different kinds of stones to give the wall variety in colors, textures and shapes.

To give the wall unity and to keep it from looking like a rock collection, Liddle avoided stones of peculiar shapes and colors, and tried not to place too many like stones together. The stone of maximum size was, of course, determined by one man's lifting capacity. He didn't use small stones on the face of the wall, because he didn't want it to look too fussy.

Stone walls *are sound bulwark against winter snow. In addition to its ruggedness, stone's natural insulating properties make cabin warmer in winter, cooler in summer*

The complete cabin will work as a smooth machine with all the convenience and comfort of the all-year house, yet the building goes together in five distinct stages—each of which, complete in itself, can be lived in while the next stage is being built

With this camp cabin you add a part each year

Here is a way you can make "some time" mean "five years from now"

ONCE UPON A TIME building a *cabin* was a much cheaper and easier undertaking than building a *house*. In the back country you could find men with the know-how to put up simple structures with the materials at hand, at a cost less than half that of a town or suburban house.

Under such conditions the Western family took the cabin in stride. Planning a cabin, a summer vacation shack, a place in the country, was a normal and familiar activity. Now, high building costs threaten the whole idea. If the custom is to continue, some way must be found for families to get around the cost barrier.

Let's check through the possible differences between cabin and house to see what they offer in the way of a solution:

1. If the use of the cabin is concentrated in the summer months, costs of providing space for sleeping and entertaining can be held to the minimum.

2. Skilled workmanship is not necessary in the cabin. Rough construction is in tune with cabin living.

3. Many steps in cabin building are in the capacity range of the amateur builder.

4. More than a house, the cabin lends itself to piecemeal building — a stage-by-stage development with livability at every stage.

To exploit the differences and advantages in cabin use and construction we pooled our experiences with those of Architect George T. Rockrise of San Francisco and took on this problem:

Our hypothetical family (two teen-age boys) have bought three acres of woodland. They hope to build a cabin-lodge. A cost estimate on their rough plans has just come in and they find that financing is not to be had. What to do? Shall they build a permanent camp this summer? Or try to build a cabin on a pay-as-you-go basis?

Here are the answers Architect Rockrise gave them:

1. Let's set up a five-year building program aimed at a cabin which we will draw up in complete detail now.

2. Each of five stages of development will be complete in itself. If at the end of the second year you wish to postpone the next step for a year or more, you will have a usable and livable summer unit.

3. Each yearly addition will be made without remodeling or re-doing any previous work.

4. The cabin design will not call for special construction skills. Building methods will be standard and universally understood.

5. All materials—windows, doors, glass, kitchen and bathroom equipment—will be generally available in economical stock sizes.

6. Expenditure will be budgeted in equal yearly payments.

Interior at the final stage—with cabin finally complete. Balcony which serves as entrance hall to the bedrooms also diminishes the height of the inside wall to the more intimate scale of the fireplace and the hearth. Room is generous 15 by 27 feet.

FIRST STAGE

Kitchen comes first for many reasons—economies in food, time saved in preparing food for hungry and busy builders. Kitchen is large enough for a storm refuge or for family gatherings. It serves as a storage room for camping gear. Kitchen plus fireplace plus canvas adds up to a lot of convenience.

If you favor the half camp, half cabin idea, you may stop your building here, or after any succeeding stage.

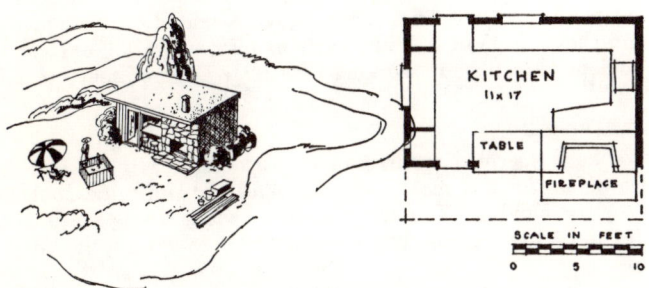

1. In the first year the cabin is little more than a camp with a de luxe family-size kitchen. However, a smart use of canvas roofing extending from the kitchen with canvas walls at one or two sides would give adequate living space in summer months

SECOND STAGE

With the addition of a water system and a bathroom the camp becomes civilized. In this stage of development the problems of water supply and storage, water heating, septic tank, and electrical power system must be solved.

Hot water coils in the fireplace give you one source of hot water. If you have a better than average supply of sunlight look into solar heating as another source.

The bath is compartmented to handle three people at a time. It is wise in this second stage to complete a concrete slab foundation that will give you a smooth dry area in front of the fireplace, and add to the livability of that area.

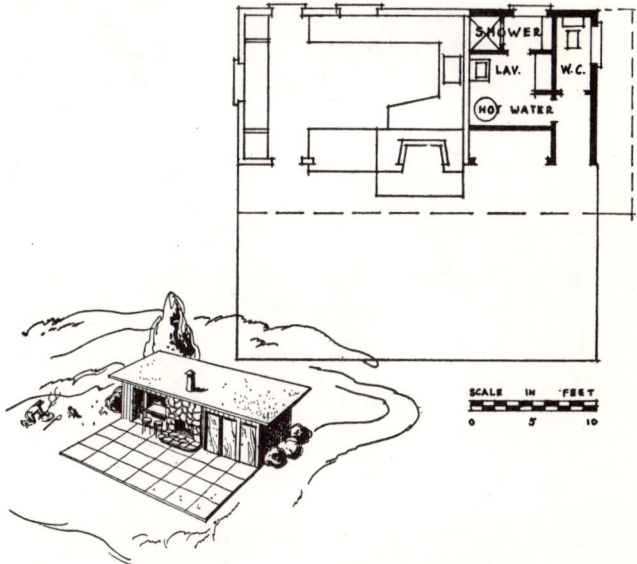

2. With a bathroom added to the kitchen, the utility core of the cabin is complete. The water, heating, and lighting systems don't show on the plan, but they are a large part of construction at this stage. Concrete slab is base for additional shelters

THIRD STAGE

The progress plan of the building was designed to allow either the living room or the bedrooms to come first. Which should

51

be built in this stage is purely a family preference. (See below for details in construction.)

If you do choose to build the living room first, the wall between living and sleeping rooms will be your outside wall until those rooms are built. Chimney flue will be left exposed.

FIFTH STAGE
Whether the final additions of car port and storage space are necessary will depend upon your use of the cabin.

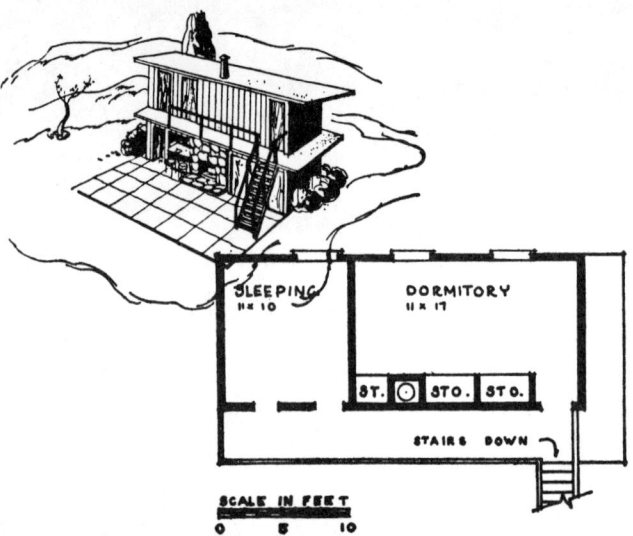

3. You will note that two doors lead into the sleeping room shown at left above. The one farthest left is for access from bedroom to a future closet. This will be built on end of balcony when you go into the fourth stage of construction, the living room

FOURTH STAGE
The overhang of the first kitchen unit now serves as a balcony hallway to the bedrooms. Amount and size of glass would depend on the maximum size you can handle. Crystal sheet will be satisfactory in the 6-foot 6-inch spaces indicated in plan. However, wood members can be adjusted to provide for smaller glass units.

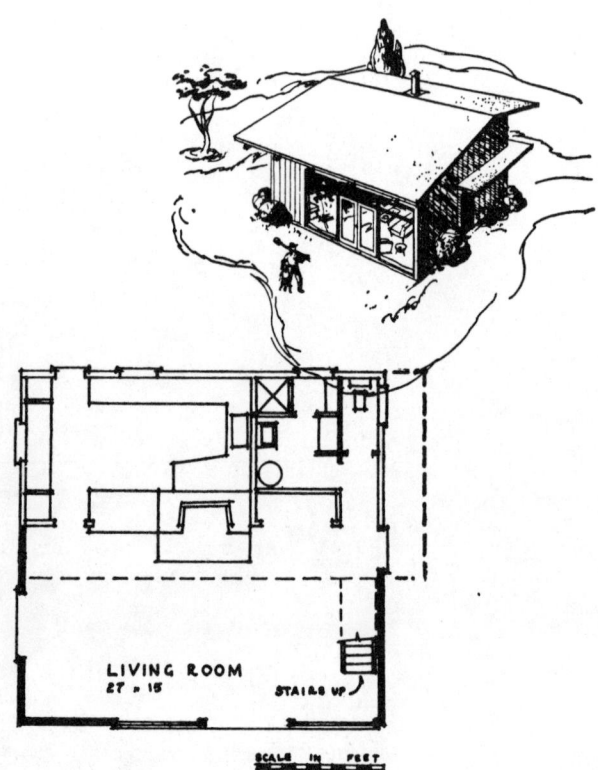

4. After the completion of this fourth stage, all the interior living space is finished. This much cabin could give you most of the comforts of home. The site, and your cabin living habits, will determine whether or not outdoor additions will be desirable

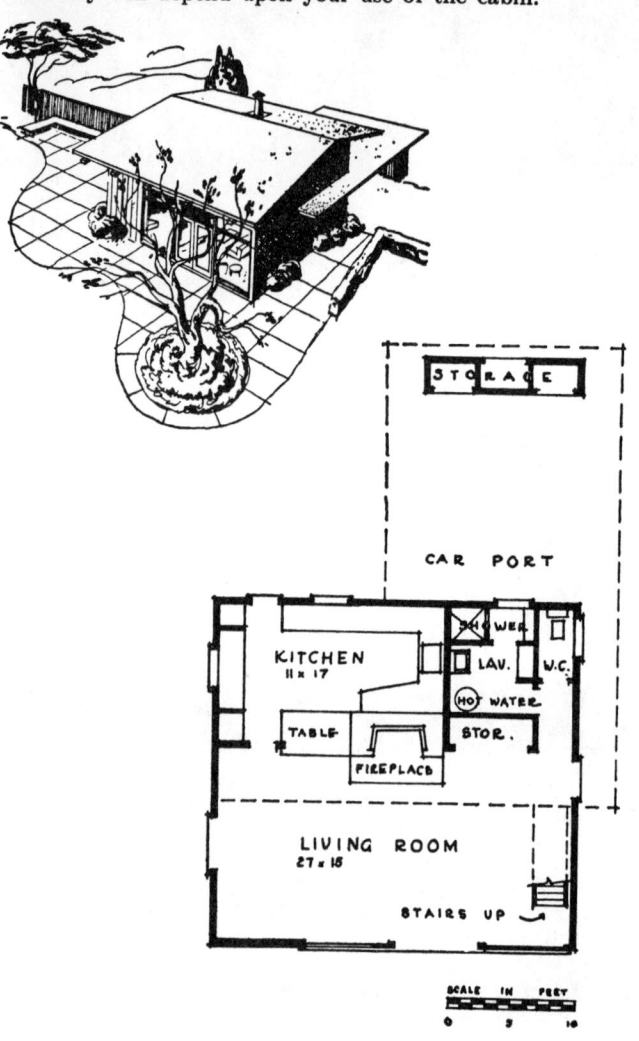

5. Carport and storage make fifth addition. Terrace is optional

CONCRETE SLAB
If the site is fairly level and transportation not too expensive, a concrete slab simplifies construction. A rented concrete mixer and the division of slab into sections by headers will overcome obvious objections in working with large areas of concrete.

FIREPLACE
We have specified a patented fireplace form with circulating warm air for the reason that it takes the difficulties out of fireplace building. You aren't likely to make a mistake in the design of the working parts of the fireplace with such a unit.

CANVAS
Throughout the first stages of construction, canvas is overhead shelter. It will convert large areas into usable space for sleeping quarters. Even entertaining large groups of guests need not be too much of a problem. (Give priority for working skills.)

SIDING AND ROOF
Your selection here will depend on availability of materials. Rough 1-inch boards from the ever-present small sawmill will serve well if used with battens or weatherproofing. Nail building paper directly on the studs. There are many grades of building paper, some with a metal finish on one side, which are not unattractive left exposed. If more insulation is desirable, finish later with boards, plywood, or composition panels.

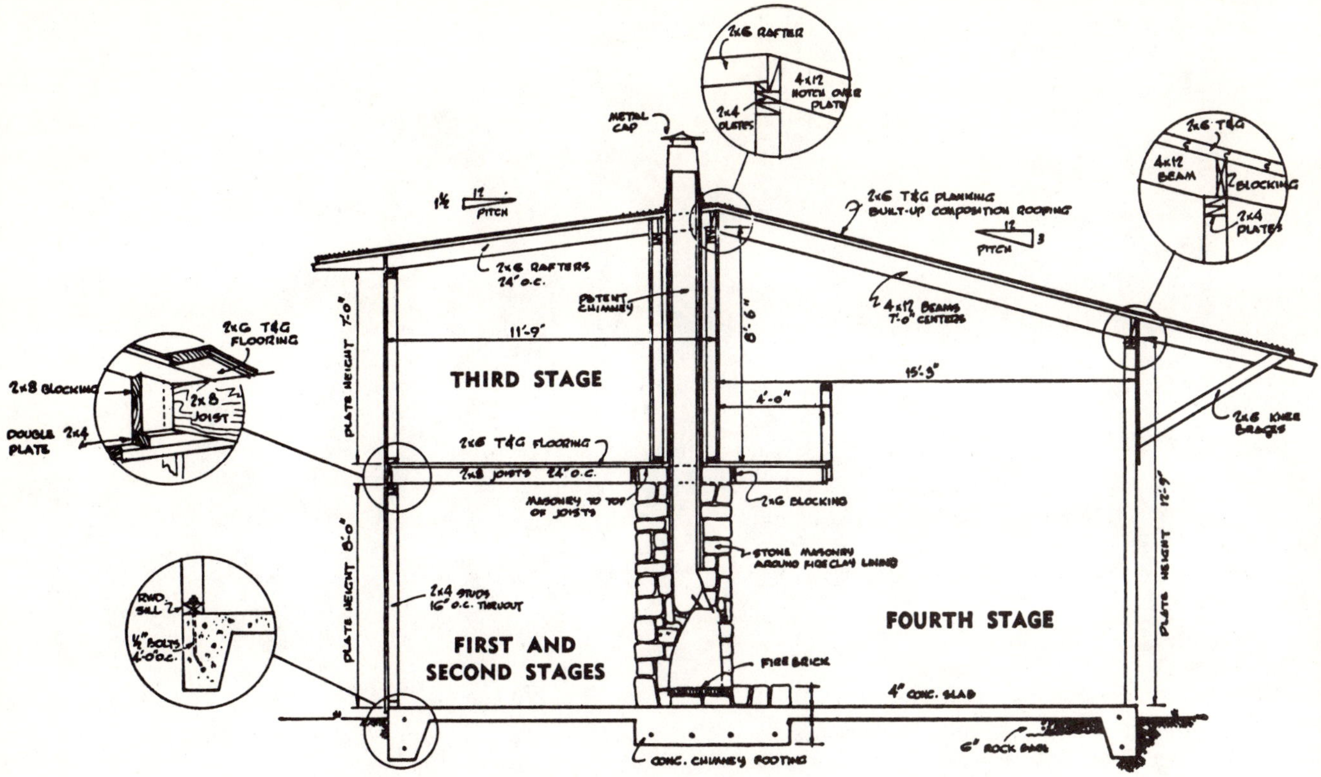

Cross-section, sliced through the fireplace from front to back

HOW THE FRAME IS PUT TOGETHER

These working diagrams are designed for the amateur carpenter who plans to put up his cabin himself. With few exceptions, the first three stages could be handled by one man working alone. (A power saw would be highly desirable.) But in the fourth stage, extra hands will be needed for 4 by 12-inch beams.

In the first and second stages, 2 by 6-inch tongue-and-groove planking serves as the roof. Rolled roofing laid on top will be adequate for two or three years. Then when you add the bedrooms, just take up the roofing and this planking is your floor. Tongue-and-groove gives such strong bracing that there is no need to apply it on the diagonal.

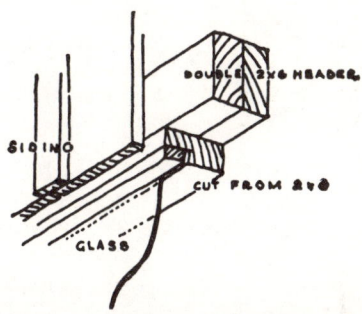

How the windows are framed, detail of the top. Cut out corner of 2 by 4 to receive the glass. Nailed strip holds in place

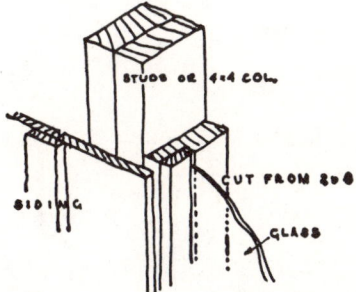

Same notch-and-strip detail for side of window frame. Double stud or 4 by 4 alongside. The siding is board and batten

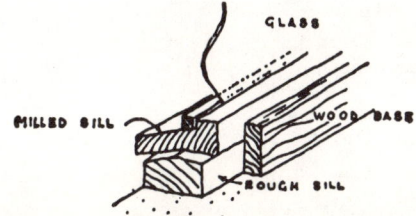

Same detail at the bottom of window except that in place of 2 by 4 you use stock mill piece, slanted to let water run off

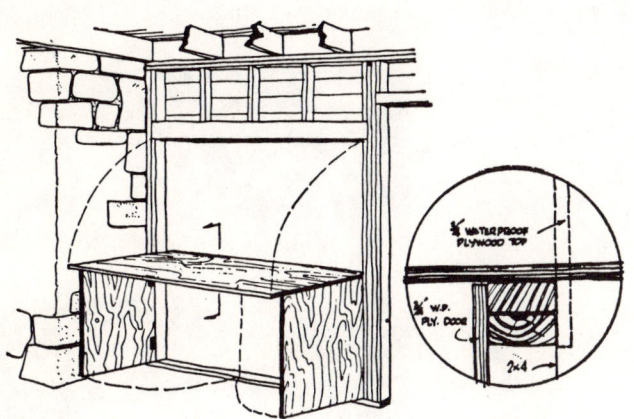

This table top and its gate legs should be made of waterproof plywood. Until you complete the fifth stage of the cabin, they are exposed to the weather both when open for table use and when the kitchen and cabin are closed up for winter. In all stages it can serve either as pass-through or as dining table

Wooded valleys, pine covered hills and sky above San Bernardino mountains are three walls of this cabin. Ceiling follows pitched roof and glass disappears into ceiling without interruption. The chimney is set at an angle to keep snow from piling up behind it

Glass walls in a mountain cabin?

BEFORE YOU tell yourself 10 reasons why this mountain cabin is the most impractical thing you have ever seen, know these facts about it.

It was built as a guest house for a larger all-year home. The owners lived in it with great comfort while they waited for the completion of their larger house, located just up the slope overlooking the dam at Lake Arrowhead, California.

How does it perform?

The architect, Lucille Bryant Raport, likes the way the glass disappears into the roof, opening even the peak of the cabin to trees and sky.

The structural engineer, Gordon de Swarte, likes the honest open use of the steel tie rods which serve both as curtain rods and as the lower chord of the roof truss.

The photographer, Julius Shulman, likes the careful placement of the house for sun and view, the handling of the overhanging eaves so that sun is controlled without destroying the view. His photograph, top right next page, shows this.

The owners enjoy the free feeling of the mountains. They like the radiant heat from the warm floor panel and the ease of housekeeping regardless of number of guests entertained.

How does it perform in the snow? Aren't the glass walls cold? Won't glass be broken by tree limbs in storms? How about snow against glass? What about vandals?

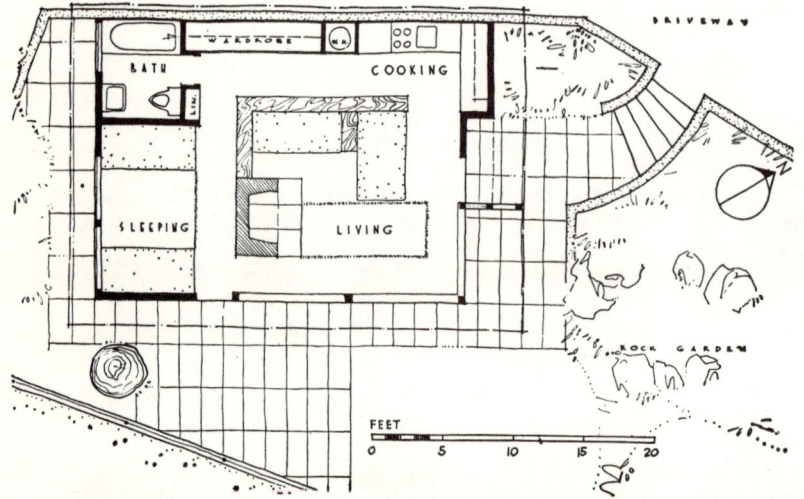

Overhanging eaves serve as sun visor. They project far enough to prevent glare at normal standing height inside and still permit a full view of mountains in distance

Glass in end walls extends to ceiling ridge. Glass panel over door opens for ventilation

The glass traps the heat of the winter sun and keeps the cabin warm regardless of outside temperatures. At night and when there is no sun, drawn curtains help intercept loss of heat to cold glass.

Floor warmed by hot water, in wrought iron pipes in concrete slab, and heat-circulating fireplace are more than sufficient for the coldest days.

To protect glass from heavy drifts of snow, portable shutters can be hooked over the walls. So far these have not been needed, for when the snow slides off the roof it is carried by its own weight out and away from the house.

The shutters also protect the glass from tree limbs or from possible damage by vandals whenever the house may be unoccupied for any length of time.

If you forget cabin requirements for a moment and consider the application of the design to a small house in the country, several features are of especial interest.

The arrangement of space is flexible. One room is not unusual in a vacation house. But flexible arrangement in this 525 square foot area is not obtained in the usual manner by scattering beds, tables, and kitchen equipment along the walls of the room.

Notice how the fireplace and built-in counter give definite control of living, utility and sleeping space without lessening the spaciousness of the room.

The bedroom behind the fireplace is private, separated from the living quarters by curtains.

Interior was treated as one large room but curtains can be drawn for complete division between the sleeping and living quarters or to create three separate areas

Kitchen equipment, including hot water heater, washing machine, dishwasher, sink with automatic garbage disposal unit, and refrigerator, is lined up against the rear concrete wall of the house. The rear wall also stands as a retaining wall against the slope of the site.

To provide privacy when there are several guests, curtains are drawn between different sections.

All plumbing vents have been taken up between roof rafters to the ridge. They are concealed by horizontal louvers running the length of the roof.

Low counter separates living and kitchen areas. Double beds slide under from living room side, are couches during the day

Fireplace is buff-colored brick set around heat-circulating form. Interior walls are combed plywood; the ceilings are fiberboard

Glass-walled *living room juts out toward Squaw Creek, exposing view on three sides. Although cabin is square, roof gables (one in each corner) provide sharp textural pattern, unusual shape. Cedar board and batten exterior construction. Tongue-and-groove cedar used on inside walls; foundation walls are concrete block*

Mountain cabin by a rushing creek

Nestled in a mountain valley, with a rushing creek at its feet, this year-around vacation house is surrounded by exceptional natural beauty. Owner-Architect George Rockrise has made certain that seeing and enjoying the rugged scenery is easy—from anywhere within. Generous use of glass is evident in the photographs. And even the roof's gables, in each of the four corners, point to a view.

Working with builder Lee Van Wetter of Squaw Valley, California, architect Rockrise shaved costs to gain a pay-back in space. The results were highly successful; this is a *spacious* cabin. Its 1800 square feet can "swallow up" a cabinful of guests and not bulge at the seams. (The unfinished basement offers a future additional 600 square feet.) The two main floor bedrooms have their own hall and door for quiet and privacy; upstairs there are two bedrooms, placed at the east and west corners to catch views of valley, mountains, and ski slopes. Two bathrooms (one per floor) are compartmented for multiple use. A study area on the balcony forms the fireplace alcove below, and looks out over the living room to the pine trees and the stream outside.

Despite its size this is a house for fun, comfort, and easy upkeep. Both floors have perimeter heating. Electricity is used for cooking, and an oil heater provides hot water. The large deck, just off the kitchen and dining area, is a sunny activity center in summer.

Deck *on southeastern side of cabin forms sunny lounging area during summer months, children's playground in winter. All-season entry to right; stairs to beach now covered with snow*

View from southwest *shows basement under south corner of living room. Built to fit creek bank, basement is accessible through trapdoor in living room, contains firewood, workshop*

Above: *Balcony stretches diagonally across living room. Slats in railing could be closer together for maximum safety of small toddlers. At far end of the room, kitchen's serving counter seats four.* **Right:** *View from balcony looks out over observer below who watches from "best seat in the house"*

Spaciousness *of cabin can be seen in plan at right. Four bedrooms are placed for maximum quiet and privacy. All corners of the cabin, both upstairs and down, have windows for view. Narrow catwalk at base of floor-to-ceiling glass makes it possible to wash windows on the outside. Dotted lines show the roof's generous overhang*

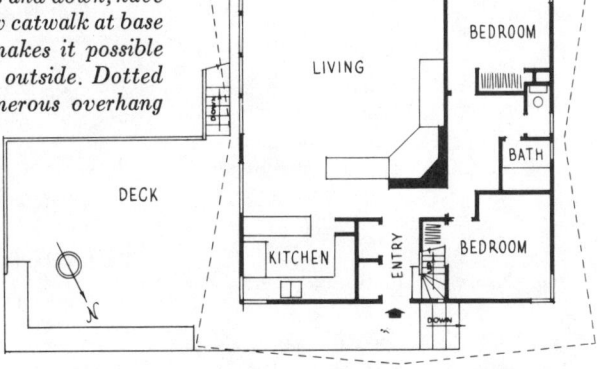
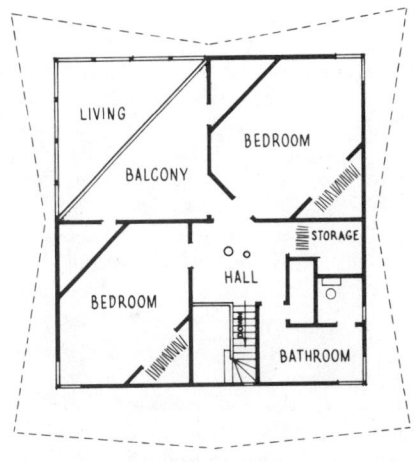

First Floor Plan   Second Floor Plan

Upstairs bedrooms *are nearly identical, with ample closet space and floor space. Corner windows give excellent view, admit light from two directions. None of bedrooms are side-by-side*

Fireplace *with raised hearth is in north corner of living room, in low-ceilinged alcove beneath balcony-study area. Built-in settees on both sides can double as additional sleeping space*

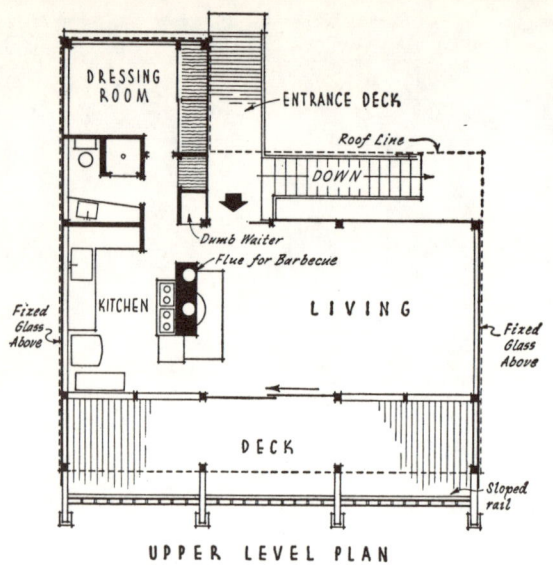

Upper floor has no bedrooms—sleeping in living area, on deck

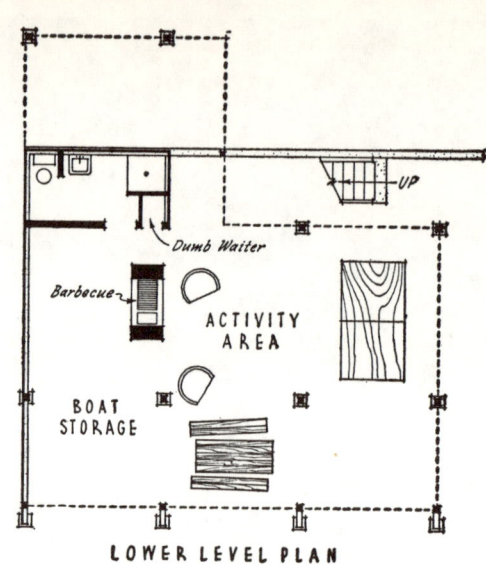

Lower level, open on three sides, is cool living area in summer

Unusual...and fun:

Lake cabin with a "floating roof"

A house can be exciting just because it is built to be a vacation house. It can be exciting because it is built on a lake shore, or because it is built on a wooded hill. It can be exciting because of the way it encloses space, or because of an inspired roofline. This vacation house, designed by Architect Francis Joseph McCarthy, derives its marvelous quality from a combination of all these things.

When the owners first began to consider the possibility of constructing a weekend and vacation house or cabin on their lot at Clear Lake, California, they carefully thought out the kind of living they wanted from it. They decided that it should definitely be a cabin. Although most of the neighboring houses are almost suburban in character, they wanted a place

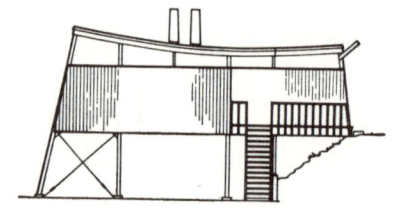

Curve of roof shows in side view sketch

that would not be like the one they left at home. They wanted a cabin that would not only reach out to embrace the trees, the sky, and the lake at its feet, but also one that would stimulate a holiday mood.

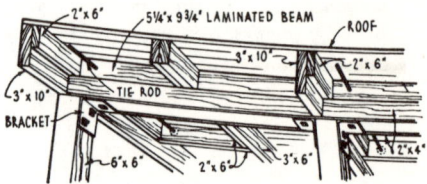

Roof detail. Glue-laminated beams used

And that is just what they got. If they were somewhat taken aback at first by the thought of a roof that floated like a

ERNEST BRAUN

Relation of deck to main living room is shown here. Off-the-vertical posts suggest tent guys to hold roof down, not up

Shaded open space below—barbecue, picnic and table tennis tables, storage space, room for boat. Rear stair to main entry

canvas canopy and a structure that sloped from front to rear, they soon got into the spirit of the building the architect proposed. They quickly realized that, in addition to designing a sound building, an equally important function of the architect is to compose space, not only to fit a family's present way of living but to be a background for new experience in living.

The plan of this cabin is simple, as befits cabin living. The walls are seven-foot privacy screens on three sides and glass on the fourth, facing the lake. Glass fills in the gap between the seven-foot walls and the roof, so that you see the trees and sky all around and the full, gay effect of the roof's upthrust curve.

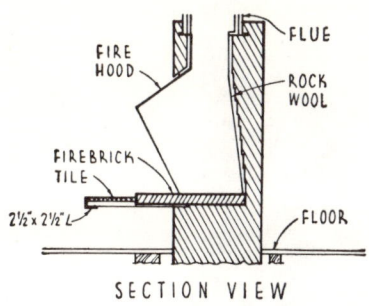

Sketch shows reinforced concrete hearth

Brick fireplace built around patent form has raised concrete hearth for seating. Flue at right comes from barbecue below

Kitchen has refrigerator, freezer, built-in range and oven. Transoms for ventilation above fixed glass. Owner did the paneling, cabinetry, some wiring; laid floor

Twin chimney flues above fireplace act as space divider between the kitchen and main living-dining area on other side

Side view shows how much privacy is afforded by walls up to eye level, also reveals full impact of the unique structural form. Trees left on site provide extra shelter

Downhill view shows open lower level area, sloping framing members and deck rail

Here you see *how the floor and decks make a platform. This was put up first—on posts and piers. It was then used for a staging on which the framing members were built and raised*

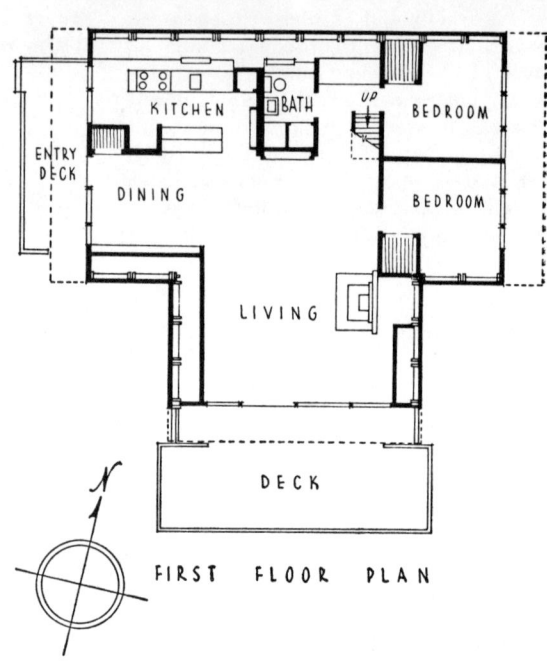

FIRST FLOOR PLAN

High in the snow country...a triangular

Kitchen and dining room *make efficient use of triangle's awkward corners. Appliances are against sloping wall on the right. In dining area, far left, a built-in seat fills this space. Ductwork, plumbing, and the wiring runs are in the bottom corners*

"**A wonderful cabin**" is what the owners call it. It fits them like a good ski boot. They chose the triangular form for two reasons:

One was the magnificent cabin site they found on the north slope of Squaw Valley in the Sierra Nevada near Lake Tahoe. The shape makes excellent sense where snow loads are heavy.

The second reason for the A-frame choice was cost. Architect George Rockrise knew from the start it had to be a two-story building, to hold the required four bedrooms and two baths, and to keep costs in line. Space costs you less when one roof and foundation serve two floors. Heating is more efficient, too.

A-FRAME CONSTRUCTION PROBLEMS

Here is how the architect and the builder met the special problems posed by A-frame construction:

Awkward, sharp bottom corners. Notice in the plan and photographs how these spaces are used for appliances, for sleeping, for storage units, with foot traffic confined to areas with adequate headroom.

Sloping windows. Because of the leak problem, these require more careful handling than vertical glass. Here there's minimum glass on the slope. The T-shaped plan and

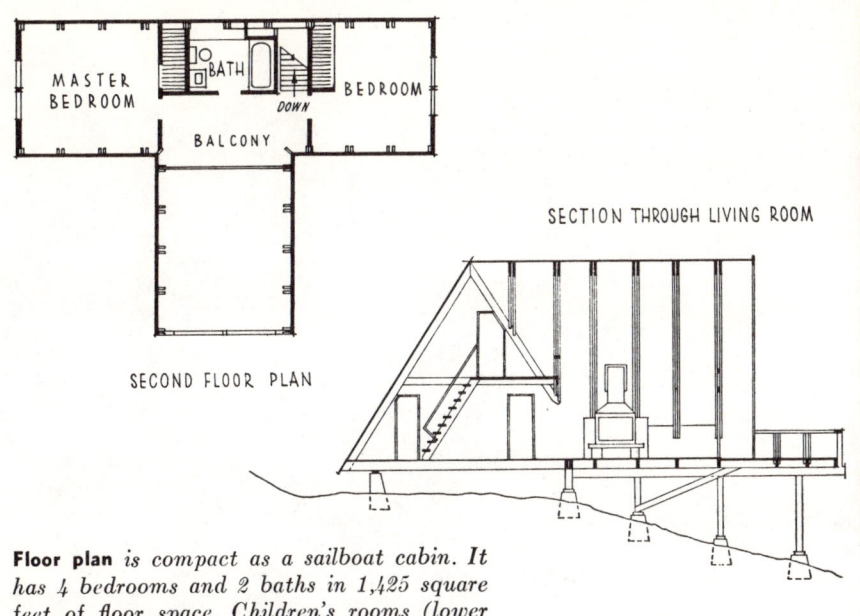

Floor plan is compact as a sailboat cabin. It has 4 bedrooms and 2 baths in 1,425 square feet of floor space. Children's rooms (lower level) have bunk beds and cot. House sleeps 10 in beds, and 2 in sleeping bags on balcony

Inclined, paired, 3 by 8 fir beams are mitered and bolted to a 4 by 12 tie piece at roof peak. At the base these beams straddle the 4 by 12 floor joists. The roof decking is 2 by 6 T&G fir

ERNEST BRAUN

ski cabin

vertical end walls of glass provide cross light.

Engineering the A-frame itself. Since he was dealing with an unusual shape, with unfamiliar stress problems, the architect called for professional help with the structural engineering. Builders, too, have had little experience with this kind of construction. Here, the builder actually made a scale model of the cabin for close study of joinery and construction problems.

Making real savings. The builder also made a thorough study of costs, before the architect started working drawings. However, potential economy of labor and materials in A-frame construction may never be achieved unless the building goes up simply and quickly. The builder and architect together worked out a way to use the foundation as a staging platform for building and erecting heavy A-frames.

The final results, as a dwelling for people to enjoy, can be summed up in the words of the owners: " . . . your eye follows up the beams to the tall roof peak, and out across the valley. . . . The house changes mood with the weather, and as you move from under low ceilings to the chapel-like living room. . . . It's fun to sneak up on the balcony and watch the kids playing quietly in 'their' corner between the fireplace and window."

From the deck the cabin interior looks like this. The top of the T-shaped plan—see sketch above—has a full second story. The metal fireplace, designed by the architect, adds radiant heat. Kitchen-dining room is on left. Bedrooms on right

Rough-timbered, roomy

IT ISN'T THE SIZE of this cabin on the redwood coast near San Francisco, or the number of rooms which make it work so well for a growing family (there are five children) and their many friends. It's the plan.

Essentially, the cabin is all only one room—with bath and dressing off at one end. But generous overhangs give more than three times the space under roof as there is in the enclosed core, offering a surplus of extra sheltered sleeping space.

Lumber costs were cut at least half by buying from a nearby mill which supplied 8 by 8's, 6 by 6's for framing, rough sawn two-inch-thick stock, random widths —24 to 39 inches—for roof and sides.

Builder and owner is Architect Robert Ratcliff of Berkeley.

The six tall hinged shutters, shown open here like louvers, fold shut across floor-to-ceiling windows to lock cabin. Heavy diagonal timbers outside eliminated any need for internal diagonal bracing

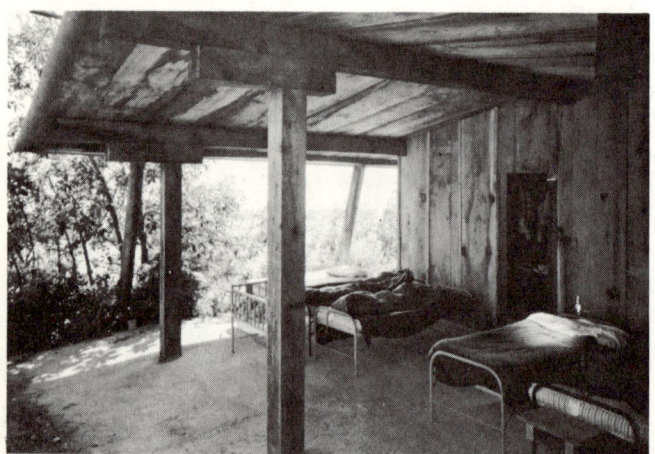

Deep overhang at one end of cabin makes sleeping space. Slab slopes to ground beyond roof. Door leads to dressing room

One end of big room divided by counter, with cooking on right, dining on left. Fireplace at far end has skylight above it

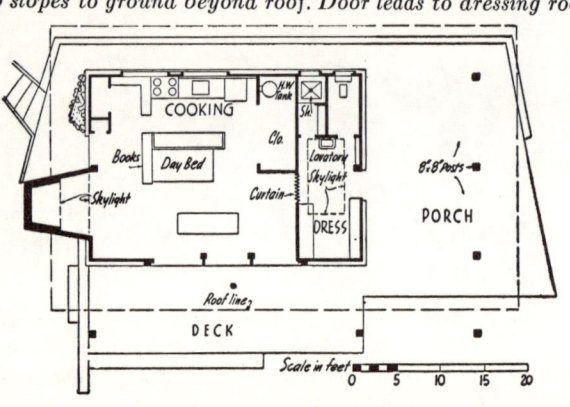

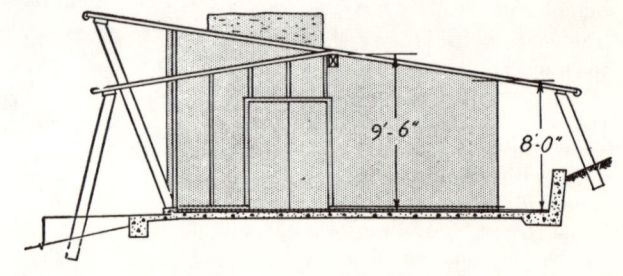

End elevation shows bracing, and how roof juts up to open side. Cabin has about 2,000 square feet under roof, 600 enclosed

Beds swing out to be made. Linen is stored in corner locker. Circle around fireplace is volcanic stone. Back and sides, firebrick. Wrought iron hood finished with stove black reflects heat

The wall at right, hung on barn hardware, slides over opening, closing cabin with minimum of effort. Overhang gives shade from noon sun. Thin rail and posts don't block view of lake

Cabin with a view

THIS CABIN goes so far beyond merely carving shelter from the wilderness that it makes us wonder how it was created.

It started when the owners camped on every part of their site, learning it first-hand, so they could save the best spot instead of building on top of it.

Then, the designers asked the owners what they wanted of California's High Sierra, and the answer was: simply to be in it. So every view which could be seen from the cabin was worked out in the planning.

The sun was treated as both friend and enemy. Morning eastern sun may come in through an open wall to warm the cabin and wake sleepers, but by noon it is kept in its place by the deck's deep overhang.

There was no strain to seek unusual materials which would be used for their sake alone.

The result is a cabin which fits the owners as well as it fits its site. The design was by Ruth Gerth and George Kosmak.

Storage under the deck is for a boat. Timbers were made extra heavy scale to support possible 18-foot snow load, or 300 pounds per square foot. The wall which is shown open can be closed to the wind by a sliding glass panel

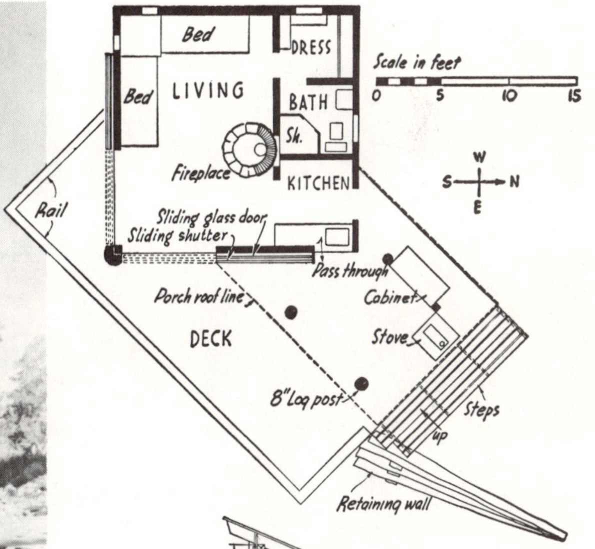

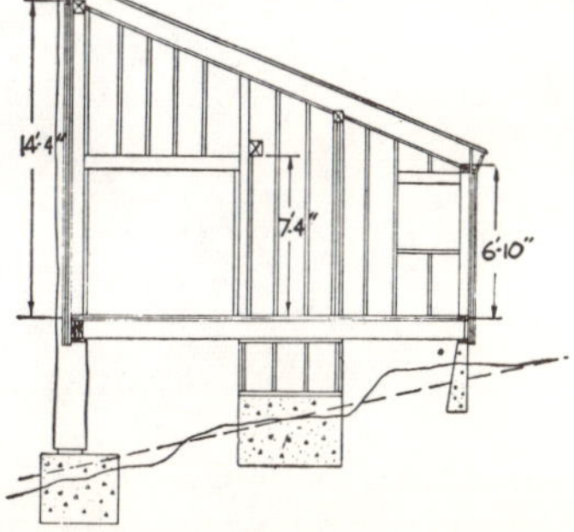

Elevation shows foundation set on slope

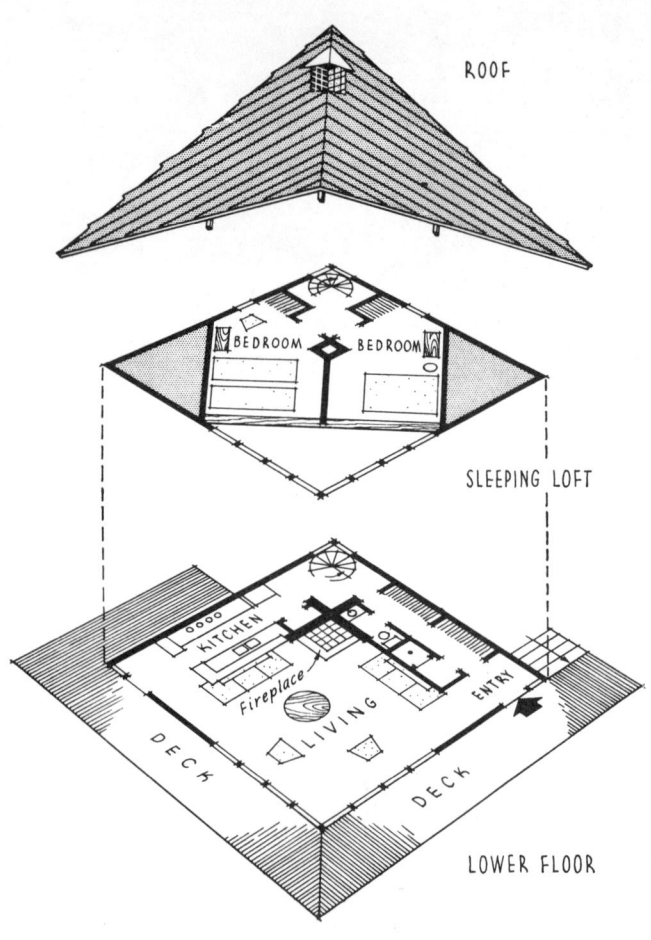

Summer. *Front of the cabin juts into the sky. Wide deck (would require railing if used by children) provides a place for sunning, sheltered from summer winds. Note pattern of the roof stringers and deck*

Cabin *is compact—576 square feet below, and 400 square feet in loft under roof peak for sleeping space. Basement (for wood, ski storage) has outside entrance*

IDEA CABIN: *With its unusual*

You feel as if you're in a high mountain look-out when you peer through the tall corner windows of this cabin.

This proves a point worth noting if you are planning or dreaming of your own mountain cabin: It needn't turn its back on the scenery just to get protection from the elements.

Basically, this cabin is a square box placed so that one corner juts from the slope. This corner—all glass—faces out over Squaw Valley near Lake Tahoe and it also faces into some of the winter storms; yet it deflects winds as the prow of a ship deflects water.

The diamond-shaped roof folded diagonally over the cabin leaves room for a sleeping loft. Underneath it and back from the high view windows is a small, snug, cave-like living area around a fireplace. As our photographer remarked, "This is the roomiest *little* cabin I've seen."

The cabin was designed by architect Henrik Bull. The owner proceeded to build it himself, with little previous construction experience. The final result reflects both men's interest in materials that fit into the changing moods (and disciplines) of the mountains. For example, untreated redwood was used as outside siding because it weathers (at high altitudes) to a rich, rust color, reminiscent of buildings in the Swiss Alps. The doors and other inside walls that are not untreated redwood are painted a bright sky blue.

Looking down *on cabin, slipped in unobtrusively among trees like a tent, you can see how lines are harmonious with mountain scenery. Note diamond shape of roof, redwood battens*

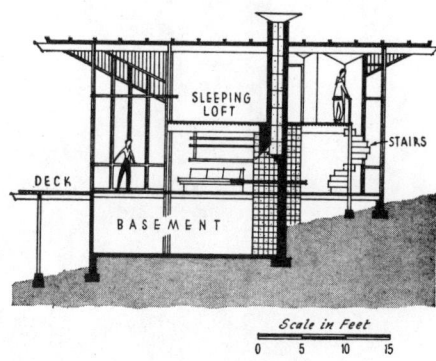

DIAGONAL SECTION

Note position of stairs to the loft. There is full headroom at center of loft, 4½ feet at the sides. Basement opens to outside

For extra strength *and* comfort...
All rough construction is Douglas fir. The ceiling and loft floor are alternating 2 by 3's and 2 by 2's, nailed together. This makes a pleasant pattern, but what's more important, it makes a strong roof—strong enough to carry the weight of the heavy Sierra snows, and strong enough so that no heavy cross beams are necessary for support (note in the drawing above how beams to support the roof above the loft would be inconveniently low).

Note how the heavy central roof beam cuts diagonally across the square cabin—giving the illusion (with the diamond-shaped roof) that the cabin is not square.

Winter. *Cabin seems to float above snow that piles around it. Windows face the view to south, trap enough warmth from the winter sunlight to compensate for heat loss at night. Owners enjoy watching snowstorms by light of a spotlight on deck at night*

folded roof... the feeling of a mountain lookout

Cave-like, *low-ceilinged living room (under sleeping loft) is pleasant retreat from the sweeping view. Centrally located fireplace heats the whole cabin, but forced air furnace is in basement for more heat*

Kitchen, *informal, compact, with contrasting colors, reflects the mood of whole cabin. Open to the living room. Black tile is unglazed; copper pots add color*

Open space underneath is handy for the storage of firewood. Note the enclosed storeroom at the far right, lower corner

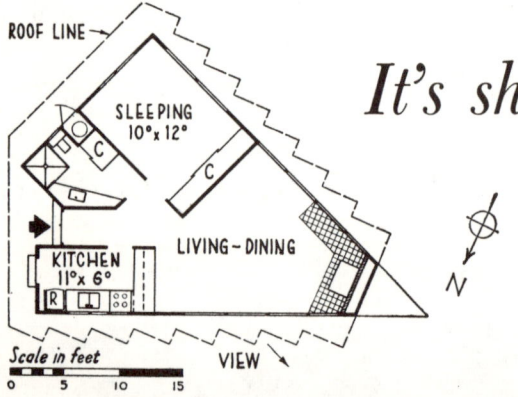

It's shaped like a piece of pie

Plan arranged so bathroom, fireplace absorb awkward angles

Cabin planners with economy in mind may get some pointers on use of a hillside site if they study the plan for this compact house in Monterey, California. To cut foundation costs, Designer Robert H. Hartman used a triangular floor plan. Thus the cabin needs support at only one point on the downhill side. A single board and batten wall, and a 2-inch tongue and groove floor over joists set on 5-foot centers accounted for further savings.

Looking from fireplace toward the kitchen pass-through. High ceiling—11 feet at ridge poles—makes small room seem larger

Walls of three-cornered living room converge to make place for fireplace at far end of the room. Raised tile hearth also a seat

Screen of 2 by 4's separates living area from dining room. Panels closing off bedroom areas (right) are perforated wallboard (insulated for sound control). Built-in lighting panels in ceiling

Cabin's exterior is brightened by burnt-orange plywood panels, black beams, and natural redwood at the corners. Wide overhang blocks the afternoon sun. Entry room (see plan) is at right

This cabin sleeps 16

This four-bedroom cabin, designed as a vacation house or for possible rental to small groups, has some good ideas for two or more families who plan a joint venture into cabin ownership. When the owners went to architect Henrik Bull, they specified that four bedrooms and two baths were required, and that the living areas be as economical and maintenance-free as possible. The resulting 1675-square-foot plan presents a roomy cabin that sleeps 16 people (each bedroom accommodates two double bunks) without infringing on the living areas.

The plan is based on a 4-foot module for economy of construction and maximum use of sheet materials. The floor and ceiling are of $1\frac{1}{8}$-inch plywood, supported by a grid framework of 2 by 4's and 4 by 4's on 4-foot centers. The flat roof eliminates the complicated connections and expensive construction techniques found with gable or shed roofs, and also gives the cabin a handsome low silhouette that doesn't spoil the view for other cabin owners located higher up the mountain. Also in the interests of economy, the fireplace is constructed of concrete block, with the base extending below the floor level.

The front view wall is of double-post construction, giving a greater feeling of shelter as well as providing extra storage space below the fixed glass.

The split-level design makes the floor plan work without requiring a space-wasting central hall. The hinged wall panels between the sleeping quarters and living area open the bedrooms to the outside view; but since only the top section is opened, unmade beds can't be seen from "downstairs."

White panel to right of kitchen is open, showing how view can be opened to bedrooms; door to bath and bedrooms at right. With only high panel open, there's no kitchen-to-bedroom view

The entry room between deck and living room provides storage for ski boots and wet clothes, while cutting heat loss and easing maintenance.

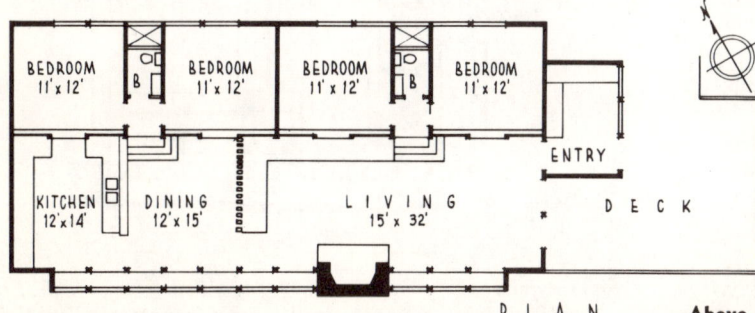
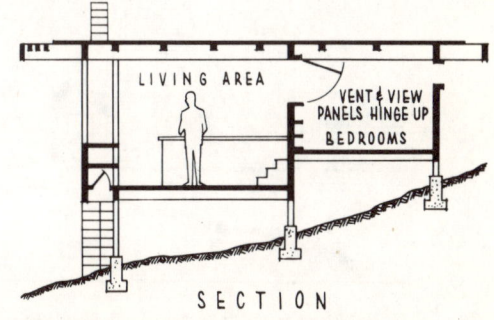

Above. Section shows how bedrooms, living room share the view
Left. Floor plan shows separation of living and sleeping areas

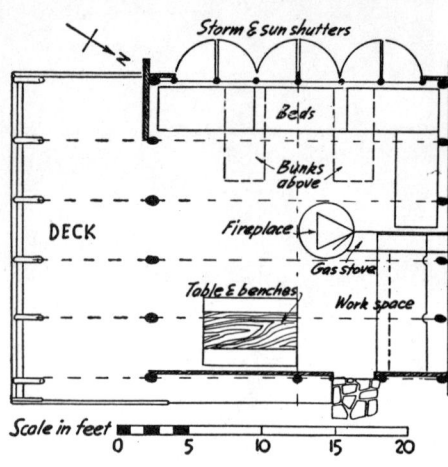

The pup-tent shape was easy to frame. All uprights were cut from trees on the site. Cabin can be closed by canvas which rolls down or by plastic-screen shutters

Triangular frame cabin

OVERLOOKING Lake Cavanaugh in western Washington, this cabin lies at the end of a narrow mountain road. It had to be built much in the same way that all cabins used to be built, using local materials wherever possible, adapted to a shape that could be completely fabricated on the site.

Heavy timbers were cut on the property, so there couldn't be too many of them and they couldn't be too heavy. Shakes were hand split by a workman who lived nearby. Finished lumber which had to be hauled in was kept to a minimum.

As a one-room cabin to sleep six, it had to be made compact and efficient. Look at the plans and elevation and you will see how this was done.

The design was by Mrs. John Prechek.

With canvas rolled up, cabin opens wide on deck. Open flooring drains water. Rail posts come up through deck from foundation

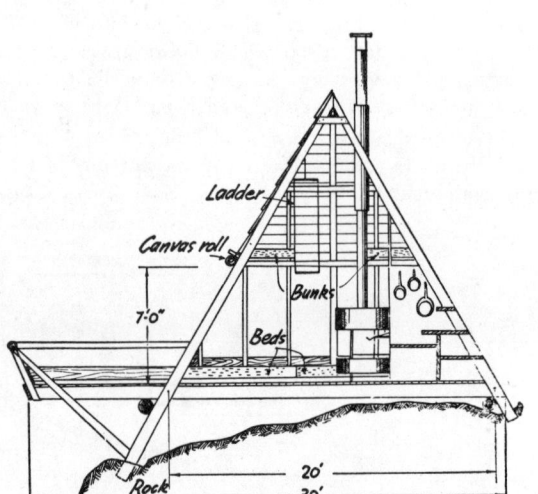

End elevation shows how pyramidal shape gives a broad base on a hillside site. Twenty-foot uprights serve as both rafters and studs, gain strength by mutual support at peak of the roof

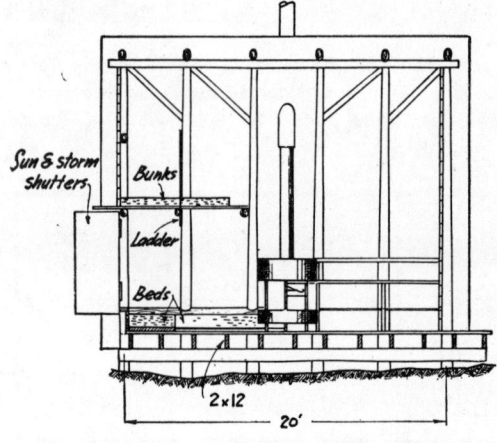

Sixteen-foot ceiling makes room for two beds placed high. Fireplace is oil drum cut in two with sand in bottom. Right side of cabin is for cooking and dining, left side is for sleeping

Cabin sits on shelf *bulldozed from sloping site. Sun deck, above car port, has canvas laced on a pipe frame for sun and wind control*

Summer comfort... on a mountain lake

On Lake Chelan in eastern Washington, this summer cabin works so well that the owners and their two children want an all-year house just like it.

Here are some of the features of the plan, by Designer Joe B. Wood, which make waterfront living simple and easy:

A masonry core with two fireplaces, one opening into the living room and the other onto the terrace.

An extra entry through the bathroom so that sand-covered sun bathers can take a foot bath or shower before entering the rest of the cabin.

Good traffic planning—several entries, not just one.

Durable, rough materials which require little maintenance.

Note, too, the snugness and the trim lines of a ship—from the flagpole in front to the sun deck over the car port.

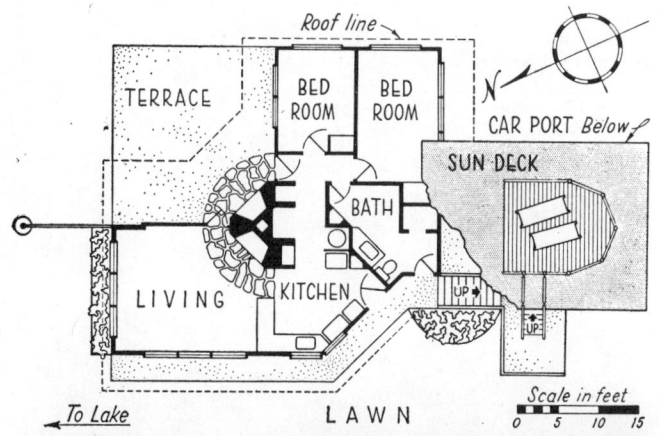

The living room *furniture can take wet bathing suits. Glass wall at right slides out on track, opens living room to terrace. The glass wall also screens the terrace from the wind*

Bar *separates kitchen from living room. Appliances are lined up against one wall so through traffic to bedrooms will not interfere with cook. Door in the background leads to sun deck*

Like a bird's nest, *this small cabin perches above heavy growth of ferns, goldenrod, tiger lilies, other Northwest natives. Windows are fixed; ventilation is through door*

Triangular deck *follows contour of land, is off main room, on sunny, private side of cabin*

360 square feet of weekend living space

All the cabin essentials have been packed inside this 18 by 20-foot cabin on Washington's Whidbey Island.

Inexpensive building materials, a simple box plan (relieved only by the roof line), and the owners' weekend labor, which included digging ditches for plumbing, installing wiring, and doing most of the finishing, helped to keep costs down.

The architect was Alan McRae.

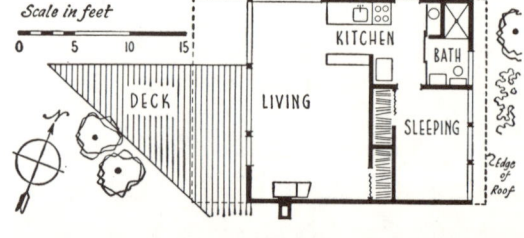

PLAN VIEW

Cooking corner *is compact. Clerestory window above runs entire width of house, balances light, lets in the east morning sun*

Small copper fireplace, *designed by the architect, is suspended from the masonry chimney. Heat, thrown off in all directions by metal surfaces, is sufficient to heat cabin on all but coldest winter nights. Slate tile hearth is laid on top of pine floor*

Cabin with a built-in terrace

The main rooms of this cabin are on the floor above, but this sheltered terrace on the lower level is really the most lived-in "room." Its basic idea could be adapted easily to a much smaller cabin, and to many hillside cabins. Partly shaded at midday, the terrace is the outdoor dining room and summer loafing area. It is the logical place for all-year storage of firewood, and can serve as a sleeping porch when bedrooms won't accommodate all the weekend guests.

ERNEST BRAUN

On downhill side *of the cabin, the snowdrifts do not pile up, and skiers can use the terrace as their staging area*

In summer, *this is also headquarters for swimming in small lake at foot of slope. Note how paving extends beyond roof*

Octagonal room captures the view

Six full-length windows around this eight-sided dining room capture views of Lake Tahoe, California, in many moods. It has windows on every side except the two sides that open into the kitchen. Outside, a deck adds to the luxury liner feeling, and takes full advantage of this site on Carnelian Bay. Because the octagon room was set into a corner, it didn't over complicate the construction of the rest of the cabin.

PHIL PALMER

Octagonal theme *carries even to bamboo dining table. The thin bamboo drapes cut glare but do not destroy the view*

A lake view *wraps halfway around this cabin. Being able to see tops of the pine trees minimizes the height of the deck*

Spacious new *outdoor living area has a tree house feeling. It opens from living room (left). Screened-in eating area at rear. Note*

A pre-cut cabin "in full dress"

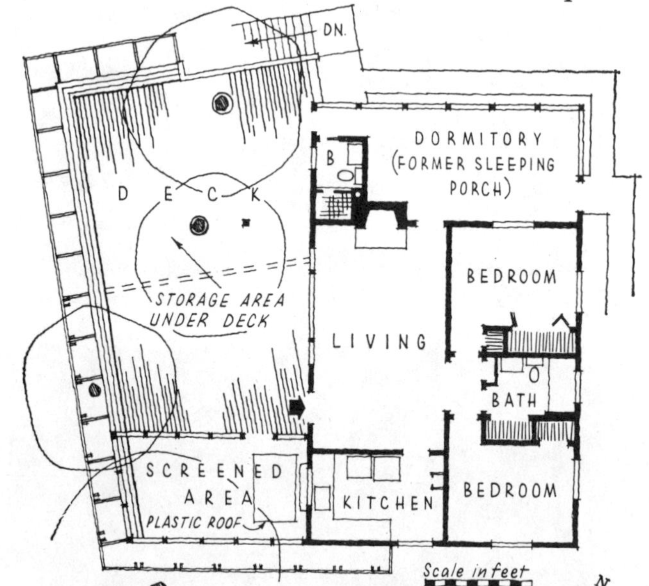

The big change came

Here's a report on how a summer house, originally a low-cost pre-cut cabin, finally came to terms with its site.

The house tops a small hill in San Anselmo, California. The owners, finding they used it less and less as their children grew, asked designer Harold B. Wagstaff for help in making it more suitable for their needs.

The major change was addition of a deck. It extends out at floor level high among the trees of the naturally wooded

Plan and profile *drawings. New deck doubled usable area of house. Old entry walk from garage (below house at right) was re-routed around north side of house. Note trees through deck*

Before. *Originally, south side of house perched high above this slope, with porch shown here. Fortunately, porch floor was about at house's floor level, so deck was added flush with it*

bench, horizontal fence in foreground **View** *from screened eating area. Evergreen trees give the deck privacy all year*

when they added a generous deck

site and gets a pleasantly varied mixture of sun and shade. Although there are neighbors, the world seems shut out.

The deck was made even more livable by screening the outdoor dining room to exclude the insects that abound in such wooded locations. Four feet of siding, a light wooden grille, and aluminum screening (which has some sheen from outside) increase its privacy from the street below.

The deck seems to merge with the trees. Its protective rail is a bench along the entire outer perimeter, with a horizontal fence that gives you a sense of safety when you are at the edge without forming a strong visual barrier to interrupt the sense of being literally up in the tree tops.

The remodeling also enclosed a sleeping porch to make a dormitory-sized bedroom, and added a small bathroom. With a few other spruce-up touches, the house became so inviting that the family now puts it to frequent use, the year around.

Low storage room *under deck is useful for locking away such things as outdoor furniture during family's absence. Light directed into trees provides pleasant nighttime backdrop to deck*

Looking out *former kitchen window. This became a pass-through to eating area, which is screened for protection against yellow-jackets and other insects, has plastic roof for light and shelter*

Glass walls... a wide deck

The wide deck, about four feet above the water at high tide, doubles the living area of cabin. The picture on the right explains the plan of the cabin. The living area, with a high ceiling, is across the front. Kitchen is on the right, bath and one bedroom are behind the fireplace, and two more bedrooms are upstairs. Except for the rear foundation, Architect Marshall W. Perrow supported the entire cabin over the canal on piling.

Serene and lovely, Hood Canal, seen through glass walls, is a part of this cabin owned by the Episcopal Diocese of Olympia. Wire-reinforced glass between beams lets light through, protects deck. Note seat rail on deck. Steps down to beach on left

Beach cabins

Most of the cabins on the next 18 pages are small and compact... a few are "big fellows." Some sit up high... others rest right on the sand. But all have one thing in common: They are built for waterside living

It "floats" above the sand

Low to the ground, this cabin gives you a definite feeling of "living on the beach." Here you feel closer to the sand, the ocean, and the fog than in a house that looks down on the beach. Notice on the plan that a swimmer coming from the beach can go directly to the bath without going through the cabin. Circular stair leads to ground level from the back porch. A fireplace provides the necessary heat.

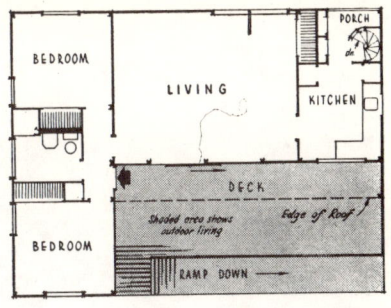

WILLIAM APLIN

Generous deck serves as an outdoor living area in this cabin in Carpinteria, California. Ramp, with its gradual pitch, is for safe and easy access to the beach. Cabin is built on wood piling driven into shifting dunes. Architects: Riggs and Shaw

A cabin at the beach is special because it's a place devoted to indolence and freedom and doing what you please. It is a place where you dare experiment with color, design, furniture, and decoration.

For all the fun and foolishness you find in beach cabins, you also find ideas that are useful in any house. There are fewer conventions and restrictions about how you should build a cabin or how you should live in it, so you feel freer to indulge whims or try experiments than you would if you were building a house. At the same time, you are usually trying to keep the budget low, so you are spurred to eliminate all non-essentials, to make the structure simple, convenient, and easy to maintain. In other words, you put first things first.

The ocean shore is an exciting place to live—any time of the year, in good weather or bad. But anyone who builds his house there must remember where he is. The beach dweller must reckon with many things; among them are sea winds, glaring sun, salt air, salt water, violent ocean storms, sand, and fog.

When the brilliant ocean sun drops away at day's end, its horizontal rays will reach farther under any overhang, pierce deeper into any unprotected house than anywhere inland.

Ocean winds are sharp, cutting winds; they carry with them the abrasive power of sand and the corrosive action of salt. In winter, the storms blowing in off the sea can be pure havoc.

The beach cabins here and on the following pages are in many shapes, sizes, and situations. All have proven their worth.

75

"Glass house"

Along entire length of living room in Malibu Beach, California beach house are panels of heat-reducing, glare-reducing wire glass set in puttyless copper-frame skylight. Outside, glass fence with wind deflector along top. Vertical section of fence is six feet six inches. Deflector is one foot. Designer was J. E. Costello

JULIUS SHULMAN

Here is a check list for beach house planners...

Sun control. If you face due west, overhang won't keep out sun entirely. Turning the big windows in another direction helps, but it may mean some sacrifice of ocean view.

Wind control. A glass fence cuts winds, and still saves the view. Use puttyless installation and check to be sure you are using heavy enough glass for wind pressures in your area. A house shaped in an L or a U, if not faced properly, creates a windy pocket where sand is blown in over the roof. Two outdoor areas give one protected place while the other takes the wind (See decks designed for the house at Neskowin, Oregon).

Sand control. Use duck walks over decks, especially around entrance areas. Have floors that can easily be swept free of sand. Give shower and bath an outside entrance, or install a shower head over duckboards outside.

Storm control. Don't have doors open directly in the direction of the biggest winds. They are hard to seal. Protect them with overhangs, but better still, keep openings on the lee side.

Corrosion control. Build with materials that improve in salt air. Redwood and cedar turn a silvery grey, and save you constant repainting. Ship hardware is built to take the action of sea air. Get it used at a salvage yard, or new at a ship chandler's. If you use landlubber's hardware, buy brass and you won't have to replace it in a few seasons.

CHARLES R. PEARSON

Log cabin on an island

All-year beach cabin on Guemes Island, Washington's San Juans. Rough structure is built of local materials. Logs for the walls came from trees on the property. The beams for the house and planks in the patio paving were driftwood

Sun and weather controls

Left. *Beach house at Neskowin, Oregon, has two decks; one deck gets shade when the other deck gets sun. Designer: W. F. Severin.* **Right.** *This seven-foot wind fence at Wecoma Beach, Oregon, is set right on the beach. It is protected from the full brunt of ocean storms by a bluff to the south*

This beach house lets its owners relax

CARROLL C. CALKINS

House faces due west, relying on deep overhang and wooden roll blinds to cut out afternoon sun. Front wall is indented for protection from southern storms. Trees cut off the northwest wind

Simple wood walls, easily swept floor, deep leather chair are for comfort, easy maintenance. View out window shows rail along edge of bluff to guard against steep drop to beach of cove below

This comfortable beach house at Whale Cove, Oregon, is warm and ready for its owners the year around. Electric heat holds the temperature at 60° even when the house is empty. On a practical level, this prevents mildew. It also prevents the uninviting chill that comes with entering a cold, clammy house.

Built and furnished so that it almost takes care of itself, the house does not have to be "opened" for a weekend.

Set up on a slab, using the natural protection of a cove and trees and the planned protection of a deep overhang over broad areas of glass, the house is guarded from water, wind, rodents, and insects. There is no battening to contend with, even though the house must withstand storms with 100-mile-an-hour winds. Freed from having to spend their weekends maintaining their beach house, the owners have found time to relax in it. They've had the leisure to gather rocks for lining paths, to transplant nearby salal and wild huckleberry in a small garden of shore natives.

With this kind of a beach house, they enjoy fully what draws man to the rugged Oregon coast: walks along the water's edge, gathering driftwood, watching waves, and hearing pounding surf.

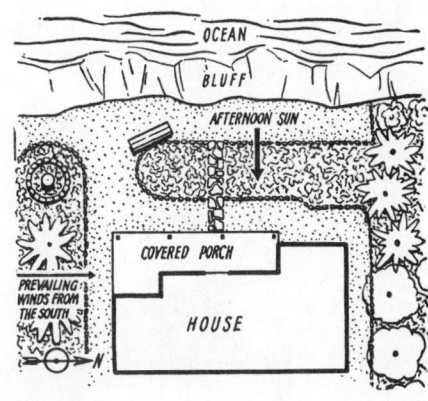

Raised wooden walk *curves around a tree to connect the parking area and entry in this Carpinteria, California, beach house. Walk, kept clean by the wind, cuts down on the problem of sand tracked indoors. The architect was Lutah Maria Riggs*

GOOD IDEAS: *On these two pages are just a few of the many ways you can make beach living more enjoyable*

Certain tried and true beach conveniences are worth the consideration of any family planning its own beach cabin. Here are some of them:

An outdoor drying rack for wet beach towels and bathing suits. Sometimes the rack is simply a generous porch railing. Where sun is not always dependable use a hand laundry wringer mounted on a sawhorse.

•

A storage locker for beach umbrellas, beach chairs, inner tubes, life rafts, and water toys.

•

A "beach kitchen," often just a deck area between kitchen proper and the sand, with a barbecue pit for open cooking fires beside the deck.

•

A navy or army surplus telescope on a swivel mount.

In Hawaii, *windows on the ocean side are often fogged up. This built-in spray system solves the problem. Sketch on right*

Hydrographic charts of your immediate beach area for wall decoration.

•

Flagpole with signal flags to send messages to children down the beach or offshore in a boat.

•

A boat horn is another good means of calling children up from the beach.

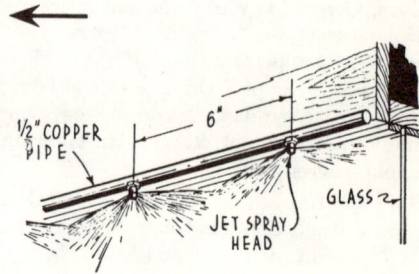

Jet sprays *on copper pipe make window cleaning a simple matter. Architect-designer: Dennis and Whitaker, Honolulu*

For wind protection *on the Oregon coast, old window panes are set in frames made of 4 by 4-inch posts, 2-by-4 crosspieces*

Half-log steps *hang from rods on a post and beam frame. Cabin is shown on page 74. The lower steps are submerged at high tide*

Car port roof *is hung from piling. (House also set on pilings, to lift it above the shifting sands.) Lower beam notched into side of piling. Note plant bench, parking bumper, cover over the walkway, and how the piling extends up through the roof of the car port*

Shower *on outside wall of bathroom in cabin on left has nozzle spray for shower, low faucet for foot washing; water drains through deck. The architect was George Vernon Russell*

This California beach house, a rectangular platform set on piles and girders, is constructed of glass and redwood shiplap

All-weather beach house

The linoleum floor can be swept free of sand in no time, which is essential for easy weekend maintenance of a beach house. The living room day beds are also for sleeping. The fireplace and portable electric heaters provide all heat

IN CALIFORNIA the beach is often better during fall and winter than it is during the summer. The sunshine can often be clear and bright, the air sharp and bracing. But since the days are apt to be unpredictable, you need a permanent structure to which you can retreat in case a wind kicks up, a fireplace for friendly warmth, and some kind of sheltered, walled-off trap to catch the sun.

This weekend house satisfies the needs of a year-around beach shelter with the directness of a propped-up tarpaulin. It was designed by a San Francisco architect, Francis Joseph McCarthy, for a Stinson Beach location.

A wall opens to the view of the ocean. In front of this wall is a deck surrounded by glass to shut out wind. Overhead is a partially opened roof, like the sunshine-top

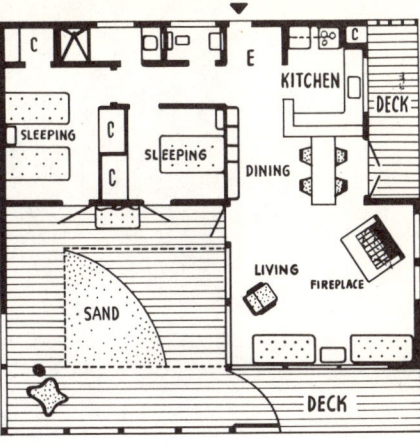

Kitchen is partially screened off from the living-dining area by a counter which also serves to define the space for dining

Sunshine top of the roof over the deck has a wide enough overhang so that it leaves plenty of shade from ocean glare

on an English automobile, to act as a sun trap. Shaded corners of this roof, however, leave plenty of room to retreat from sun glare.

The floor of the deck has been cut away to expose a protected, natural sand-box for the owner's grandchildren.

The floor of the house, set on piles and girders, is simply a rectangular platform several feet above the natural line of the sand dunes. Constantly shifting sand makes an ever changing pattern along the edges of the house.

Although the interior of the house may appear somewhat austere, it is well suited to easy weekend maintenance. Simple, unadorned furniture, linoleum floor, pine and redwood interior trim are rugged enough to stand the constant heavy wear of sand and sea air.

Deck as seen *from bedroom wing. Steps go down to sloping path leading to the lake. Notice the boat at edge of lake. Seat rail extends around the corner of the south-facing deck. Cabin has a shake roof and cedar siding*

They move on and off the deck with the sun and rain...

This cabin is built where the weather is whimsical

Generous size *of living area and dormitory is shown here (the larger bedroom is on left). Note how bedrooms open directly onto deck, so returning swimmers need not walk through living area*

Along this stretch of the Oregon coast south of Bandon, it may rain steadily for a week or so, and it may be overcast and foggy for even longer. But between these periods, the sudden appearance of blue skies, warm sunshine, and a gentle breeze can make it as delightful a place as you'd ever hope to find.

This vacation cabin, designed by Architect George Rockrise, is planned to make the most of the moody climate. When it's sunny there's a deck for lounging. It is only a few steps to Floras Lake, and a hundred yards across the sandspit to the surf. When it's cold, cloudy, or rainy, the activity moves inside. Much of the cabin's success is due to the generous open space for rainy-day recreation. The absence of partitions in the living-dining-kitchen area and in the dormitory keeps the cabin from seeming cramped. It also reduced the per-square-foot building cost.

High ceiling, *glass walls—and the deck beyond—make the room seem even larger than it is. The beams are fir; inside paneling is hemlock. Cabin is cheerful in any weather. Tree gives protection from the west sun*

Fireplace *is faced with native stone that was gathered near the cabin site. This circulating fireplace, with intake and outlet vents on the sides instead of in the face, provides heat for the cabin. Couches at corners of the living room double as extra sleeping space*

Opposite end *of room from view at left. Couch is only separation between living, dining areas; counter sets off kitchen. Benches, stools by counter provide plentiful seating. Door from parking area is just out of picture to right*

83

Looking into cabin, two sliding glass doors open. Buoy-shaped metal fireplace, in center of room, radiates heat on all sides. Floor is plywood. Deck laid parquet style in 3-foot squares

Two large doors with built-in shelves open off big room. They reveal small kitchenette with sink and stove. Shelves are "lipped" to prevent the staples and condiments from falling off

The deck is surrounded by 15-inch-high seat rail made from 2 by 8-inch boards. Large brazier on deck is for a barbecue or a warming fire. Pillows are covered with bright terry cloth towels

From inside the cabin, you look out across deck and bay to green hills and the Olympics. Inside furnishings are kept to minimum. Deck has lightweight movable chairs and cushions

The deck is bigger than the cabin

This small summer cabin boasts more deck space than inside living space. Without bowing to tradition or style, it blends with the scenic beauty of Horsehead Bay in Puget Sound.

With their main house higher up on the hill, the owners wanted a place to sleep house guests, entertain, and relax near the water. The cabin provides swimmers and sailors with a dressing room and bathroom, and a small kitchenette for preparation of informal meals.

A large deck surrounds the glass-walled front of the cabin, and wide sliding doors open from the main room onto the deck. Beyond the deck an area of lawn, just large enough for croquet or badminton, merges into the meadow grass and underbrush of the hillside.

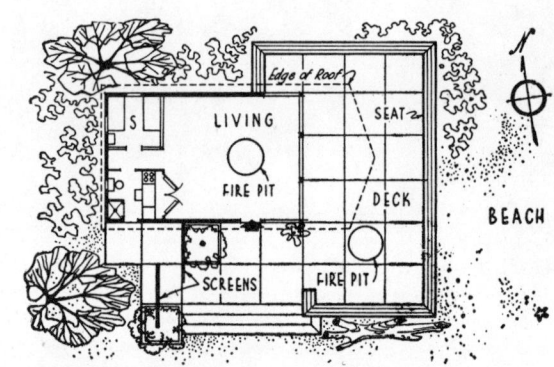

Fireplace *is wide, warm, and friendly; the deep-set niche above holds plenty of firewood. The interior walls are birch plywood*

Designed for beach living

Without the slightest hesitation or confusion, this house goes about its business of providing for beach living as its owners want it. Yet, its directness is never harsh or without grace.

No tricks relieve the simplicity of the house, yet it provides for as many moods as there are weathers. You can see the ocean through a wall of glass or through the woven reed draperies. You can turn your back on the ocean and enjoy the mountains. You can follow the sun by choosing the deck. You can enjoy a "garden" of cypress branches, or a natural mountain side, or nature's sand garden.

Architect Lutah Maria Riggs and her assistant, Arvin Benjamin Shaw III, designed this Carpinteria, California, beach house. They incorporated the family's ideas into the finished house, assuring it a casual quality, a comfort, that is inviting and real.

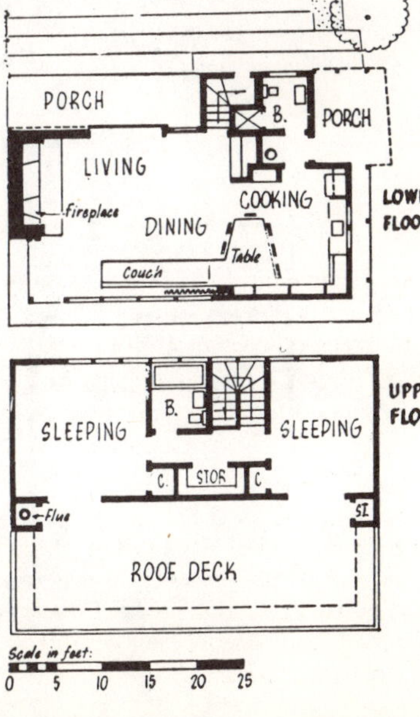

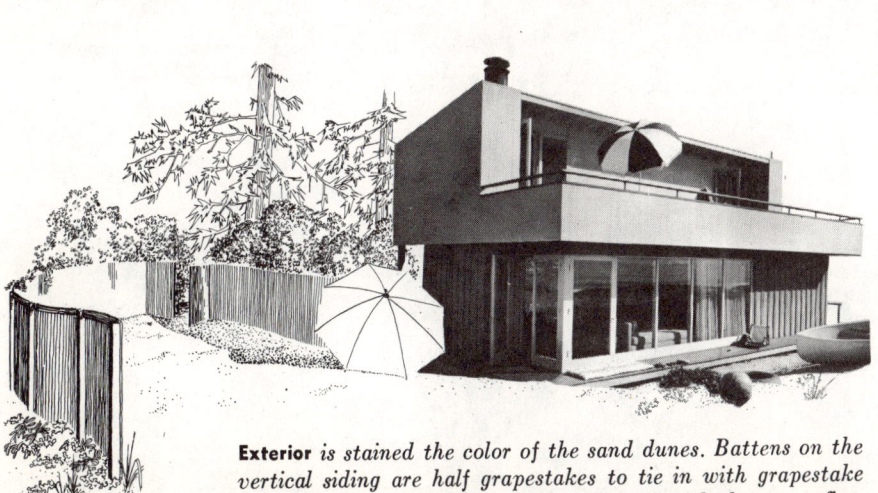

Exterior *is stained the color of the sand dunes. Battens on the vertical siding are half grapestakes to tie in with grapestake fence. Deck on the upper floor opens off of bedrooms, offers sunbathing and a sweeping view of the coast and channel islands*

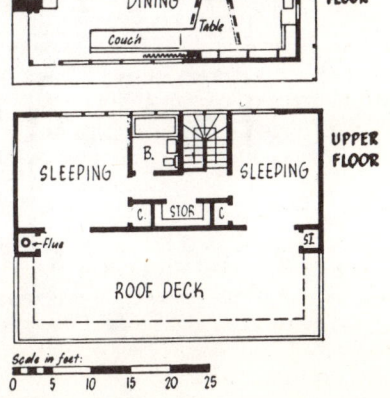

Above. House from beach side. Overhead glass door at right. Redwood single-wall construction; shake roof

Right. Dining area with cooking nook behind screen. Meat hooks hold pots, pans. Roll-up cabinet doors over sink

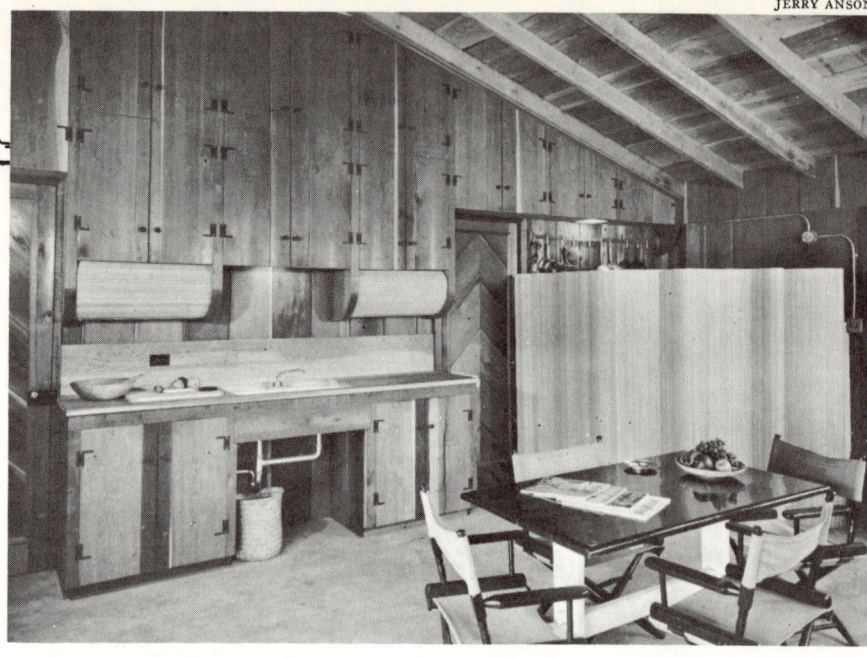

Beach house now... garage later

SOMEDAY this house will revert to the use for which it was built, a two-car garage and boathouse, with plenty of space for gear storage. The wall is framed on the entrance side so that double doors can be installed without constructional changes.

Designer Lockwood de Forest of Santa Barbara did his usual thoughtful job in detailing the garage for home comfort.

The glass-panelled overhead door, similar to garage type, was used to open living-dining area to ocean (to bring in boats later). Portable screen conceals cooking alcove. Storage space considers both present and future use. Separate storage room is not waste space.

Left. Bed at right swings out beside other. Table stores bedding. Lights operate on pulleys, height adjustable

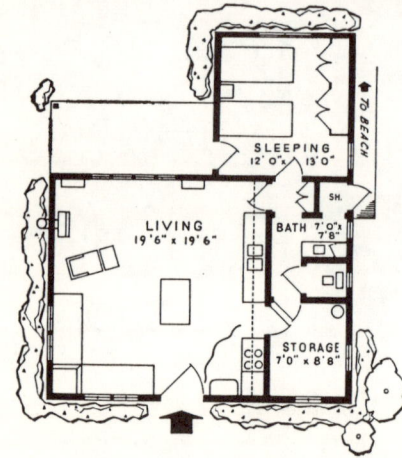

Through overhead door to ocean. Franklin stove, at left, is only heat

Right. *Though wide open to the sun, wind, and waves, this beach house at Newport, Oregon, is snug even when winds blow*

Below. *Cutaway of beach home with roof, north wall removed*

Built to take coastal weather

THE CLIMATE along the Oregon coast is scarcely tropical, but the view is terrific. The Newport, Oregon, owner of this trim small beach home built it to prove to himself and skeptical friends that large areas of glass and open planning were quite as feasible there as farther south. The winter sun helps warm the house; the bluff at the south protects it from the strong winds common in winter storms.

The house is engineered for heavy weather. The framing is of continuous 2 by 6 studs; there is extra sheathing on the roof. To cushion and offset the vibration set up by the pounding of winter surf, the large sections of glass are set in rock wool.

The materials used are pleasingly simple. The exterior is finished with natural wood, treated with spar varnish. Pale green insulating board covers the inside walls. The floor is made up of one-foot squares of pressed wood. Doors are solid panel veneer. Ceiling finish is in knotty pine. Draperies are of unbleached sheeting.

The ocean view is enjoyed also from the sleeping balcony which overlooks the living room. The balcony can be cut off with roll-up bamboo blinds.

Future plans call for the addition of a glassed-in sun deck over the garage.

Right. *Relation between indoors and out is frank in this house. Clouds, changing surf, low green beach growth are part of living*

Far right. *Ocean view may also be enjoyed from sleeping balcony overlooking living room. Dresser, built-in between closets*

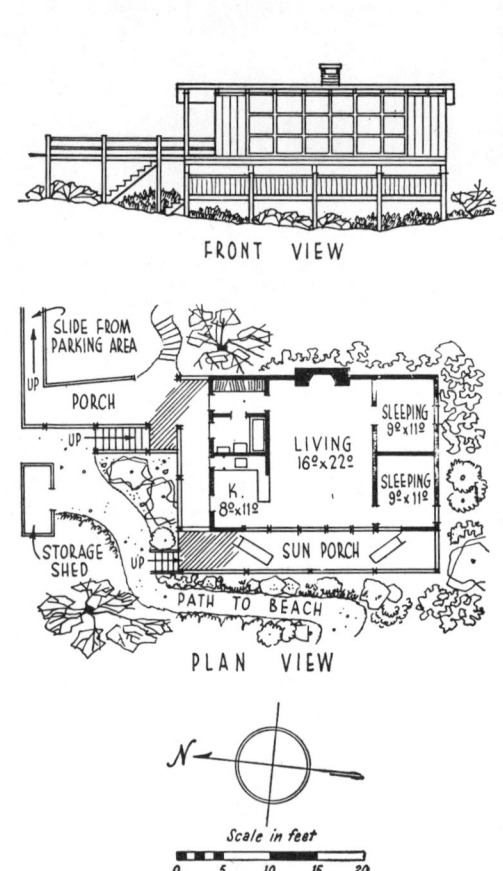

The exterior *is fir board and batten. The cabin is unpainted and looks at home in its setting of Shore pine, Douglas fir, salal, and Coast huckleberry*

At the bottom of a steep bluff...

This inexpensive cabin enjoys the ocean's fun

Deck *is below window level and doesn't cut off beach view from living area. Rope through screw eyes completes deck rail*

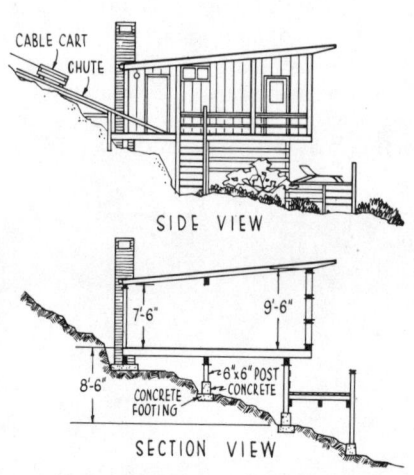

Side view *shows how simple structure fits side of steep hill. Sun porch, below the house level, makes a detached living area*

Because they built this cabin at the bottom of a steep bluff, directly over the ocean, the owners can sit snugly behind their glass wall and enjoy the full fury of winter storms. On good days, it is merely a few steps outside the door to explore the beach or gather driftwood for the fire.

The cabin is no more pretentious than hundreds of other beach cabins. It is built simply, inexpensively, to take the beating that wind, sun, rain, sand—and beach-goers—are likely to give it.

It is distinctive because it has a general air of elegance without sacrificing the necessary qualities that it shares with all good vacation houses: comfort, convenience, easy maintenance.

Architect Walter E. Church of Portland designed the cabin at Arch Cape, Oregon, for his own family.

Dining area—*always a focal point for vacation life—has a strategic location next to the large window. Kitchen is behind the bamboo screen. Screen rolls up to allow serving across the counter. Window ledge holds a collection of shells and rocks*

...and even its fury

Cable cart *is used to move supplies down to the cabin from the road above. The box has wheels and is kept on the track by the sides of the chute. It is operated by an electric winch at the top*

Fireplace *is a simple plane of brick. Interior paneling is unfinished cedar. Floors are plywood painted to match the color of sand, which is inevitably tracked into any beach house*

Native plants—madrona trees, Scotch broom, wild roses, tall grasses—were carefully protected during building. As the owner explains, "This is a no-gardening, no-housework summer house"

Back wall is tilted inward. The architect considers roof and wall as a unit, folded around the room to increase the sense of shelter. Fireplace screens off the kitchen. Entry door is on left

Plywood panels used for exterior siding. One coat of wood preservative grays it to driftwood color. Deck cantilevered from 4-foot foundations; height required because high tides lap steps

"A no-housework

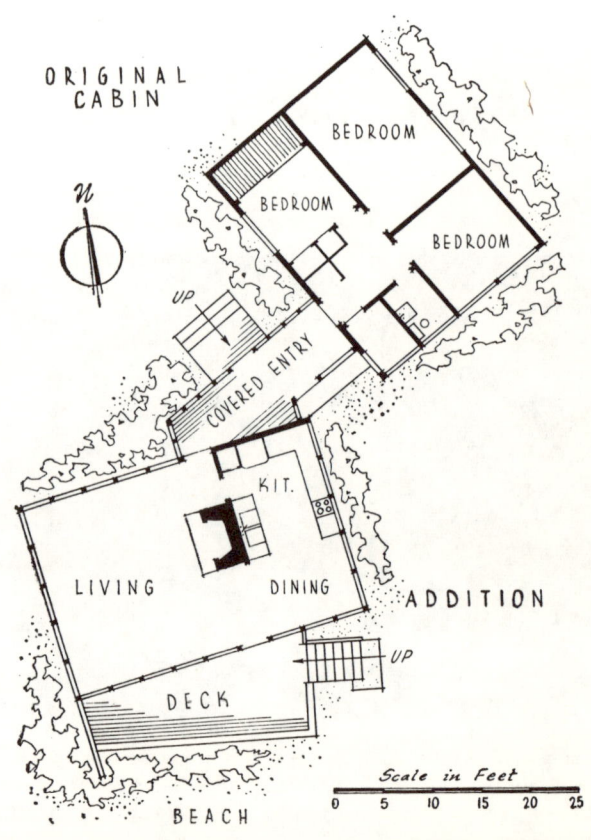

Living area *seen from entry door. High ceilings make room seem larger, help keep it cool in summer. Electric wall heaters (one by couch) and circulating fireplace furnish heat for the cabin*

DEARBORN-MASSAR

View of canal *from living area. Cabin oriented to provide view from kitchen and from original cabin (sketch above). Note overhang for afternoon shade; screened vents at roof and floor*

summer house..."

Cabins are fun, so you build them or buy them in the location where you see the most fun in store for you and your family.

The owners of this spacious but "easy-does-it" vacation house chose a stretch of Washington's Hood Canal as a good place to spend their summers. It was near friends, easily accessible, and right on the water. But there was neither an empty lot nor an attractive cabin for sale. So they bought a lot, accepted its inadequate cabin, and chose to remodel.

With the help of Architect Victor Steinbrueck, they decided to build a separate cabin containing living room and kitchen. The original cabin was converted to bedrooms, and the new and old were connected with a covered walkway. This breezeway does double duty: it also serves as a front entry.

The open breezeway between bedroom and kitchen, in a bracing climate, might not appeal to everyone. But there's a lesson for all remodelers in the way this project's design was unhindered by limitations of the original building. The main effort was on the facilities needed most.

Kitchen ideas: *With generous work space, offers of help can be accepted. Maple counter top, for sandwiches by the dozen. Extra storage allows infrequent shopping. Vinyl floor tile, natural cedar wall, black hardboard below windows are easy to keep clean*

Small docks on Toluca Lake in Southern California have been tailored to fit boats. The same idea can work for larger craft.

Float, anchored to pilings at each end, moves up and down with water. Note short gangplank between walkway at left and float

If there's a boat in your cabin plans . . .

How to build piers and floats

To the prospective shore dweller, everything that has to do with water is a new challenge. If you have a boat, you'll want a place for safe moorage; perhaps you'll want a take-off for water skiing; maybe all you want is a place to swim and sun bathe. Whatever your interest, you will soon find that developing a waterfront involves building a dock or float.

Although, accurately, a "dock" is the water that lies between piers or wharfs, the term in waterfront talk also means the pier or wharf itself. In this case, a dock means a permanently fixed platform  set up over the water, resting on pilings driven into the bottom. A float is an anchored platform which rests on the surface of the water.

Because the dock is solidly fixed and relatively permanent, it can be more flexible in design than a float, and is easier to build for a specific need. But a dock is nearly always higher above the water than a float.

A float has the advantage of a deck which is always the same distance above the surface of the water. Many floats have the disadvantage, however, of becoming waterlogged within a few years, so that their decks are awash.

BUILDING A DOCK

Distance between dock and water at high tide is usually 22 inches. Over rough water, it must be higher (at least 30 inches) or the waves will wash over the deck and cause it to rot.

Depth of water at the end of the dock should be no less than six feet at low tide. This is the shallowest depth for safe diving. A deep-keeled sailboat, however, may require as much as 12 feet of water.

Dimensions. The deck or platform of a dock should be as long as the boat you intend to moor. A 12-foot-wide dock leaves enough room to pull a rowboat out of the water and turn it. For swimming, the dock should be wide enough for sun bathers and people who are dressed to stand or sit without getting wet from take-offs. For handling a variety of activities, a T-shaped design may be the answer.

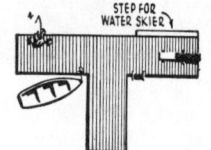

Moorage. Since a dock should be designed to give boat protection in rough weather, moorage should be on the lee side, with the bow of the boat headed into the prevailing wind. Pilings can be left high, above deck level, so that a moored boat can be tied to them.

Pilings. Heavy pilings usually must be driven by a professional. Piles are usually driven on 12-foot centers with 6 by 8-inch cross beams between the piles. The beams are capped with 3 by 8's and decked with 2-inch lumber.

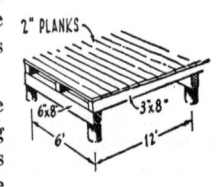

Everything above the pilings should be perfectly flush. Anything projecting would tear up a moored boat. The piles themselves are set slightly back from the edge for looks.

If you want a small dock in a lake which freezes over in winter, you might be able to drive the pilings yourself. The ice offers a firm platform on which to stand while working. Simply cut holes in the ice, slip the pilings down and drive them by hand with a heavy sledge hammer as far as you can. Don't worry about the ends of the piles not being even. The important thing is to drive each one as far down as it will go, until it reaches a solid footing. Then you can cut off the ends so that a level deck can span them. You probably won't be able to hand-drive anything but a light pier. Also, you may not be able to use this method where the rise and fall of the lake is very great, for the ice freezing around a dock in rising water can easily pull up the piles. Ordinarily, the lake bottom will set like concrete around the piles. (It is this setting quality, incidentally, which may make it cost as much to pull existing piles as it does to drive new ones.)

Piling and other timber will last longest if it has been pressure treated with creosote. Only under pressure is the creosote able to penetrate far enough into the wood cells to be really effective. If a piece of timber which has been previously treated is cut in two, the ends immediately should be given two coats of creosote heated to about 150° F. You won't want to use creosote on decking or anywhere else where it might come off on clothing or swimmers. Untreated piles are often used in fresh water, but it is the consensus of opinion that pilings in salt water should be creosote treated.

Place the deck on one corner of your property if you don't want to obstruct a view of the water. However, if small children are using the dock, better have it in view of the house at all times. Railings aren't a good idea, as they restrict activities—such as jumping in and out of boats. If you are worried about children falling into the water off your dock, probably it is wise to fence the approach from land.

FLOATS

Float shapes can vary. A float might be square or rectangular. It might be "U" shaped. The U shape has a special advan-

tage in giving protected moorage. It also makes it possible to get in or out of a boat from the bow or either side. To protect a boat from the sun, it is easy to pitch a canvas canopy right over the U. A small, square float can be attached to shore by two logs, and one log can be deck covered to make a simple, narrow walkway.

Flotation material will depend upon what is available in your area. Buy the least expensive material which will have the most sustained buoying powers. For example, logs, balsa wood, empty 50-gallon drums, plastic pontoons all make good flotation.

The best logs are cedar fire-killed snags. They are completely dry and will float high for a long time. Other logs will soak up water so the float will be awash within a few years.

Surplus balsa wood rafts, when you can get them, also make excellent flotation. The 60-man size (12 by 8 feet) is somewhat easier to find than the 25-man size (4½ by 9 feet). These rafts are covered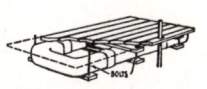
with a waterproof canvas coating, but a coat of tar increases their life and cuts maintenance considerably. Stringers are bolted together across the top and bottom of the raft, and a decking is nailed across the top. A float of this type can be secured by driving a pipe through it into the bottom.

Fifty-gallon drums quickly corrode in salt water, or in fresh water if left the year around. They are not, however, too expensive to replace. If you want a float only for the summer and pull it up on shore for the rest of the year, the drums will last a long time. Use as few drums as possible or the float will be overly buoyant and tip easily. Some boat owners float their platforms first, then place as many drums underneath as needed to get the desired buoyancy. The drums are loosely corralled by the edge of the float.

A foam plastic now on the market is reported to be impervious to water and not affected by salt, fungus, dry rot, marine life, or most of the other flotation problems. It is also fire resistant but will burn or melt if subjected to intense heat. However, it is dissolved by gasoline. Pontoons of this material can be covered with a special coat which offers additional protection.

Securing. The float should be held in place, allowing only for up and down movement with the rise and fall of the water. Floats can be secured by pipe, steel bands, or lumber around a piling.

GANGPLANKS

In order to walk from shore or a dock to a float, you'll need a gangplank. One end usually will be hinged to a dock. The other end which rests on the float can have rollers or wheels if there is constant motion between gangplank and float. It's best if these rollers or wheels move against a steel plate or in channel iron tracks—otherwise the gangplank can wear through the float's deck in one season.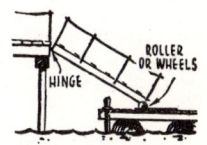

WALKWAYS

For either a walkway or a small dock, you might use a line of single piles joined by a three-foot-wide walk. This lacks much stability, however, and storm debris tends to collect under it.

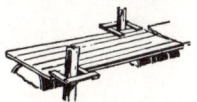
A three-foot-wide walk might also be laid over a single floating cedar log which is made non-tippable by anchorage to the pilings.

PERMIT REQUIRED

Legally, you must get a permit from the District Engineer, Corps of Army Engineers, before building a dock or float in navigable waters. The Engineers publish a pamphlet outlining what is required. This includes an engineer's drawing (which may cost $40) of the proposed structure. Only exception to rule requiring a permit from the District Engineer is in localities where a "pier-head" line has been established, determining the limit to which a dock or float may project over the water. In this case, you must get permission from a local authority.

This simple boat slip might be all you need...

Hoisting this small boat out of water for storage under a tarpaulin keeps it from being buffeted by waves and protects it from rain and sun. By fastening the ridge pole, which supports the tarpaulin, with such flexible connections as ring bolts and shackles, you can swing the davits in and set the boat on the dock. Standard 2-inch pipe is bent for davits that support 300 to 400 pounds each. For heavier loads, the specifications for davits should be checked by an engineer. Designer was John M. Bates, of Lake Grove, Oregon.

Boat slip *is 20 feet long and 6½ feet wide*

S. B. KNOLL

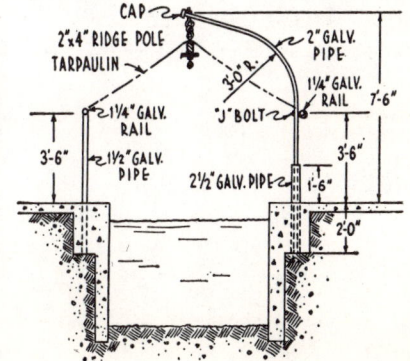

Desert cabins

Have you dreamed of a low-cost retreat in the desert? An increasing number of families are learning to enjoy the cactus country

Heat, wind, no water—these are the tough realities when you build a cabin in the desert. Yet a surprising number of Westerners, most of them Southern Californians, have learned to meet these terms in their own ways to enjoy desert cabin living. (The Federal Small Tract Act makes it possible for citizens to file on small tracts of land up to five acres. If the idea of a desert retreat appeals to you, turn to page 8.)

We recently visited cabins and talked to cabin owners in California's Mojave Desert areas, from Palmdale to Twentynine Palms. We were looking for those lessons from experience worth passing on to prospective desert cabin builders.

One desert problem we found still unsolved in many areas: A collection of small cabins (frequently the minimum 400 square feet) scattered across an expanse of open desert frequently has a ragged "shanty town" look—unless owners take special pains to make their cabins blend in naturally with the landscape. On more practical building matters, however, the "desert rats" gave us many useful suggestions for prospective cabin builders.

LEGAL PRELIMINARIES

Once you've obtained a desert tract, your first responsibility is to improve it according to the requirements applicable in your particular area. In addition, be sure to check with the county or municipal authority that has jurisdiction over your property. San Bernardino County, for example, requires that any structure be set back 65 feet from any property line—25 feet from the 40-foot easement now required for county roads.

Your first step will be to get an accurate survey.

In almost every desert area, you can find a local surveyor who is familiar with the neighboring country. Insist that he stake the four corners of your property so that there can be no mistake in your mind as to the boundaries of *your* tract. He should also provide you with a descriptive map locating your property in relationship to *permanent* markers.

Since a surveyor is legally liable for his computations, an accurate survey may save you many headaches that could be created by building on someone else's property. A survey for an average 5-acre tract will run from $100 to $150 unless you arrange with neighbors to have a number of tracts surveyed at one time,

---

CABIN IDEA NO. 1: *You build with cool concrete masonry*

First stage of cabin could be walls and roof with roughed-in provisions for plumbing and wiring in concrete slab. Adding a bedroom would require only one wall and a section of roof

Concrete slab, masonry shell, and roof of this cabin could probably be owner-built for about $1,000. Basic idea: to provide a simple desert shelter, open to view and breezes on one side, with wind-protected court for outdoor living on the other.

Where sliding doors are indicated on the plans at the right, they might consist of stock sliding garage doors and screen doors or sliding glass doors, depending on your budget and how you plan to use the cabin. Ceiling height should be calculated so that stock doors or door frames could be utilized without waste.

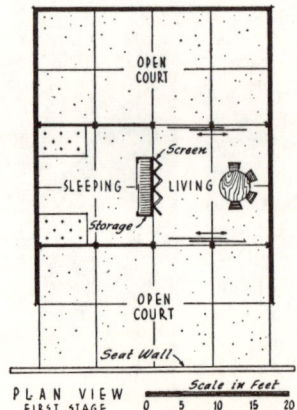
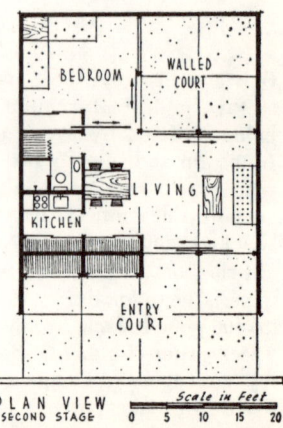

DESERT DIRECTORY. *Just as informal as cabins and houses built on 5-acre tracts. This intersection of graded dirt roads lies within one of the oldest planned desert tracts, the New Horizons Desert Acres, located near Yucca Valley, off the Old Woman Springs Road leading to Victorville and Lucerne Valley. Not all the cabins in this area are to the left—we could not get all the signs into this photograph*

in which case you can bring the price of your own surveying job down to about $25 to $35.

BUILDING A ROADWAY

Unless your plot lies right on some already cleared access road, you will have to build your own. If you must cross other undeveloped tracts to reach your own, the land office recommends that, if possible, you contact owners of these properties and arrange to build a common access road. If this is impossible, any road you grade across other properties should be located along property line boundaries and any main access road should follow a half section or section line. To establish boundaries of neighbors' tracts, you may obtain a section map from the land office showing property divisions within the section.

Unless the land is too rocky or sandy, you can usually grade a simple roadway yourself by making a drag out of angle irons or I-beams, attaching it to your rear bumper, and dragging it along the desired path. If you have to work in very loose sand, it is wise to obtain a jeep or other

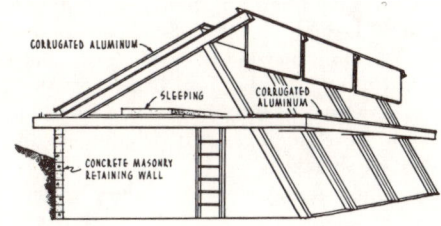

With a shed roof *cabin, consider making the roof steep enough to accommodate a loft sleeping-platform for overflow guests*

4-wheel drive vehicle for the pulling job.

Once the road is cleared of brush and rocks, the tires of your car and the inhospitable climate will usually keep down plant growth and take care of the maintenance. To hold down blowing sand or keep an adobe soil from becoming gummy during a rainstorm, you can pour a light film of used crankcase oil over your roads and parking area.

(Several tract owners reported that to establish a roadway, they merely pointed out the desired path to the concrete truck that delivered concrete for their slab. Eight wheels loaded with several tons of concrete did the job for them.)

If your land is too rugged for an owner-builder project, or you'd simply prefer to hire the job done, you can have a roadway cleared to your site by a grading

---

CABIN IDEA NO. 2: *You build one stage at a time*

For desert tract owners *whose site might be a sloping piece of land, backing this cabin into the hillside would provide some of the built-in air-cooling properties of a basement or cellar. Adding new space would be simple—like playing dominoes—with each new unit tied on to either end of the basic structure.*

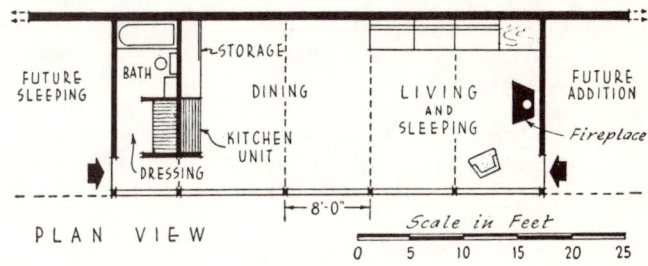

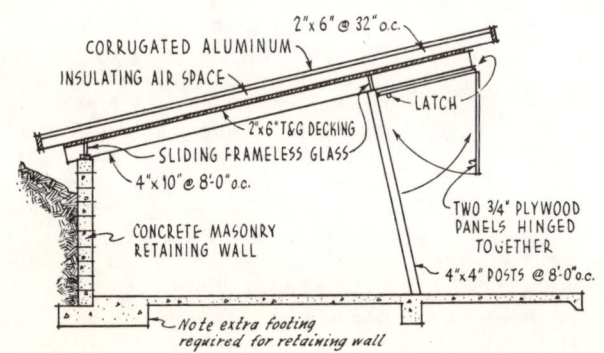

View would be in one direction only, with cross ventilation provided by high narrow ribbon of sliding glass in opposite wall. Through system of hinged panels (which might be glass instead of plywood) the cabin could be totally closed, partially open with one flap down as a sun shield (as shown directly left), or wide open for view. Cabin ideas on these two pages are from Architects Buff, Straub & Hensman, Los Angeles

company. Since most such firms charge a minimum day-rate, again you'll find it less expensive to share these costs with neighbors if possible. A grader costs $120 to $150 per day for crew and equipment and can grade up to eight miles in a day's time.

Road drag *is a triangular "plow" made from 4-foot lengths of angle or I-beam steel, should weigh about 200 pounds. Build center brace to support the added weight—box of sand, or crew of children*

LOCATING YOUR CABIN ON THE SITE

You'll want to consider view, topography, accessibility to a road, and prevailing wind when you locate your cabin. Don't build in any low spot that looks as if it may have been a run-off wash at some time for desert storms. Rain in the desert can be as unpredictably heavy as it is infrequent. A higher site will probably give you a better view, and it will invite the desert breeze. You might also look at surrounding acreage and try to guess where your "next-door neighbors" would be most likely to place their cabins. On the open desert, 5 acres is a relatively small site when you want to give a cabin a certain degree of isolation.

GETTING THE CABIN BUILT

Least painful way to comply with the minimum improvement requirements listed in your lease is to have the cabin built by a local builder specializing in this type of construction. Some builders will give you a 400-square-foot minimum cabin for as little as $1,200. For this figure you get a floor, four frame walls, and a roof. Obviously, for a price of only $3 per square foot, finishes are far from luxurious.

If you prefer to do most of the work yourself on weekends or perhaps on a vacation, you can bring the cost of a minimum structure down to $600 or $700 —or spend the difference on a more exciting and interesting cabin. "Kits" containing the essentials to build a minimum acceptable structure are available in several desert communities.

Most owner-builders have a local contractor lay their concrete slab (average charge: 75 cents to $1 a square foot) and then build the superstructure themselves. They haul materials out from town on weekends. Many recommend that you pre-cut most of your structural members before you haul the lumber to the site.

If you want a cabin that is both attractive and easy to build, you might invest in a few hours of an architect's know-how and imagination. Ask him to help you work out a plan and construction scheme designed for pre-cutting and on-the-job assembly.

HOW TO BEAT THE HEAT

Without water or power, your only air-conditioning will be the breeze. You can do a number of things to shield a cabin from the heat and capitalize on this breeze.

• First line of defense is your roof. The lighter its color and the more reflective its surface, the more natural insulation you'll build in against the sun's rays. The brilliant white coating that many desert home owners apply to inexpensive roll roofing is a good choice.

Recently aluminum roofing seems to be gaining in popularity. (One warning: Install it so there are no openings where a strong desert wind can work its way underneath and sail the lightweight metal sheets through the sky like sheets of paper.) Aluminum roofing casts a glare that may bother neighbors on higher ground, and it doesn't exactly harmonize with the desert surroundings; but on the credit side it is inexpensive, fireproof, relatively free of maintenance, and should give long service.

• Be sure to provide for cross-ventilation to take advantage of the desert's built-in cooling system. But you also want to be able to shut out the desert storms. Windows and doors should let you throw open your house when you want to enjoy the desert at its best and tightly seal it when the desert elements are at their worst.

• Paint with caution—the desert sun is very hard on paint. Chances are that you'll want to use cool or natural colors on both the inside and outside of your house. Reds and brilliant primary colors seem out of place to most people who love the desert and live in it. Wind-blown sand is also one of paint's worst enemies. The more natural surfaces you can leave without painting, the less maintenance your house will require.

• Try to provide some overhead shade outdoors, preferably filtered so that the breeze can get through. Several umbrella or cottonwood trees planted now, for example, can give you a cool green parasol after about 6 or 8 years.

• A screened porch is a desert favorite. It will provide you with an outdoor living-dining area free from flies and bees.

• Insulate your roof and also your walls if this is within your budget. It will certainly pay off in comfort, both in the summer and on cold winter nights. Concrete masonry is one of the very best desert building materials since it provides a good amount of built-in insulation, requires little or no maintenance, and is completely fireproof. (Remember that fire protection in the desert isn't what it is at home; if your cabin or house should catch on fire, you might have to stand back and just watch everything combustible burn.)

WHAT DO YOU DO ABOUT WATER?

Few desert five-acre homesteaders will have water available on their tracts. Many who use their cabins chiefly for weekends will simply bring their own in cans or tanks, then drive to the nearest service station or community "water hole" and refill them as necessary.

Those who plan on longer stays or want the added convenience of tap water, will probably want to invest in a water tower and tank and have their water delivered. Cost for a typical steel tank and tower runs from about $250 to $400 installed to provide gravity flow to your house or cabin. At present, water costs about $7 to $10 per 1,000 gallons depending on delivery distance to your site.

Even before *you have modern plumbing inside your cabin, water tower and tank can be fitted to provide simple clean-up facilities for desert grime. For winter use, wrap pipes with an insulating material*

If you plan to be your own builder, you'll need water for construction. If you plan on building a tower and tank eventually, it would be well to build them first.

In most desert areas that have been classified for small-tract development, drilling a well is not feasible. Drilling costs are high—about $8 to $10 per foot for drilling and casing—and sub-surface water depths are too great. With a strong community organization, however, you might be able to consider drilling a community well and sharing the costs.

WIND PRECAUTIONS

Besides providing a close fit on doors and windows, about the only other wind precaution is to be sure your roof is secure. Both roll roofing and built-up roofing, especially, are relatively immune to wind damage. Both aluminum roofing and asphalt shingles should be carefully applied so that gale winds won't pry them loose. Be sure to get asphalt shingles that are specially designed to withstand high and gusty winds.

ELECTRIC POWER

This is another rare desert commodity unless you live close to a developed year-around community. In most areas presently being filed on and leased, a power company is so far distant that even if an organization of many home owners were to apply for service, the cost of bringing the power lines to the area would still be prohibitive.

Recently, however, private power companies have been considering extension of lines in some areas, and in others home owner organizations have received promising attention to applications placed with the Rural Electrification Agency (R.E.A.).

In the Joshua Tree-Twentynine Palms area, the R. E. A. agreed to loan a local organization $930,000 so that it could erect 299 miles of line to serve 897 members. Members agreed to pay an initial $10 fee and $10 per month for the first year of operation of the new power service, following which the charge was to be based on usage.

Where power is not (or probably never will be) available, some desert tract owners have installed their own small gasoline-operated generators to provide for a limited power system. A small 3-kilowatt generator (capable of producing 3,000 watts of electricity) will cost from $300 to $500. You have to be selective about what you turn on at any one time, but this size generator will actually operate a television set (provided practically everything else is turned off).

No bricks *to lay, no concrete to pour; hard-baked earth makes a natural patio floor. In planning this patio, owners accepted what they found—clear air, bright sun, natural desert plants. Rather than try to close off the vast dry desert, they have learned to enjoy living with it. View from dining window looks out to Arizona's Catalina Mountains*

Electric refrigerators or freezers are not recommended since the continual on-off cycling of the motors wears out generator brushes in a very short time. If you do want a refrigerator, it would be wisest to install a gas-operated model. If you want a freezer, one desert home owner recommends that it be locked and unplugged during the day; then turned on and allowed to run for several hours during the evening to restore a safe temperature. When necessary, open it just long enough to load it or transfer items to the freezer section of the refrigerator.

One couple who live year around on the desert pay only about $4 per month for the fuel that is needed to operate their small generator. Larger families or late-at-night readers would undoubtedly have to pay more.

COMMUNITY ORGANIZATIONS

One of the best ways to make your desert community more hospitable is to initiate a tract-owners' organization. In almost every desert area, we found that these organizations, modeled after typical urban home owners' associations, had proved very valuable—not only in helping to provide needed services for the area, but in maintaining concern for the appearance of their area and in providing a common bond of interest among owners.

Often these organizations are limited to owners of all tracts in one or more defined sections. Sometimes this is a pre-organized group who all filed on adjoining lands in a section so that as a group they might develop their own desert retreat.

In the New Horizons Desert Acres, 1 N., 5 E., Sec. 12 in San Bernardino County, one of the organization's initial projects is to obtain one tract for recreational purposes and build a community recreation hall. In another area, a tract-owners' organization formed primarily to obtain service roads for their section. The county agreed to do the grading if the owners would provide the money for materials.

Canvas cover *keeps sand, animals out of pool during storms and at night. Pegs go through grommets into holes in curb*

Four-foot-deep "dunking pool" *at this home in California's Yucca Valley is just right for a cool bath on a hot day. Water, which comes from a tower tank, is used for irrigation when the pool is drained every two weeks during the summer months*

The owners' words best describe this retreat: *"You get up . . . you have breakfast . . . you sit out in the sun. Pretty soon it begins to get hot. You move into the shade. Then you begin to notice things. A squirrel moves. You see a little wildflower. It takes a little while before things come 'into focus' . . ."*

Built for under $500...

A wooden "tent" for the desert

This "wooden tent" was built in the Monrongo Valley near Palm Springs, California, where the owners found they could obtain a 5-acre desert camp site under the Small Tract Act. Since theirs was to be used for "recreational" purposes, there were no requirements on length of time they had to spend in actual residence on their property.

They paid a nominal filing fee, and then were assessed a rent of $5 per year for 3 years. The lease stipulated that at the

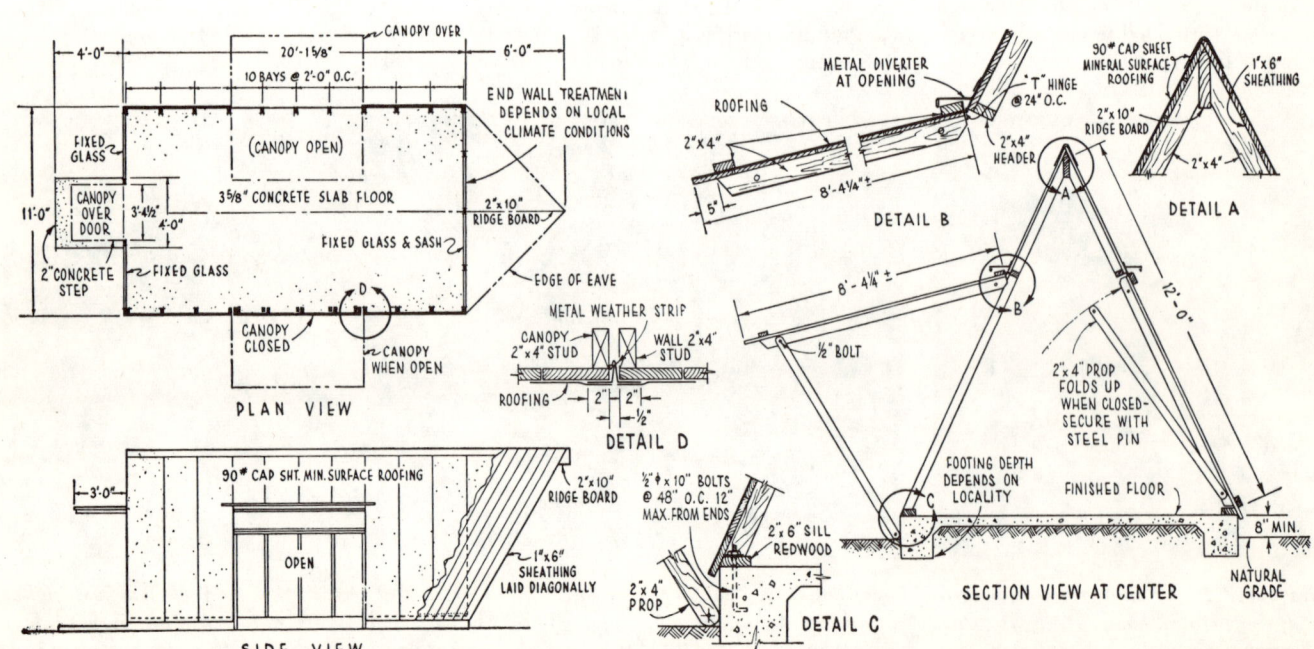

Diagonal sheathing and 2-by-4 structure are visible in this view through the interior of the small cabin. When side flaps are raised the amount of usable floor space is greatly increased

Head-on view of the A-frame wood tent shows its potential with "full wing spread." With the major portion of both of the walls lifted, cross-ventilation and shade are provided

end of the 3 years, by which time they must have constructed on their land "improvements appropriate for the use for which the lease was issued," they could buy the 5-acre site for only $20 an acre. In this particular case, the only actual building requirements were the minimum requirements of the county building code —a structure that could be locked up, built strong enough so it wouldn't blow over.

Although this structure was designed as a low cost shelter for the desert, it obviously could serve as a permanent headquarters camp in other sections of the West: in the mountains where you generally go deer hunting or close to your favorite fishing waters.

Situated in the desert, this structure had to provide maximum ventilation and shelter from the scorching heat of the sun when occupied. It also had to be a rockbottom, minimum cost project that could be neglected when unoccupied.

Since it would have been costly to isolate the blistering heat entirely by mechanical or structural means, the owners chose to make it comfortable through shade and free movement of air. Their design provides as much space as possible, while minimizing every possible lumber cutting and assembling job.

From a construction point, it would be difficult to build a simpler, less expensive structure that would satisfy all the demands we have mentioned. All the materials used are commonly available and are relatively easy for the inexperienced builder to handle. The only "outside" labor required was for laying the concrete floor slab (which, incidentally, accounted for two-fifths of the total cost).

POSSIBLE VARIATIONS

There are unlimited ways you could alter the original cabin in materials and in shape and design. The variations depend primarily on the climate, where you build, and what materials are available and inexpensive locally.

Perhaps the most logical variation might be in the floor system.

By using a conventional floor framing system, then applying wood decking to the floor, you could avoid the expense and inconvenience of a reinforced concrete slab. Build the frame on pre-cast concrete piers, and you are ready to apply the roofing material.

The other variation on use of materials would be in the choice for a roof. Here are only a few suggestions:

Use shingles rather than composition roofing (nailed to diagonal sheathing).

Replace diagonal sheathing with plywood or hardboard; cover with roofing.

Replace diagonal sheathing with wood lap-siding laid horizontally.

For a translucent roof, use corrugated plastic panels.

You might want to design the cabin to gain even more ventilating area. Another hinged section, high on the roof, or louvers on the wall opposite the entry might allow for better circulation.

In a cooler climate or where there is a strong prevailing wind you might close one side altogether or make the opening on that side smaller. Or you could add a stove or prefabricated fireplace for warmth.

If you liked, you could make the cabin more symmetrical, providing a shaded area and protection for the window walls on both ends.

On a hillside site, you might want to carry the structural pattern to a logical conclusion with a deck on one side and protected space below.

At the beach or in marshy land, you could prop the cabin up in the air and provide decks on both sides.

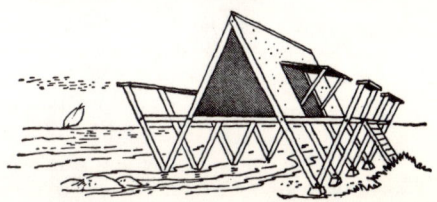

PHILIP FEIN

An old black pot-bellied stove, given prominence in the room by a backing and platform of used brick, substitutes for a fireplace. Copper and brass hearth accessories add warm accents

DEARBORN-MASSAR

Pass-through window from the kitchen to the deck helps to tie in the interior with outside living areas. Open shelf storage makes things handy for the cook. Architects: Terry and Moore

Arranging the interior

With careful planning, the special charm of a favorite vacation spot can be brought right inside the cabin. Choose the smooth blues of the ocean, the textured greens of the forest, the sandy desert browns for your decorative scheme, and build an atmosphere of informal comfort at a leisurely pace of living with all out-of-doors as a backdrop.

Everyday tasks are streamlined and minimized only as a result of thoughtful organization of the vacation household. The routine of cooking, housecleaning and entertaining will try the patience and endurance of even the most adventuresome housewife if the stove won't heat and there is no place to keep extra bedding — if she must wash by hand and set a table with odds and ends of cast-off utensils. Provide the convenience of properly functioning equipment, adequate and accessible supplies, and the dignity of tasteful furnishings, and the change to country living will be a welcome rest.

Consider your family's varied interests, ages and schedules. Arrange the furniture — which should be simple and sturdy — in flexible groupings for these activities: for conversation, a game of cards, lazy refreshments, and for the junior grade cowboys who whoop it up all day long.

The fireplace grouping, the very heart of the cabin, can be worked out in combination with bookshelves and fireside seats, a cheerful corner for dining and reading, and plenty of space for the tired sportsman to relax in warm, dry comfort. A rack for wet clothes, a handy supply of wood and perhaps a chopping block on the hearth will save many steps. The *Sunset* book, "How to Design and Build Your Fireplace," suggests many pleasing arrangements.

Furniture that "can take it," that can be wiped clean in an instant, is far more practical than overstuffed pieces that are inclined to musty mildew and require frequent dry cleaning. Paint and ingenuity will coordinate the unmatched units and contrive space-saving arrangements that serve more than one function. Hutch benches, studio couches, folding tables and chairs all increase cabin flexibility. The handyman can easily construct sawbuck tables and barrel chairs, and cane chairs of Mexican or Chinese manufacture are well designed and inexpensive.

Remember that varying floor levels, although adding interest, will make it difficult to move heavy supplies and to wheel furniture outside. Rugs should be reversible and small enough to shake clean — for the vacuum cleaner usually stays behind. Sandy footprints will sift through straw matting, which is an especially good floor covering at the beach.

Don't make the mistake of competing with the scenery by putting up too many curtains. Paneled walls are often pleasing frames for the view in themselves, and folding shutters will assure privacy and security when needed. Sometimes a simple valance of fabric, wood or metal is sufficient. If you prefer draperies that can be drawn closed on traverse rods, keep them plain. It is wise to have the rod built into the window frame at the time of construction if it is to bear an especially heavy load of fabric. Bamboo shades, fitted vertically or horizontally to the windows, filter the sun by day but do not give complete privacy.

Denim, burlap, monk's cloth, ticking, sail cloth, canvas, muslin, plastics—these and many other sturdy materials are well suited to vacation wear and tear. Corduroy tailors well and needs no ironing, and

Indian rugs and animal hides are effective as either upholstery material or floor coverings. Cushions should be at home indoors or out. The clever decorator will keep a sewing machine at the cabin, and get an entire bolt of bright gingham to be made into aprons, pot holders, table cloths, and laundry bags as special needs arise. Thoughtful coordination of even these small items adds immeasurably to a pleasant interior.

Color, of course, is the keynote to the whole scheme. A dark interior can be lightened and a small room made to seem larger when bright colors are tastefully introduced. Don't be afraid of bold primaries, but above all keep to the tones echoed in the vacation surroundings. In general, plain fabrics, plaids, stripes and the primitive geometric designs of Indian rugs, tapa cloths and the like are more appropriate than large floral patterns.

Lamps and other accessories may be plain and unobtrusive—or special points of accent and interest. Don't flounder at a half-way point. If you have any flair with a paint brush, have a little fun spoofing your friends and family with wise little mottoes, interesting peasant figures and other whimsical designs as decorative panels and borders. Tack up sketches of the cabin locale, whether by a talented adult or a crayon-wielding three-year-old. Other pictures are best used with restraint, in favor of good maps and photographs of the area.

CABIN BEDS AND BUNKS

The vacation home must boast regular and emergency sleeping accommodations for a greater number than would be expected of a house in the city of the same size. This means careful planning to utilize all available space as economically and attractively as possible, without sacrificing comfort. Double-purpose areas are usually the answer — beds in combination with sofas and storage units, or so designed that they may be brought out of hiding at a moment's notice.

Bunks may be built one directly atop the other, or staggered to provide extra cupboard and drawer space as well as more head room at the lower level. Sofas that also serve as beds are particularly versatile, whether single or double. Good casters—hard-wheeled, ball-bearing types are best—make it easy to move large units. Conceal one single bed under the other, to be rolled out when needed; or plan a corner arrangement of these two, perhaps with a square chest for blanket storage at their heads. A double bed may be pared down to sofa width by a back-rest storage unit; or the full size may be used as a wide lounge.

Count on porches, decks and lofts for good sleeping spots, and remember that Army bunks and cots are sturdy and inexpensive. Inner spring mattresses may be obtained in sizes to fit these cots, and the investment in extra comfort is well worth while. Metal bunks are cumbersome to move, but metal cots with folding legs and also those which fold in the middle are easily moved and stored. Canvas cots, though they are inclined to be cold and require extra padding for "insulation," can be knocked down into a bundle no larger than 37 by 8 by 4 inches. Sleeping bags and air mattresses are handy extras.

Don't forget the housewife in your plans— she should be able to tidy up in the morning without struggling against an inaccessible mountain of bedding. Have you ever tried to straighten out a double-width, double bunk that is set into a corner or alcove? Think twice, and plan to keep all sides of the bed within reasonable reach.

Consider, too, the early-morning comfort of the dressing area, and provide a little electric heater or a portable kerosene stove for quick warmth in the bedroom or washroom. For the cabin without running hot water, a stand for a hot teakettle near the basin is a "must," and remember that even without regular plumbing, surface drainage can be provided for a standard sink or basin. A marble dresser top, if you are lucky enough to find one, can prove a sturdy, splash-proof standby to your dressing room equipment.

CHARLES R. PEARSON

This one-room cabin shows carefully budgeted space for cooking, sleeping, and storage. Ladder which hooks up out of sight leads to extra sleeping quarters on balcony. Cook can visit with guests, but kitchen work counters are screened from view

The convenient cabin bunk appears in many variations. Here are some of the best installations we have seen.

In the following plan, arrangements have been made to sleep five persons—not bad for an 18 by 24-foot cabin.

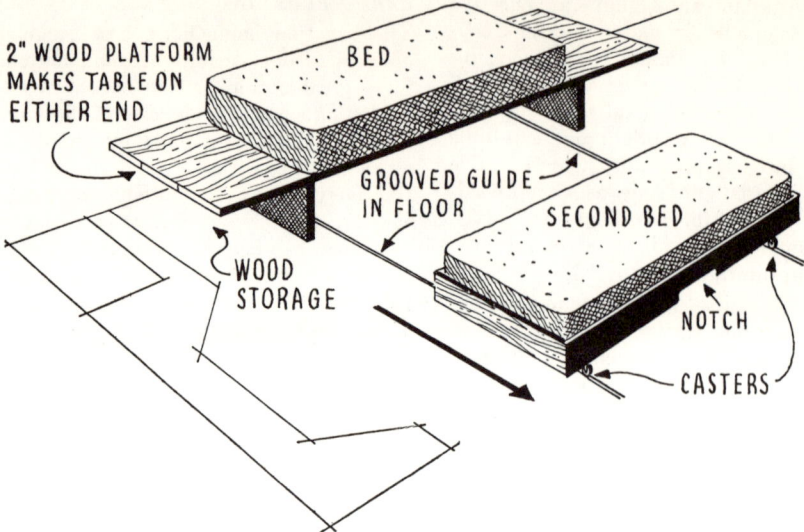

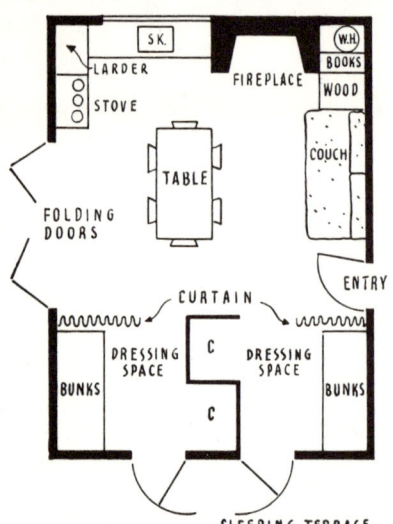

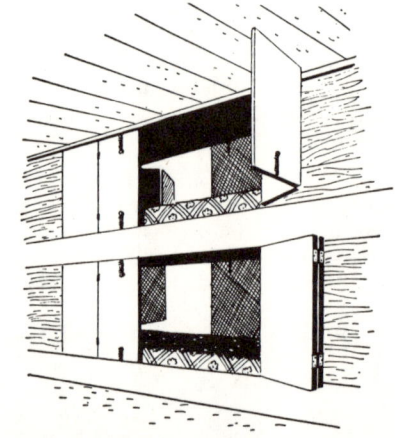

combination is to store a pull-out frame under a couch. The extension of the base of the couch is a tried and true way to build excellent substitutes for end tables.

The hinged bunk has a space saving advantage over the built-in type. The labor involved in closing and opening is a disadvantage, however.

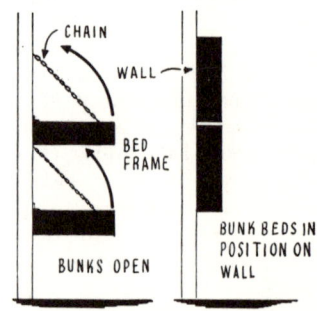

The sofas-by-day, beds-by-night take up more space than bunks, but their use as furniture during the day compensates for the loss.

The bunk-wall has several advantages. The bunks are both in the room and on the porch. Because they can be closed off from the room, bedtime can be optional, regardless of general activity in the living room. This type of bunk is appreciated by those who like outdoor sleeping.

Another way to avoid the upper-lower

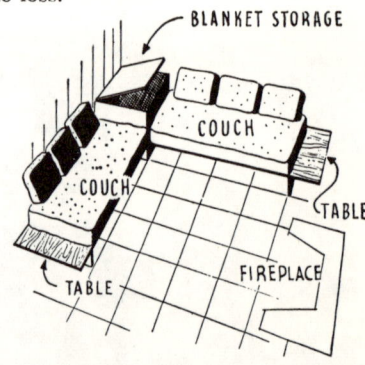

Corner, blanket storage cabinet serves as night table; and it works out the most logical two-couch arrangement.

A bunk variation on the two-couch idea is the hybrid shown here. Its advantage is the increased storage space.

Combination storage wall and bookcase makes a serviceable bunk background.

JERRY A. ANSON

This interesting cantilevered arrangement permits maximum storage in drawers below bunks and in cupboard at the head. Bedspreads and curtains are made of red plaid

For those who hate a closed-in feeling, here's a simple solution: stagger the lower and upper bunks and if you wish to have a view when you wake up, locate a window above the head of the lower bunk.

In the view above, the kitchen alcove is open and the beds are in their daytime position. In photo at left, the mechanics of the bed-davenport are displayed. When the beds swing under the built-in cases, the width of the bed is reduced to comfortable seat width. Note pillow and blanket storage space.

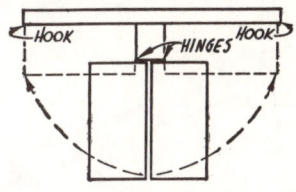

Below is a rough sketch of an in-a-wall bed. Two-by-four frame is bolted to cross-

pieces of the door; springs are bolted to it. The knotty pine wall actually forms the platform for the let-down bed. Hinged legs, cut in tapered form, fold flat when not in use, and add a decorative note to the plain paneled wall. Extra storage for bedding and clothing is built into the alcove. Photograph of the bed, at right, illustrates it in the closed position, allowing extra room for daytime living space.

R. WENKAM

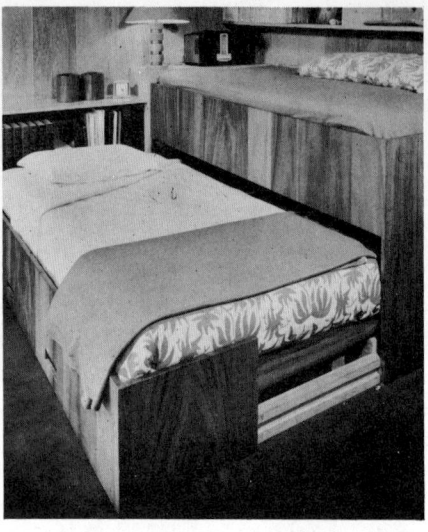
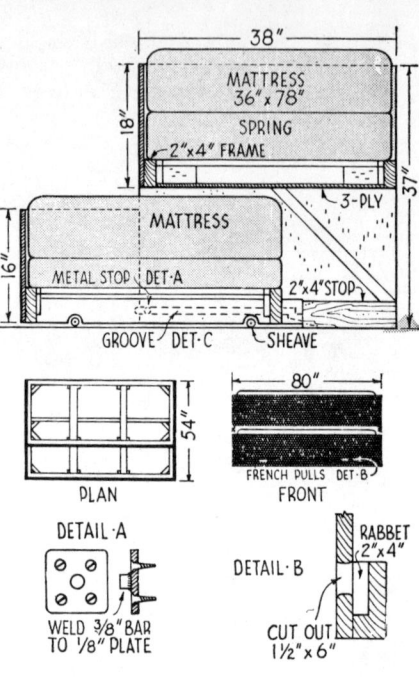

Bunk bed *with stair-step arrangement saves space in small bedroom. With bottom bunk pushed in, side of top bunk becomes a backrest for "sofa." Plenty of headroom. Wood is natural South American monkeypod. The architect was Philip Fisk*

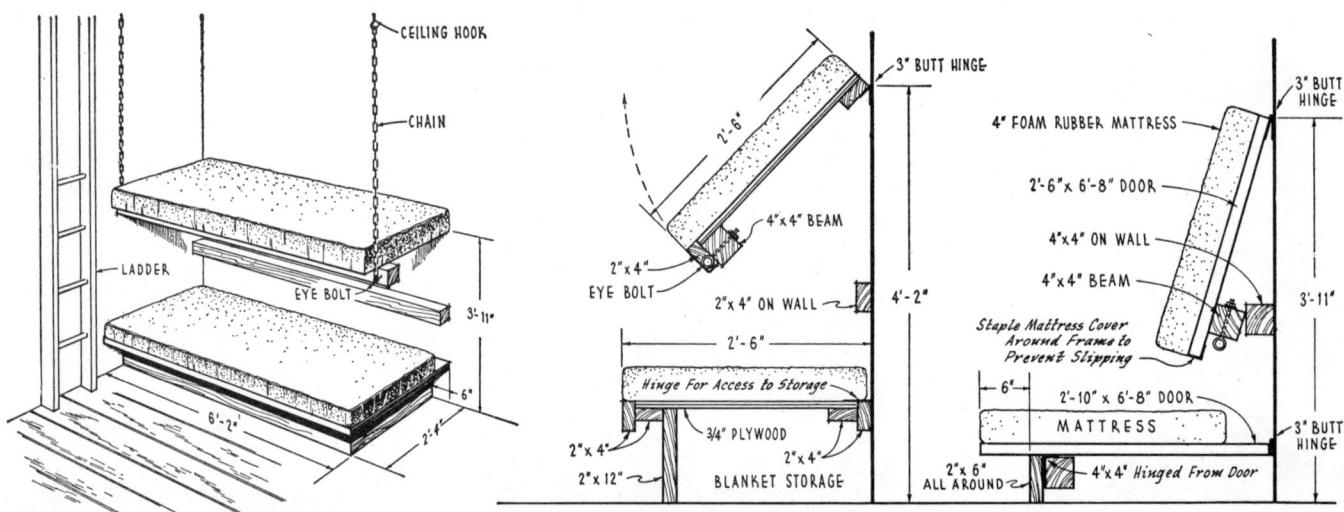

Variations *on combination fold-down, chain-supported couch-bunk as designed by architect Henrik Bull for overflow sleeping in mountain cabin; adaptable to boys' room. Fish net stretched from ceiling to edge of the top bunk could be used for safety*

ERNEST BRAUN

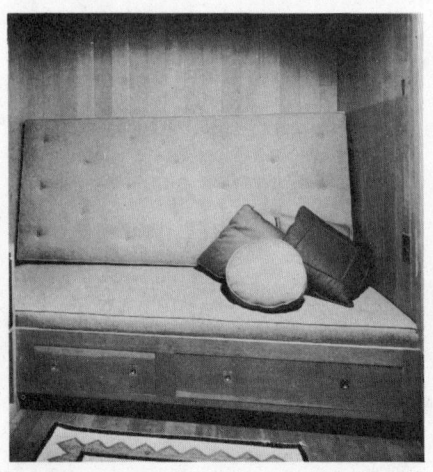

Left. *When bunk is down, this is a seven-foot lounge.* **Right.** *Bunk in raised position is fastened to wall with heavy butt hinges, locked in place by two ¾ by ¾-inch square spring bolts which fit into the wall. Top custom-built mattress is held in place with tabs attached to the plywood base. The architect was Joseph Esherick*

DINING ARRANGEMENTS

Mealtime should be the time for relaxing and visiting, for family conferences and leisurely entertaining. Even though this ideal is too often shattered by busy individual schedules and hasty snacks at irregular hours, a pleasant, convenient dining area is high on the planning list.

Arrange first to make the most of your

Mountain scenery *can be seen from dining table with this "picture window" arrangement. View here is of Lake Tahoe. Between meals, family games and projects take over*

For small cabin, *this disappearing table is a real space-saver. Handy for games or meals, out of the way when out of use*

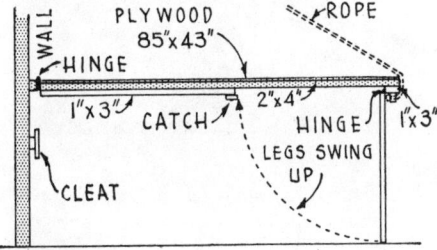

Cross-section *of the table in down position*

Legs *fit under frame, are locked in place with swivel catches. Ropes, pulleys hold table up; metal or wood catches would do.*

vacation surroundings: to sit near a window overlooking a favorite view, or to enjoy eating near the warmth of the cabin fireplace on chilly evenings. If you have a table that can be moved about, indoors and out, in keeping with the season and the guest list, so much the better. Tables whose heights and seating capacities can be ingeniously varied add to the cabin's flexibility, but they must be strong and simply constructed to be practical. A good drop leaf design is always dependable. Dining chairs and benches should harmonize with the rest of the room for between-meal use in other areas.

Some families may prefer a breakfast bar arrangement, particularly when space is at a premium. This fixed counter, which also serves as a low partition and storage unit, can be equipped with blinds or shutters that will completely screen the kitchen area between meals. One caution: remember that it is much more pleasant to be able to lean back in a standard chair than to perch atop a high stool, so plan for a comfortable compromise.

Your cabin deserves its own set of dishes and silver, instead of a collection of rejected items from the urban buffet. Consider plastics, restaurant-weight china or good pottery, and stainless steel utensils. Mugs serve as both glasses and cups, and eliminate saucers. Have plenty of trays on hand, and keep linens at a minimum.

The dining table, after meals, doubles as work table, desk, and game center. For this reason, as well as to lighten the vacation laundry load, the surface should be sturdy and easily cleaned. Linoleum is a very satisfactory table top, and can be wiped clean and dry in an instant. Natural wood, carefully finished and waxed, can be made to resist heat and stains; and there are many excellent plastic surfaces on the market. Wrought iron garden tables with heavy glass tops are particularly adaptable to a beach house, and have the added advantage of being relatively unobtrusive.

Convenient *serving counter shown open to kitchen in the lower photo can be screened from the living areas by a Venetian blind*

CHARLES R. PEARSON

Dining end of all-purpose room, windows uncurtained. Neat, colorful storage in Dutch cupboard adds interest and convenience

Open fire provides cheery background for rainy-day meals. Sturdy colonial treasures are especially suited to cabin living

JERRY A. ANSON

Disappearing table, 8 feet long, is 2-inch slab of laminated, circular-cut oak, painted black. Support mounted on wheels

Set up in the kitchen, black table top makes an attractive breakfast counter. Walls are lemon yellow; the trim is a dark green

CHARLES R. PEARSON

Low partition separates kitchen from dining area, provides storage for dishes without detracting from openness of room

Dining shelf, opposite side of photo at left, built at standard thirty-inch height, affords maximum enjoyment of the view

CONVENIENCE IN THE KITCHEN

The vacationing housewife may be willing to leave her cares behind her, but not her kitchen conveniences. No matter how rustic and informal the rest of the cabin, the kitchen must be as up to date as possible if the cook, too, is to enjoy herself "away from it all."

Gas or electric appliances are, of course, ideal, and compact all-in-one units, including refrigerator, sink, stove and storage are available for the small kitchen.

Be sure of a constant ice supply if an ice box must substitute for a refrigerator—ice houses, stocked during winter months, are located in many northern lake-side regions. Coolers are still popular; just be sure to locate it so that the air inlet is on the shady side of the cabin. Never store food where animals might get at it.

Without standard utilities, kerosene and butane stoves operate efficiently, and the old-fashioned wood stove is a cabin standby. The wood stove with a water reservoir assures a supply of hot water for dishes and washing, eliminating the need for constant kettles atop the stove when there is no other water heater. Remember that the walls and floor around the stove should be protected from flying sparks by brick, tin, or asbestos, and that you will need a conveniently placed and well-filled woodbox.

Where electricity is available, a useful combination is a wood stove for kitchen warmth and general cooking, plus an electric hot plate or small stove for a small, quick meal or a single pot of coffee. It is handy, particularly on moving day, to bring a complete hot meal to the cabin in an electric roaster. Barbecue cookery also adds variety; in cabin country, douse coals afterward, and take every possible fire precaution.

If you are tight on space, consider an apartment-size stove (20 inches wide). Under-the-counter refrigerators also save space.

Portable appliances can help make cabin life easy: Electric fry pans, sauce pans, pressure cookers, griddles, rotisseries. It is a simple matter to bring one or more of them from home for a weekend or vacation.

The vacation larder is often beset to provide impromptu meals for guests of elastic numbers and appetites, and infrequent shopping trips make it necessary to plan carefully for well-rounded menus and convenient storage of staple goods. Canned foods, prepared baking mixes, dried fruits and vegetables will go a long way toward supplementing a few fresh items. A kitchen blackboard facilitates a constant inventory of these supplies, which should be kept in airtight metal or glass containers for maximum protection against rodents and insects.

R. WENKAM

The three hinged panels of this free-standing all-purpose unit will seat up to eight people, fold to conceal storage of camp stools and other equipment. Sliding-door cupboards, drawers at end and other side of cabinet contain dishes and silverware

CHARLES R. PEARSON

This combination of wood stove and small electric unit is ideal for many cabins, provides quick emergency heat as well as old-fashioned comfort. Ample storage for kindling under hinged seat at right. Brick wall is both decorative and practical

JERRY A. ANSON

In a rustic kitchen you can let yourself go without being bound too much by rules of interior design. Owners welcomed rough finish of cabinets, painted Pennsylvania Dutch designs on wood, used knots as handles. Linoleum counters match the floor

JERRY A. ANSON

Small compact kitchen is equipped with few—but well chosen —utensils. Shutter doors can be pulled across tiled counter

JERRY A. ANSON

Stove in picturesque setting heats dining area, doubles as warming oven, serving buffet. Brick extends the counter surface

MORLEY BAER

In this small kitchen space, canned goods and staples are conveniently stored overhead. Light box illuminates the shelves

"Kitchen in a closet" has combination sink, range, refrigerator (below), plus counter. Architects: Burde, Shaw, and Kearns

MORLEY BAER

Extra bed, always handy for emergency use, folds in middle for compact storage. Plenty of room also for bedding in closet

Closed, the storage unit shown at left becomes a paneled wall. Light-weight Chinese peel chairs harmonize with knotty pine

STORAGE FACILITIES

Safe, convenient storage of the myriad articles of special and standard cabin equipment should be a part of the basic building plan. Space must be carefully allocated for the quantities of food and other supplies necessary during occupancy, as well as for those items that are to be left at the site between vacations. The best plan is to list, then measure, all of the articles that are to be stored, seasonally or permanently; and to design the storage spaces around these specifications.

Be liberal, and use your imagination, for careful forethought and organization at this stage can preclude the need for hodgepodge extra cabinets as time goes on.

There are many ingenious ways to build easily accessible storage units into the rooms where they are needed, and the wooden interiors of most vacation homes lend themselves ideally to the carpentry camouflage of doors and drawers that harmonize with the lines and materials of the walls themselves.

Plan an inside storage wall where possible, one that opens on both sides of the partition. Doors should be scaled to the spaces within, to bring every shelf and rod within easy reach and eliminate groping in dark corners. "Snuggers," strong spring fasteners for cupboard doors, permit maximum access space with a minimum of hardware. Drawers of all sizes can be made to slide directly into the wall.

Some storage "walls" may be only partial partitions, free-standing units that do not extend to the ceiling to detract from the open feeling of the cabin. Bookcases and breakfast bars are commonly designed with this dual purpose in mind. Window seats with hinged tops double as chests, and many small "extras" may be cached in the shallow space between the studding. Simple open shelves and racks can be decorative as well as useful, but remember to keep the equipment stored here arranged to an orderly and pleasing plan.

The following main storage needs for an average cabin can be adapted to your own requirements:

1. Clothing: Family vacation wardrobes should be protected from mildew, rodents and moths and other insects. Assign a special section to heavy work clothing and sports attire, where it will not crush or soil other garments, and keep an extra assortment of wraps and bathing suits on hand for guests.

2. Linen and bedding: It is a good idea to line one bunk or closet with metal for permanent storage of all mattresses and blankets. Linens should, of course, be kept near the point of use, and special compartments can often be built under bunks or into headboards for these items.

3. Food and utensils: The kitchen and pantry will be overloaded with more food and probably even more utensils than are required for an urban family. Storage for heavy sacks of vegetables and cases of canned and bottled goods should be provided near the unloading point, and everyday staples and utensils should be conveniently placed near work centers.

4. Tools and special equipment: Cleaning equipment; a tool chest fitted with at least an axe, saw, hammer, pliers and wire cutter; and paint, kerosene and stove fuel should all be kept in a utility section. Every cabin needs a fire extinguisher and first aid box, and instructions for their use should be clearly posted.

5. Sporting equipment, hobbies, entertainment: The sportsman will want to clean his gun or wax his skis or arrange his flies as he stretches before the fire in the evening, and his equipment will inevitably be dropped and propped haphazardly unless neat racks and compartments are designed especially for these family hobbies. Plan to display instead of

discourage the youngsters' constant collections of shells and other interesting local treasures, and keep toys, crayons, and drawing paper on hand in drawers, tubs and chests. Many long hours are spent writing, reading, and playing cards, and you should be able to set up several card tables in a jiffy, quickly find cards, rules and score pads without frantically ransacking every cupboard in the house. Have a good supply of writing materials handy: ink, stamps, and stationery that is especially printed with your cabin's name and address and perhaps even a simple map of your vacation area. Avoid the musty collection of outdated literature that is too often relegated to the cabin, and keep current magazines and books carefully arranged. The vacation library should contain books on the history, flora and fauna of the area, woodcraft and hobby manuals, a first aid handbook, a few late novels, and several interesting anthologies and collections of classics and lighter works. Remember that radio reception is very often poor in remote areas, and provide space for a phonograph and record collection for musical entertainment.

6. Between seasons: Boats, outdoor furniture, and other special equipment should be brought under cover and stored during the months it is not to see service. Some articles should be disassembled, cleaned, and oiled—be sure to follow the manufacturers' instructions. A basement or other safe space under the house is ideal for storing heavy equipment, which should be raised off the ground by ropes, cradles, or racks to avoid damage by cold and moisture. Place a drip pan under the outboard motor and other machinery that may stain the floor. For more storage ideas, see the *Sunset* book, *Storage in Your Home.*

MORLEY BAER

Dishes stored on open shelves below kitchen work counter. Drawers, running full length, store silver, kitchen tools

MORLEY BAER

An interesting and practical little spice cabinet with shelving also built into the door. Guard rails help keep cans in place

MAYNARD L. PARKER

Bins for vegetables, shelves for staples alongside pots and pans. Door space has been utilized for flat pan covers, pie tins

MORLEY BAER

Cleaning tools, ironing board share left cupboard, canned goods over hamper in center. Washer at right in storage wall

Closed view of wall behind serving bar shown in left photo. Storage also built into the counter. Shutters at the windows

TOM BURNS, JR.

Quantity storage for case lots increased by stacking cans on sides; lip on shelves holds cans in. Architects: Hamlin and Martin

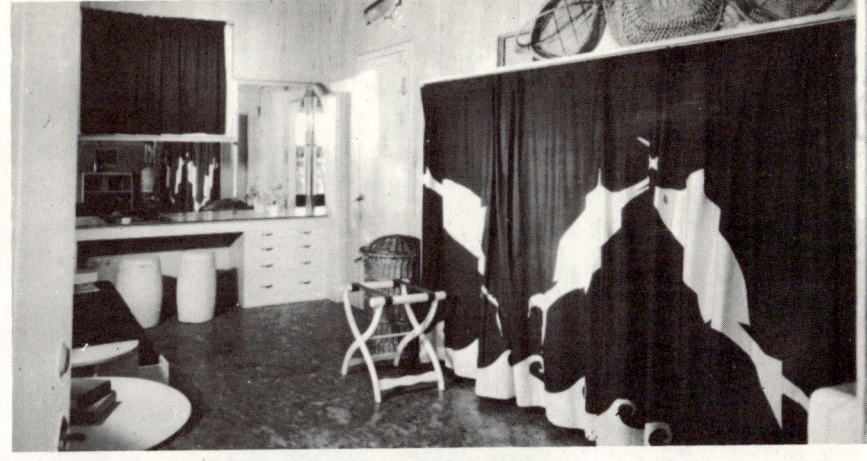

MORLEY BAER

Top left. *Headboard of bed is hinged at base, lets down for storage of pillow, blanket. Books in handy open shelves*

MAYNARD L. PARKER

Top right. *Storage must sometimes be concealed behind curtains for reasons of expedience. This bedroom at the beach meets problem attractively with oilcloth designs appliqued on duck, adequate fullness and rings that slide smoothly on brass curtain rod*

ERNEST BRAUN

Above. *Series of inexpensive pine chests of drawers, uniform in height, was purchased unfinished and fitted with new hardware for a custom appearance. Bedspread is bright burlap. Harmonizing draperies of paisley print close on traverse rods*

PHILIP FEIN

Right. *Card tables and game accessories swing out from living room wall for a game of bridge or canasta at a moment's notice. Adequate storage cupboard is cleverly concealed behind five-ply redwood panel*

CHARLES R. PEARSON

Above left. *Logs are smoothed and waxed. Floor is random width planks, pegged*

MAYNARD L. PARKER

Above right. *Wood ceiling and walls, concrete floor combined in beach house. Texture interest in sofa covers, straw rugs*

JERRY A. ANSON

Lower left. *Two-foot lengths of combed plywood are arranged like checkerboard*

JOHN ROBINSON

Lower right. *Knotty pine is perennial favorite. Stairway leads to dormitory in the loft. Note exposed beams, iron hardware*

INTERIOR FINISHES

Economy, ease of maintenance and construction, and harmony with the vacation surroundings will all determine the selection of an interior finish. The walls of a true log cabin are hard to beat for rustic charm, whether hewn flat and smooth or left rounded. Construction is laborious, however, and most builders will prefer the simpler, quicker method of nailing wooden or insulation board panels to the studding. Walls of knotty pine, knotty cedar, redwood or other boards of uniform or random widths are a pleasing background for cabin furnishings. Plywood is available in 4 by 8-foot sheets in a variety of finishes; insulation board panels also are made in this standard size, and one firm manufactures a plaster-type board covered with simulated wood grain.

In the rustic cabin, wiring and beams may be left exposed, and simple strap hinges, wooden knobs and other inexpensive hardware used throughout. A linoleum or composition tile floor is easiest to clean, while wooden planks and blocks require more frequent polishing. Concrete and tile floors are good in regions of no frost.

Building your own stretch of road

Locating, engineering and supervising the construction of a drive is really the province of a professional engineer or landscape architect. This is especially true if your land has tricky slopes, as so much of our Western land has. Cost for this kind of surveying is much lower than where the surveyor must work from corners and lay out boundaries. However, with some extra study and time, this is one part of road building you can do yourself.

If you are going to contract for either grading or surfacing, have a definite plan. Most paving contractors prefer that you not leave the locating and design up to them. A finished plan, a staked-out course, or a graded road bed gives them something to bid on. When they have to take the time to engineer and design the road, it is included in their price.

If your property slopes in several directions or is tilted in general, a landscape architect or engineer first finds the rise and fall of the land at certain intervals, locates trees, rocks, and buildings, and plots all of this on a survey map. He then lays out the road on this map, having it follow the line of least resistance, and keeping in mind points listed here. You can do some of this yourself, and these general rules may help you.

Consider placing your drive to one side or the other of your property if possible, leaving just enough room on the property line for a screen planting. This will give a maximum of free space, important on smaller places.

There should be nothing to obstruct the driver's vision for at least one car length into the private road. Even this far back, it is wise to keep planting or native plants low—no higher than the driver's eye level.

Along your drive, no planting of trees should be close enough to bother the driver of the car. Drivers go more slowly if tree trunks are close to the road. But if yours is a long road, you may want to use this device to slow traffic.

If possible, provide an unrestricted line-of-sight of at least 200 feet at all points along your road.

Be sure there is a solid reason if you curve your road. Some good reasons for making curves: to by-pass a stand of native trees; to ease a change in grade by going diagonally across a hill; to go around a high spot rather than over or through; or to avoid extra cutting and filling.

Remember the axiom that moving dirt costs money. If you are working on a tight budget and you have a choice, by all means go around or over a high spot rather than through it. It's nearly always cheaper. Bulldozer rates are usually by the hour or by the day. They vary by locality and by size of equipment. Roughly, however, you can figure on it costing you 75 cents per cubic yard to move soft earth, up to $4 a yard to cut into rock. This is figured on rates of $15 to $20 an hour, including operator (1959).

Keep in mind that both routes are curved —over a hill or around it. General practice is to go around.

It is better to traverse a very steep slope diagonally than to come straight down.

Don't build roads across slide areas. You don't have to see a fresh slide to be in a slide area. An old grass covered slide—a depression where the slide came from and a hummock where it came to rest—is just as sure a sign.

Also avoid seep areas—water comes from underground. Water under a pavement will soon cause it to fail. You can install drain tile to take the seep away, but you'd better get an engineer's help.

Plan on side-of-road and under-road drainage (culverts and gutters). Prevent any run-off water from washing across or onto your road if you possibly can. In a case such as the one illustrated here, where you go up a hill in two shots, you would probably need at least one culvert as marked.

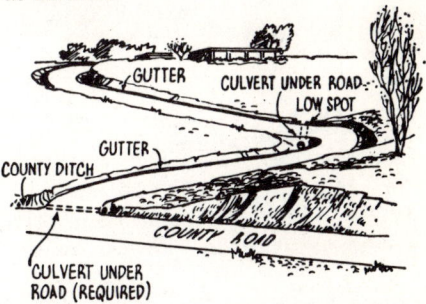

When a road crosses low spots, or when low sides alternate, you will need culverts

Locate culverts so that the discharged water will not cause gullying. You can use lined ditches, but they are quite expensive. You can use an earth ditch, if it follows a grade of about 1½ per cent.

If you must cut deep into a bank, don't overlook the problem of sloughing from the bank into the road, particularly if your soil is sandy.

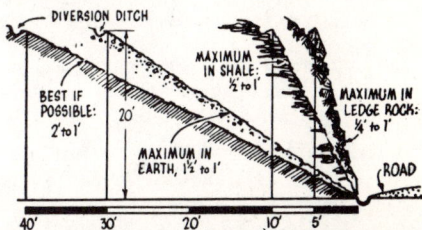

Standard maximum back slopes for roads in soil, shale, rock are set up like this

FIGURING GRADE PERCENTAGES

Percentage of grade represents steepness. See chart at left for a list of what grade percentages are within reason for country roads.

You can do a fairly accurate job of finding percentage of grade with a pair of stakes notched or nailed at five feet (or at a mark close to your eye height), a hand level, some stakes, and an assistant.

A hand level is easy to get, simple to operate. It is a small telescope through which you can sight an object and simultaneously read a bubble which tells you when you are looking along a level line.

You can figure grade percentage for any likely looking slope by several methods. The following two, using the equipment listed above, seem most simple to us.

Method 1. With white tape paint, or any other easily visible material, mark one stake a foot below its top, or a foot below the notch. Stand on the slope and

Grade Percentages

A one-foot rise in	Means grade per cent of	Which, for a road, means . . .
100 feet	1%	Usually minimum for drainage, less would be a problem
50 feet	2%	Gradual grade, not much of a problem
25 feet	4%	Gradual grade, not much of a problem
15 feet	6.6%	Gradual grade, not much of a problem
12 feet	8%	About maximum for high gear at slow speeds in average car
10 feet	10%	A noticeable grade, but easy. Steeper than this, pushing a wheelbarrow is difficult
8 feet	12.5%	No steeper if possible. Can't push wheelbarrow up
6 feet	16.6%	Have to use concrete surface. Brake action downhill and spinning uphill corrugates asphalt
5 feet	20%	Getting into real problems
4 feet or less	25% or more	You really need help. OK for short distances, but safety factor involved. Water rushes down much too fast

rest the hand level in the eye-height notch of the unmarked stake. Sight through the hand level along your chosen course up the slope. Have your assistant move the marked stake up the course until the one-foot mark you made is on your eye level. Then measure the distance along the slope between the stakes. Match that distance with the chart.

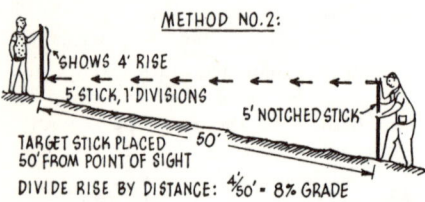

Measuring grade percentages with a given rise in unknown distance. See the chart

Method 2. Locate the uphill stake 100 feet, 50 feet, 25 feet, or any convenient distance up the hill, sight at it, and measure the rise it shows. Measuring the rise will be easier if the uphill stake is marked with one-foot divisions.

Finding grade percentage measuring rise over a known distance. Divide as shown

After you know which slopes are least steep, you can stake out a road course along them. Take a car or a jeep along a proposed course to test it, and you'll get a good idea of how it will work out.

With a little extra work in measuring angles and distances and putting them down to scale, you can roughly plot the road's course on paper. However, mapping isn't absolutely necessary. If you have the road staked out, the grading contractor will have something to bid on, or if you're doing the grading yourself, your boundaries will be all set up.

Expect some deviation when the road is graded. The tractor driver is likely to suggest minor changes, and frequently he'll be right. Even the best surveyors' plans are often subject to change, come the excavating.

If the terrain is right, a good bulldozer operator can make a good road by eye. But his roughed-out road will need to be settled and graded before paving.

ROAD DIMENSIONS

Eight feet is considered bare minimum width for a one-way drive. Fifteen feet is fair for two-way driving, and 18 feet is good for two-way (with no parking). The eight-foot minimum is for a car with its doors closed—nobody getting out. Also, it's hard to see the edges of an eight-foot road in a new wide car, especially at night. Since car treads will be near the edge of any road close to the minimum width, the tendency to crumble will be great there. The wider the drive, the less wear and tear on the material used. Don't overlook the fact that heavy service trucks may use your road. Allow some extra width for them if your road is built to accommodate their extra weight.

On a hillside, even if you are going for the minimum eight-foot width, you'd do well to start with a 12-foot width. It will narrow itself down soon enough.

A curve should have an inside radius of no less than 28 feet for a car, and not less than 41 feet for a truck.

You can make a perfect turn, with the average big car, in a circle with a 58-foot diameter. Few of us make perfect turns, and it is safer to figure on a diameter of at least 60 feet.

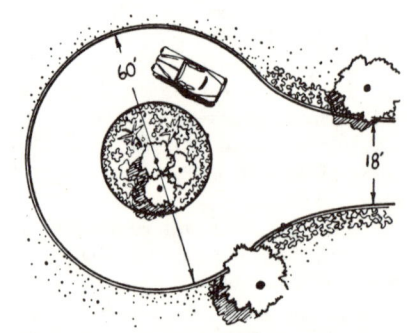

Most cars require 60 feet to turn a circle

A rule of thumb for turn-arounds goes like this: you should be able to back your car clear out of the garage before starting

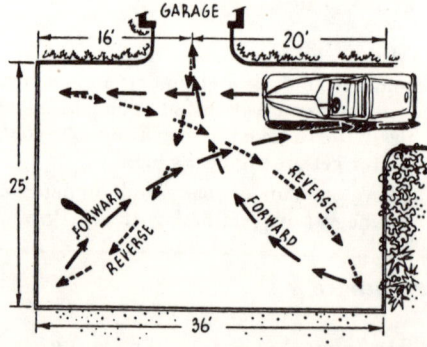

Dimensions for side-entrance turn-around

to swing. The inside radius of the swing should be 19 feet. Ideally, you should be able to back another car length before heading out your drive. In practice, such a hard and fast rule is seldom followed, and may be used only as a guide. After working out the turn-around on paper, measure it on the ground and mark it with stakes or hose. Try it with your car before putting the surface on.

Don't forget to allow for large trucks, which need added turn-around space. And don't forget to allow for guests' cars if your turn-around is also a parking area.

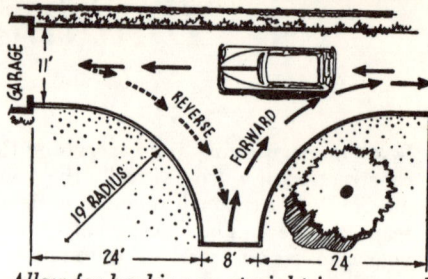

Allow for backing on straight-in approach

ENTERING THE RIGHT-OF-WAY

Whether your drive enters a county road, a state or federal highway, or a privately owned tributary road, you have to be sure that the grading you do at the intersection will not block drainage along the side of the main road.

In most sections of the West, you have to see the county engineer or the county road commissioner in order to make any changes on a county right-of-way. If it's a state or federal highway, get permission from the district highway office or highway maintenance supervisor. These men will tell you what kind of device you should use to go over the right-of-way drain. And, chances are, they also will give you some good advice on how to do it.

If the county has a deep ditch along the road, you usually have to run a pipe under the drive fill which crosses the ditch. Often the county will also ask you to install a headwall of concrete or stones on the face of the fill, to prevent undermining around the pipe. The pipe may be concrete or corrugated metal. The county inspector can help you decide what type of pipe, what diameter, and what headwall material to use. Some counties, Lane County in Oregon, for instance, install the drainage ditch crossings. You need only to furnish the material.

Where there is just a depression or slight swale at the edge of the shoulder, you can use what is called a valley gutter—the road dips down to follow the original depression. The one advantage here is that there is no possibility of plugging up. As disadvantages: when it rains the surface may get muddy; it tends to wash out if not correctly made. A pipe culvert, on the other hand, has the advantages of having no hump to drive over and of dryness during heavy weather. It has the disadvantage that it might possibly plug up.

Two ways to cross main road drains

When installing either pipe or gutter, it's wise to follow the same down grade to the lowest point as that which runs from the crown to the shoulder in the main road.

GRADING THE ROAD

You can build a usable dirt road over an average soil—neither sand nor clay extremes—if you provide for near-perfect drainage.

Drainage, for that matter, is the first requirement in any type of road.

The road must be crowned—graded higher in the middle than on the sides—so that water will flow off readily. Make the center line, or crown, higher than the sides at the rate of one-quarter to one-half inch per foot of road width, depending on the surface you are going to put on. The softer the surfacing material, the steeper you should make the crown—so water will run off faster. An 18-foot road topped with dirt or gravel should have a nine-inch crown; a hard-surfaced road of the same

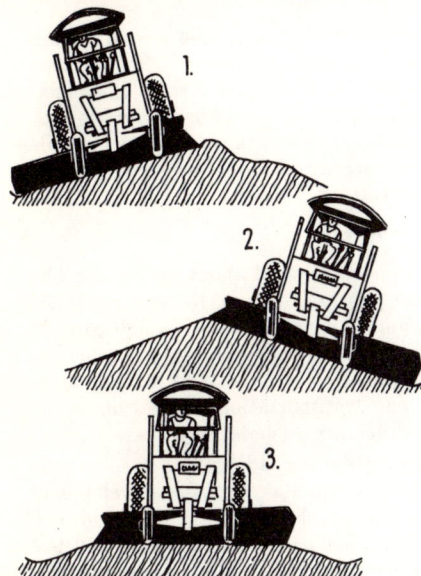

Crowned road has the center line higher than the sides at the rate of one-quarter to one-half inch per foot of road width

width would need a crown of only four and one-half inches.

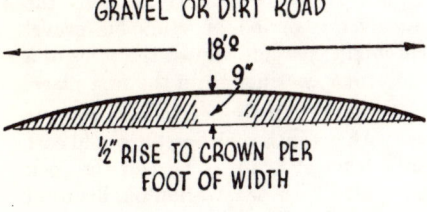

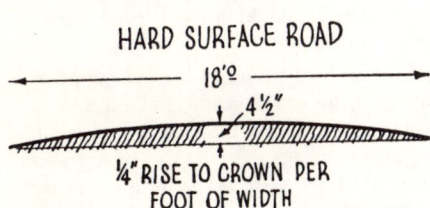

Build and maintain crown high enough to take off water. Allow for surface softness

Install ditches at both sides, and culverts to carry water under the road at places where ditches stop or will not drain adequately. Grade should be slight. If it is too steep, run-off water will rut the face of the road. Even at best, a dirt road needs regular patching.

Ideally, your dirt road should at least be held together with road oil or some other binding material.

You can eliminate wheel ruts in a dirt road that's drying out after winter rains by pulling a drag over it behind your car or truck. Use an adjustable type spike-tooth harrow with the teeth set quite flat and a plank tied on the trailing edge. The spikes roughen the surface, the plank fills in holes and ruts. Pull the implement up one side of the road and back on the other side in order to maintain the crown.

Grading and crowning a road by hand is a hopeless job. A bulldozer or a grader ("blade") can grade a lot of road in a short time.

A grader carries a movable blade underneath it; a bulldozer pushes its blade in front. The grader alone can do a good job of making grass-root cuts on comparatively level land. However, it can't work well in tight places. A bulldozer generally costs more for rental or hiring, but can make deep cuts and move much more dirt. Usually both pieces of equipment are used. The bulldozer roughs out the road, and the blade comes along to give it a crown and put on finishing touches.

GRAVEL TOPPING ON DIRT ROADS

A topping of gravel is the next step up from a plain dirt road. Gravel will bind in with a clayey soil to make a fairly firm surface that will keep you from getting stuck. Compared to other materials, it is cheap.

Sharp gravel is preferred to round or pea gravel because it locks in place to a fair degree, where round gravel rolls off.

If you are going to use the road only occasionally during the summer, a thin gravel blanket one and one-half inches thick often is enough. But for daily in-and-out traffic, figure on a covering up to four inches deep. And plan on the regular upkeep chore of shoveling or grading loose gravel back to the middle of the road.

THE ROCK BASE

If you are going to go any farther in the development of a better, longer lasting, all-year road, your next step after grading is to put in a rock base. Depth varies from four inches over sandy soil to six inches over adobe soil or in areas which get heavy frosts or snow.

There are three kinds of rock base in common use: (1) a native quarry material found in most parts of the West known variously as *red rock, rock fill, bank gravel,* or *rock-and-dirt,* used in the form in which it is dug; (2) *river bed* or *creek run gravel,* a natural mixture of aggregates with a silt that acts as a binder; 3)

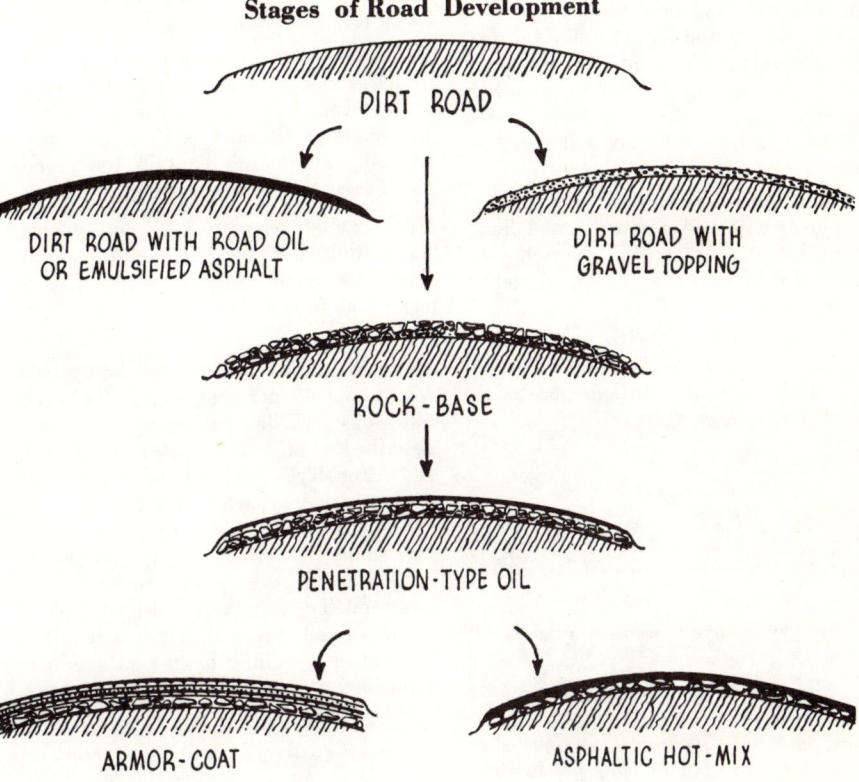

Stages of Road Development

Each stage is a usable road in itself. Crowned dirt road (top) is cheapest and also the beginning for anything else. Top it with oil or gravel or develop farther by putting on a rock base for foundation to any of the several types of hard surfaces crusher run base, crushed rock manufactured exactly for a road base. It is run through primary and secondary crushers to break rock from about two-inch size down to binder dust. Everything fits together when wet down and rolled, with the fine dust holding the larger aggregate together in a hard mass.

Any rock base will set up hard and firm when handled right and if it doesn't contain too much clay or soil.

If there's a stream bed on or near your place which contains usable gravel—a good amount of rocks and silt, but no clay—look into the possibility of hauling it to your road. If you haul the gravel yourself, you probably will need a dump truck and perhaps a mechanical loader. When you start figuring costs of the loading and hauling, you may find that your free gravel isn't so free after all. A great amount of gravel is needed to make a four-inch base over a road of any appreciable length. You have to dump a cubic yard of gravel every four and one-half feet to make a four-inch base on an 18-foot road.

If a nearby quarry offers good crusher run base, get it. In the long run, it's the best choice of the three possibilities.

Spread the material evenly over the crowned dirt road bed. You can use the road immediately after the rock base is graded out, but the road will last longer if it is rolled first. To make the base compact, wet and roll the material into place. The exact sequence of wettings and rollings is touchy and depends on how the material sets up and how it rolls. If water isn't available at the road site, you have to rent a water wagon. A roller, operated correctly, can compact the waterbound rock base so that few ruts will ever develop in it.

You can hire the grading and rolling equipment with an operator or rent light equipment and do the job yourself—although it may take twice as long if you're inexperienced.

A good rock roadway with no surfacing will last a long time. But pockets may form if the mixture contains too much clay or not enough aggregate.

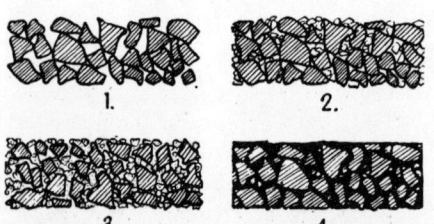

Rock bases: (1) rocks, no binding—slip; (2) and (3) silt, little clay for binding — good base; (4) too much clay — ruts

Even if your road-making budget is short, at least try to get a good rock base. If it's well made you can go back in one, five, or even ten years and pave the road. But if the base is put in poorly, you run into trouble when you want to put on a surface. A run-down rock base may have to be scarified (torn up) and rerolled. More time means more cost — perhaps more than if you had done a first-rate job on the base in the first place.

PAVING—PUTTING ON HARD SURFACE

Here are commonly used hard wearing, smooth surfaces you can put on your rock base, in order of cost beginning with the cheapest.

(Road paving nomenclature is far from standardized — a paving material often goes under one name in the San Francisco Bay area, another in Portland, and still another in Southern California. In the following sections we have attempted to use either the most descriptive or the most widely recognized names for the different paving materials.)

Penetration type oil. The cheapest of paving surfaces for roads is penetration type oil, of which there are four or five grades in regular use. This is an oil-asphalt product that will penetrate the rock base, bind it together, and make a crust on top. This treatment keeps down dust, where rock base alone will make dust.

One reason the cost is low on this kind of paving is that no rolling is necessary beyond the original compacting of the rock base. All you have to do is to have a truck come out and apply the oil. After five or six days, it will be dry and will have penetrated into the road.

Oil can go over red rock or stream bed gravel as well as crusher run base. Also, like emulsified asphalt, it can go over a dirt road—if the dirt is firm, correctly drained, and doesn't contain too much clay. Clay won't be penetrated.

Many paving contractors will put on this penetrating oil cover as a preliminary to one of the more expensive kinds of pavings which follow.

Emulsified asphalt. This is asphalt mixed with about 40 per cent water. Its possibilities as a garden paving material were described on page 58 of *Sunset* for March 1952. For dryer parts of the West—east of the Cascades, parts of the Central Valley and the Southwest—one shot of this on a sandy road makes a very good wearing surface, especially on pumice or volcanic soil. The crust of emulsified asphalt eventually sets up hard. Often, a covering of sand or screening has to go over the emulsified asphalt so it won't "pick up."

Armor-coating or macadamized asphalt. An armor-coating pavement is made this way: Oil is put down over the rock base. Right on top of it goes a layer of sharp gravel, just enough to cover the oil. It is broomed and rolled. More oil is applied, then more gravel. It is broomed and rolled again. Usually two coats are sufficient for residential roads, but you can go to three or four coats.

This is the process used for many country roads—gravel may hit your fenders when you drive over a fresh application. It has only a few disadvantages: depending on the type of oil used, it may bleed in hot weather; if used close to the house, it will track in for about six months until you can sweep it clean.

Asphaltic concrete or "hot mix." Mixed at the plant, it comes hot in a dump truck and can be placed with a blade or mechanical spreader. Hot mix is just about the ultimate in paving—just this side of concrete. It makes an excellent road, smooth and permanent. It is hard, sets up fast, and will support dead weight. It makes a very black road. A cement and water coat whitens it.

Cold mix. Cold mix is also a road paving material, but its chief use is for patching —no matter what kind of road. It's a mixture of aggregate and oils, cut back with kerosene so that it can stay loose in a pile for six weeks or more. When you patch with it, tamp it down.

ROAD COSTS

An important point about road costs: The closer you are to town, the cheaper grading and paving will be. Although costs of equipment and materials vary somewhat between regions of the West, added trucking and transportation charges make the big difference—wherever you are.

Here's what a road builder would spend at the various stages of road development (costs are exclusive of sales tax and incidentals) for a road 12 feet wide, 500 feet long—6,000 square feet—the place located 10 miles from town (1959).

He could get a crowned, dirt surface road for $240. He could have this dirt road topped with an inch and a half of gravel for a total of $420. Depending on the soil, rainfall, road use, and other factors, he might have to put a new load of gravel on the road every year. If this were the case, over a period of years his gravel road might cost him almost the price of a good armor coating job in the first place.

If he wanted a more permanent, all-year road with a 4-inch rock base, it would cost him a total of $780. If he had the rock base sealed with penetration oil, his total cost would be about $960.

For $1,140 he could have a road paved with armor coat.

Or for the most permanent road (short of concrete), he could grade, put on a rock base, have the rock base sealed with oil, and lay a surface of hot mix for a grand total of $1,380. An extra detail: header boards (at 70 cents a lineal foot using 2 by 6's, and including labor) along the sides would cost $700, for a total cost of $2,080. If he used concrete curbing instead (at $2 a lineal foot, including labor), the extra $2,000 would bring the total cost of the road up to $3,380.

WATER: *The first consideration when you select a cabin site*

Anyone who thinks about, shops for, or will soon move to a country place beyond the water company's pipelines must face these all-important questions:

Where will the water come from? Will there be enough? What kind of a pumping and pressure system will we need?

The final, detailed answers to these questions must be your own. You will arrive at them after you have figured, inquired, and talked with neighbors, well drillers, and pump dealers. Your work will be easier if you already know some of the significant facts, laws of physics, and tips on shopping that we present here.

FIRST QUESTION: IS THE WATER SAFE?

Water on your country place should be clear and free of pollution. Also, you will prefer that it be cool, colorless, tasteless, and soft.

To a certain degree, you can treat, filter, and soften water to improve it for domestic use; but you can avoid some of these extra chores completely if, right at the start, you don't buy unless the place has a source of naturally good water. If local people are satisfied with the water and if it comes from a source apparently not subject to pollution, you usually can assume that it is all right; but even here a water test might surprise you. County health officers sometimes recommend chlorination of water even though its users consider it perfectly acceptable.

Shallow ground water is most likely to be unsafe in populated suburban areas. If a shallow well (see page 118) appears to be your best water source, and if you have any doubts about the water's purity, check with the county health officer and have the water tested for evidence of bacterial contamination.

Palatable water will usually be safe to use in the garden. But some waters—especially in the Southwest and in desert areas—carry considerable minerals or salts that might eventually build up salt content in the soil to harmful levels. If you wonder about this possibility, you might ask your county agent or farm advisor what he thinks about the suitability of this water for irrigation, or have it tested by a commercial laboratory.

WATER FROM STREAM, SPRING, OR WELL?

The happiest arrangement is to have your water source—stream, spring, or well—on your own property. You can bring water from neighboring property; but even if your neighbor is a friend or relative, you should buy and have recorded a right to its use and an easement across the neighbor's land for the pipeline. This protects you against being cut off at some future date—the lands may change hands and the new owner may not be in sympathy with the former verbal or friendly arrangement.

You can store supplemental water in ponds or cisterns for livestock, irrigation, swimming, fishing, and fire protection; but such water is not generally safe or dependable for domestic use.

WATER FROM STREAMS

In the Northwest, and in a few parts of the other Western states, you may have an opportunity to obtain safe water from live streams. However, streams are always subject to pollution and muddiness.

In most Western states, property owners along a live stream have a riparian water right. This is the right to take a reasonable quantity of the water for domestic use and for irrigation. Ordinarily, you don't need a permit from a water authority. But in order to take water from a stream that does not touch your property, you have to obtain a water right through purchase of someone else's existing right or by filing application for such a right with the state water authority.

USEFULNESS OF A SPRING DEPENDS ON VOLUME OF WATER

A spring is an underground water outflow, usually on the side of a hill. If a spring flows at a usable rate the year around and is located so that it remains safe from pollution, you can often develop and protect it as an economical source of domestic water. However, before you count on a spring, check the safety of its water and the adequacy of its flow. A spring that flows late in the summer of a dry year will probably flow the year around.

Rate of flow from a spring is usually too

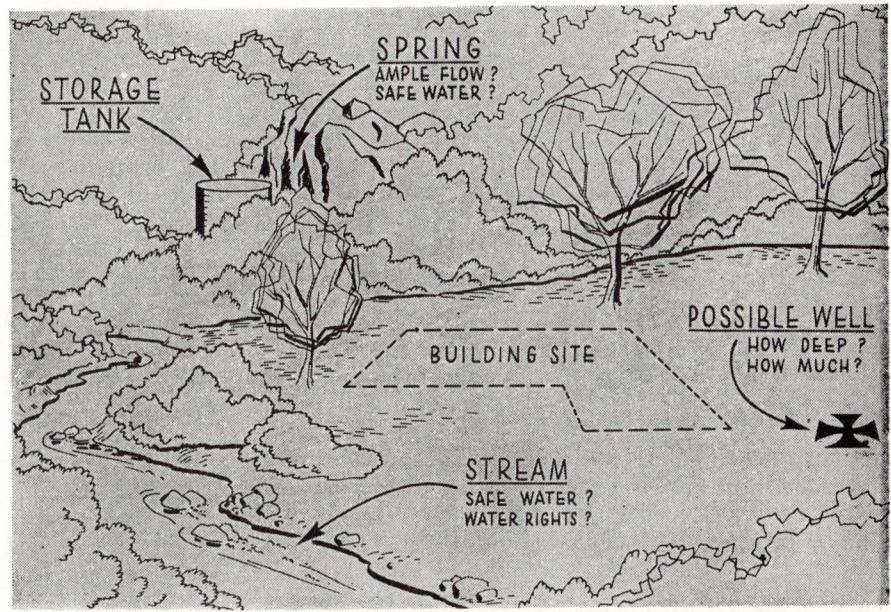

Country dweller's possible water sources, and the vital points to consider for each

slow for direct piping from spring to house. The answer is to accumulate the spring water in a storage tank that will hold enough to furnish a day's average requirement or enough to supply water at the maximum rate of use for a few hours. (These amounts explained in *How to figure your water requirements*, this page.)

If your average daily requirements figure out to be 2,000 gallons, or if the probable maximum rate of use is 900 gallons an hour, a 2,000-gallon tank would be your minimum size.

If the spring can flow into a tank that is 90 feet above your house, gravity alone will furnish you with 40 pounds of pressure at the house (gravity and pressure figures are explained on page 119).

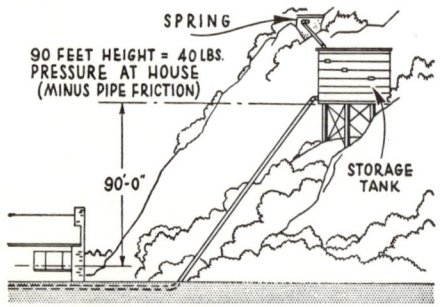

Spring, storage tank give adequate pressure if they are high enough above house

WELLS, DEEP OR SHALLOW, DUG OR DRILLED

Wells remain the most common source of domestic water for homes in the country. A well is merely a hole in the ground, dug or drilled deep enough to reach below the ground water table. It may be as shallow as 20 feet or deeper than 300 feet. There is ground water in most natural basins and valleys, but, unfortunately, it is not available everywhere.

Neighbors and experienced well drillers can probably tell whether and where ground water is available. You can have your well's location "witched" if you believe in this age-old custom; but, in the long run, the best source of local water information is always the well driller. He can tell you where wells have failed and succeeded, how deep they usually have to go in your area, how much they should yield, and how much drilling will cost. If the well driller himself calls in a "witch," as drillers have been known to do, that's his business. We leave it up to you.

In cases where good water is obtainable a few feet underground, you can dig a shallow well with little special equipment but a lot of labor. The problem is to prevent a cave-in while you are digging. If your soil is a consistent sandy loam, a team of 3 men can dig about 5 feet a day; at this rate it would take 4 days to dig a 20-foot well. Such wells are sometimes lined with redwood lumber, but a large concrete pipe does a better job—it makes a strong permanent lining. A well of any type has to be lined or cased to prevent caving-in and to keep out dirt and unsafe or impure water. If the lining extends a few inches above ground, it will keep out surface dirt and water.

Cover the well to protect children and to keep out contamination.

Because a shallow well is always open to pollution from nearby sewage disposal systems, never locate one within 100 feet of any present or potential future septic tank drainage. Deep wells that draw water from gravel strata far below surface are safer in addition to being more efficient.

Generally nowadays, a well is dug only where well drillers are not available. Where a well driller's services are available, it is usually cheaper and safer to have a well drilled and cased than to hire diggers yourself and line it as you dig. An 8-inch drilled well with steel casing costs $3 to $5 a foot, so 100 feet might cost $400; a dug well 3 feet wide by 20 feet deep, with all its hand-digging and limited water, would probably cost $200.

When a well driller makes a deep well, he uses special equipment to handle whatever conditions he may encounter. He usually installs a special steel well casing, 6 or 8 inches in diameter, along the bore to exclude unsafe shallow water. Where waters vary in quality at different depths, perforations are placed only at the level of the gravel that furnishes good water. People generally use the wider size, particularly if the well goes deep or if it may need to be deepened later. In much of the rural West, 100 feet is a common domestic well depth.

Pipes and machinery accessible for repair and replacement with this arrangement. This is a jet pump and its pressure tank

Where possible, locate a well fairly close to the dwelling, so you can use as little service pipe as possible. Cover the well and water system with a small pumphouse to protect the equipment from the weather—particularly from sand and from freezing. If you put a removable roof panel over the well, you can pull the pump or suction pipe out for service if necessary.

Electric service should go directly to the pump from a central power pole and not through another building. Thus water

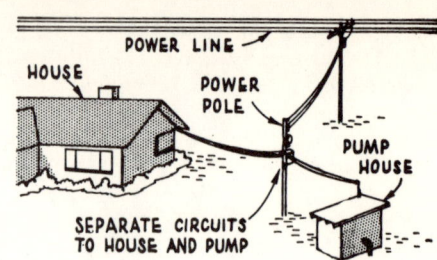

Electric circuit runs directly to pump so power will be available in case of fire

will be available if something happens to the building or to the branch circuit in that building.

ADEQUATE SUPPLY

To be adequate your water supply should meet your peak summer need. It should be adequate in two ways: (1) in total quantity during a day or a week, and (2) in the rate of flow at any one time. You measure water quantity in gallons or in cubic feet (there are 7.5 gallons in a cubic foot). Flow, or discharge, is measured in gallons per minute or per hour. A flow of 10 gallons per minute would be 600 gallons per hour.

HOW TO FIGURE YOUR WATER REQUIREMENTS

To begin with, allow 50 gallons of water per day for each person in your house—this is for drinking, cooking, washing, bathing, and flushing the toilet. In hot dry weather, a garden and lawn need irrigation that equals about 2 inches of rainfall a week. This means about 1.25 gallons per square foot, or 1,250 gallons per 1,000 square feet. Figure on the basis of a week because that will probably cover the watering cycle. Here is how to add up a weekly water requirement for a 5-person dwelling and a 10,000-square-foot garden (approximately ¼ acre).

WEEKLY REQUIREMENTS	GALLONS
5 persons	1,750
(@ 50 gals./day times 7)	
10,000 sq. ft. garden	12,500
(@ 1.25 gals./sq. ft.)	
Total for week	14,250
Average per day	2,035

Note that garden is by far the heaviest consumer. Thus, if you plan to have about half an acre in garden, lawn, vegetables, and fruit trees, you will need about twice as much as shown above.

If you want a swimming pool, figure it in too, at its capacity. However, you can save a little here by using an auxiliary pump to take the swimming pool water out for irrigation. A pool that is 10 feet by 30 feet by 5 feet deep would contain 1,500 cubic feet or 11,250 gallons and require 12½ hours to fill with a flow of 15 gallons per minute.

RATE OF FLOW

Five gallons a minute is about the least flow you can use to meet the needs of a small family home. The smallest water system sold usually delivers about 4 or 5 gallons per minute. This would obviously be too small for a home with much garden area. Allow about 5 gallons per minute for each sprinkler or hydrant that you will use at one time. Ten gallons a minute would supply 2 sprinklers and still allow enough water or pressure for use in the house; this might be enough for a small place of a quarter acre, with about 10,000 square feet to be watered.

Many experienced pump dealers recommend a system with a larger discharge, if feasible, because they have seen so many people regret not having provided for a larger system to run more sprinklers.

In case of fire the more water (greater flow) available, the better your chance of putting it out. Fire underwriters recommend an effective stream—about 10 gallons per minute—through a one-quarter-inch nozzle. Volume of water should be sufficient to make this flow available for 2 hours.

The fault with many springs and some wells is that although they furnish water continuously, it flows slowly. In this case, in order to obtain a usable rate of flow, it is necessary to accumulate the water in a tank or in the well and use it intermittently at a higher rate.

As part of his service, a well driller will pump a new well for a short time to determine its yield. Then he can tell you how much use you can get from this flow of water and what would be the proper pump. In the case of a spring, or an existing water system, you can measure the rate of flow yourself. See how many seconds or minutes it takes to fill a 2 or 5-gallon bucket, or how long it takes the spring to refill its basin after you dip out a bucketful.

If it takes 2 minutes to fill a 2-gallon bucket, the flow is 1 gallon a minute, 60 gallons an hour, or 1,440 gallons in 24 hours. This would be enough for a home and a small garden if the water were stored in a tank.

WATER PRESSURE BY GRAVITY OR PUMPING

A gravity system requires a large storage tank high enough above the water outlets to furnish the required pressure. It takes 2.3 feet of fall to provide 1 pound per square inch of pressure: if you want 30 pounds of pressure, the bottom of the tank would have to be 69 feet above the hydrant—plus a few feet more to overcome pipe friction.

The storage tank may be filled by a small continuous flow from a spring, a hydraulic ram in a stream diversion system, or by intermittent pumping from a well—the working principle of most windmills. The storage tank should hold at least 1 day's water requirement. Unless the tank can be located on a hill above the house, you need a tower, and that may be rather expensive. Under most conditions the complete system of pump, motor, tank, and tower for a gravity pressure system costs more than a pressure system.

An automatic pressure system is composed of an electric motor, pump, small hydropneumatic tank, pressure switch, and an air volume control. Air under pressure in the top of the tank presses on the water so it will flow out when a faucet is opened. When enough water flows out to reduce pressure to a certain level, the pressure switch turns on the motor which pumps water into the tank until pressure rises again to a point at which the switch turns off the motor.

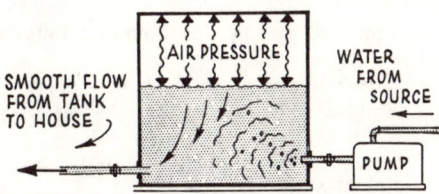

Principle on which automatic pump works. Pump goes on when tank pressure lowers

Most systems, installed, are set to turn off at 40 pounds of pressure per square inch. You can set the pressure higher if the installation requires it. A moderate size tank has an advantage over a small one since it involves less stopping and starting and will yield more water in case of a power failure.

MATCH THE PUMP TO THE JOB

The pump is the heart of the water system. It lifts the water out of the well and forces it into the tank or service pipe at the pressure required. Pumps come in many kinds and sizes, each designed to fit a particular set of pumping conditions. A basic factor that determines pump size is depth of water in the well. You can raise water by suction only 22 to 25 feet. A shallow well pump located entirely above ground will suck water up and force it on its way, but you need a deep well pump to draw water up from more than 25 feet below ground. The motor or engine is usually above ground, with the business part of the pump down the well, in or near the water.

There are several basic kinds of pump. The reciprocating or piston-type pump

PISTON AND VALVE TYPE PUMP

Outside view *of piston-type pump. Jet pump, more popular, shown on page 118*

has a cylinder and piston, or plunger, which is moved by a crankshaft. It has valves and several moving parts. The shallow well form is usually horizontal and does not need to be over the well (but should be within 600 feet of it). The deep well form has the cylinder down in the well, with the plunger operated from a shaft at the top of the well (windmill pumps and some hand pumps are of this type).

The jet pump is now the most widely used type for domestic use—both shallow and deep well. Essentially, it is a centrifugal pump aided by a jet or injector. A small stream of water is forced into a venturi tube at the water level where it creates a suction, drawing in additional water which is carried up the suction pipe to the rotating impeller. The impeller forces water on, under pressure, into the tank or supply line. Usually, the motor, centrifugal impeller, and tank are located above the well, with only 2 pipes extending down the well to the jet.

When you select a pump, it is usually best to follow the recommendations of the dealer. He has the technical information that will help fit the system to your needs in the most economical manner. It is true that you can buy a preassembled shallow well system which you can plug in like any other appliance. But if you need a deep well pump, your system should be tailored to fit the job; and that will require the help of a specialist—an experienced dealer who can analyze your problem. He will consider lift, discharge, total head, and size of pipe in prescribing type of pump and size of motor.

INITIAL COST OF A WATER SYSTEM

Cost of a complete water system for a country home will vary widely with depth and kind of well and size of system. A shallow well (costing $100) and a 10 gallon-per-minute, 1/3-horsepower water system (cost around $175) would come to $275, which is about the minimum. On the other hand, an 8-inch well drilled 100 feet deep (cost $360) and a 1½-horsepower system (cost $500) would add up to $860, a cost more typical of the average installation. Unless you know the specific conditions, you had better allow around $1,000 for the total cost of your complete system.

NEIGHBORHOOD MUTUAL

Many country people find the best answer to their water problem in a mutual water company, a group of neighbors who set up a single water system to serve all of them. In such arrangements the costs and risks in water development are shared, and each single householder usually has a smaller individual investment. Many thousands of such mutual systems, with memberships ranging from a few to a hundred, are scattered through the Western states.

How to develop a spring

MANY A MAN, new to country living, finds it almost impossible to believe that he can't develop a water supply. Despite the evidence of deserted farms and dry areas, he feels sure that if he is smart he can bring water out of the ground.

This optimist looks at any sign of water as evidence of more water. Actually, you can't increase the *flow* of spring water. You can collect and concentrate its flow —and that's all.

It sounds childishly obvious to say that unless a spring flows in the dry season it is not worth developing. But many a man has bet the purchase price of a place in the country on a mistaken belief in his ability to develop a seasonal spring—one that flows well through winter and spring and dries up in the summer.

He'll find moist spots that fool him: at the base of a rock, in the "V" of a small draw or arroyo, at the toe of a small landslide, in dry stream beds, in the middle of an oasis of green growth. In winter and for most of the spring months, these "springs" have a fairly constant flow. Come summer and autumn, this flow may dwindle away to a trickle or completely disappear, although the ground may appear moist and the growth around it may remain green while other growth turns brown. These are not true springs; they are little more than seepage of surface water. Except in rare cases, they aren't worth developing.

If time permits, you should check a spring's flow for an entire year. If it flows enough water during the dry season to supply your needs, it is worth developing. If the flow disappears, or diminishes below your need, it is not worth developing, unless you can provide sufficient storage of the wet season excess to carry you through the dry months.

One of the best ways to check a spring's worth is to talk to some of the old-timers in the area. If they tell you it has run year in and year out, in dry years as well as normal years, you can feel reasonably safe about spending money to develop it.

DEVELOPMENT

In general, spring development follows these steps:

 Excavate and clean the spring opening
 Build a wall, box, or dam to catch as much of the water as possible
 Cover the bottom with gravel
 Install piping
 Put on a cover
 If cattle are nearby, install a cattle-tight fence.

You should plan some kind of storage other than the spring itself. If you don't, you are likely to saturate the ground all around the spring so that your spring flow will become too diffused. You will end up wasting water by seepage into the hillside as fast as you collect it.

Variations in type of excavation and in type of collection basin will occur with almost every spring. Here are some of these variations:

If the water comes out of an opening in rock in an out-of-the-faucet stream, excavation is likely to do more harm than good. The best thing for you to do is clear away loose rock and dirt from the opening, and make a water-tight box to catch all the water. Cover the bottom of the box with coarse gravel, imbed your pipe in the gravel, and call it quits.

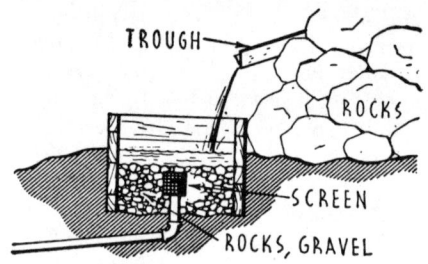

If the spring flow is diffused over a wide area, you should excavate to catch all of this seepage. Sometimes a V-shaped wall with the arms of the "V" extending back into the hill makes the best collecting method for a spring that seeps out over a 10 or 15-foot area.

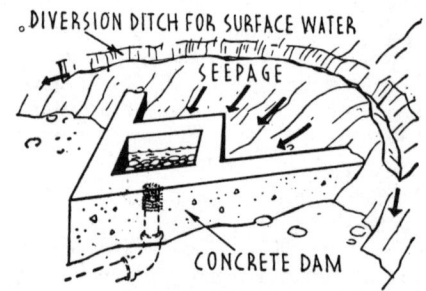

One of the oldest methods of developing a hillside spring—and one that is still recommended frequently—is to dig a tunnel about 6 feet high and 4 feet wide into the hill to a distance of 10 or 20 feet. Dam up the opening of the tunnel with a concrete wall, lodging a pipe through the wall to drain off the flow. Timber the walls of the tunnel, or make a masonry arch, to eliminate the possibility of cave-in. This

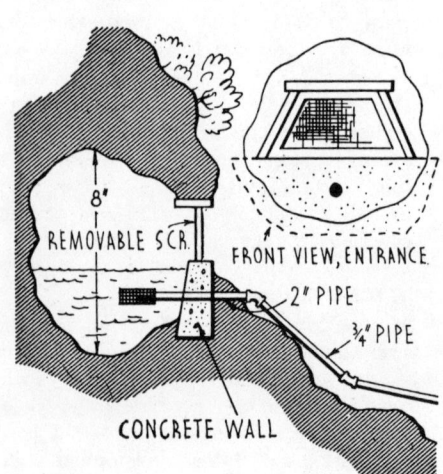

To collect *diffused flow of spring, cave was dug back into hill. A concrete wall dams up entrance. Opening is left large enough for cleaning. Spring flows about 700 gallons daily, fills 2,300-gallon tank*

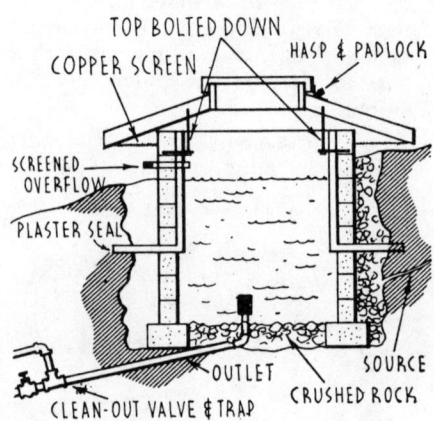

Excavation *for this spring is about 6 feet deep, 6 feet in diameter. Walls are of concrete block with vertical joints left open. Plaster keeps out surface run-off. Spring supplies enough for household use*

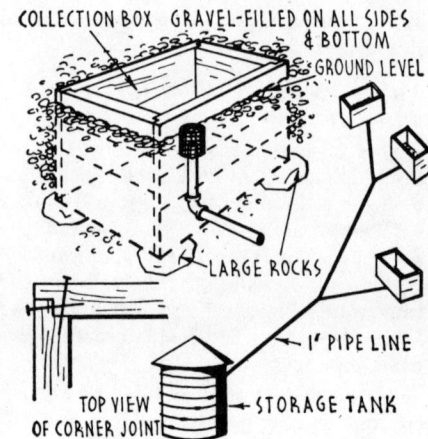

Three small springs *are hooked together by a pipeline. Holes were dug where the water emerged, and 36 by 27 by 30-inch redwood boxes were set in the holes. Plastic pipes could be a money-saver here*

type of development very much resembles a dug well that has been laid on its side.

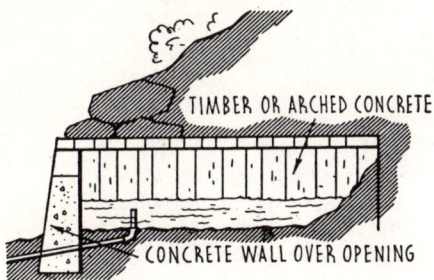

If your tunnel reaches a particularly strong flow of water back in the hillside, it is best to locate your collection basin back in the tunnel. Carry your water from the back of the tunnel to your storage area through concrete sewer pipe or regular water pipe.

A variation of this type of excavation is a T-shaped tunnel back into the hill.

Both tunnel systems work best with springs in somewhat porous ground, such as sandstone or limestone. The galleries back into the hillside provide collecting avenues that tap a large part of this porous, water-bearing material.

If a spring flow carries much silt with it, it is best not to imbed your pipe in gravel. The gravel and silt eventually will cement together to close the pipe. Either keep the end of the pipe well above the floor of the spring or catch the silt before it reaches your collection basin by a stepped series of low dams.

Where there's evidence of water near the "V" of a draw, a long trench running at right angles to the draw, about 15 or 20 feet long and 6 or 8 feet deep, usually will be the most satisfactory development.

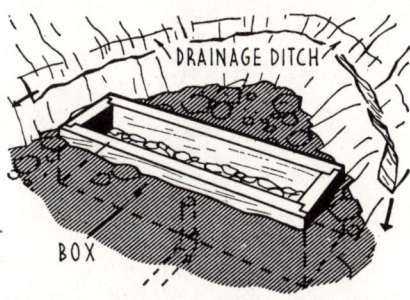

The hill should be trenched above the spring to keep out surface run-off and to hold back sliding dirt and rubble. If the spring excavation shows signs of filling-in with sand and silt, it is wise to timber the walls or set a box in the hole.

If a spring with a diffuse flow over an area of some 10 or 12 feet occurs on a relatively level spot, you should make an excavation down to fairly solid ground, probably four or five feet deep and approximately in the center of the seepage area. Make a box, without a bottom, the size of the hole you dig. This will hold the water and keep back the soil. You may have to pump your water from a spring of this type.

Whether you build a box or a concrete dam to collect your spring water, take care that you don't wall off the source. Remember, your aims are to collect as much of the flow as possible and to protect it from seepage and contamination.

If there is any evidence of mineral content, such as incrustations of salt around the spring opening, you might as well abandon it as a source of domestic or irrigation water. It's always wise to check the mineral content and the bacterial content of spring water. State Agricultural departments will give you a report on mineral content. Obtain a bacterial analysis from the county health department.

Dynamiting a spring in an attempt to "open it up" usually does more harm than good. The impact of the explosion tends to cement the little crevices through which the water travels. On the other hand the use of limited amounts of black blasting powder as an aid in excavating is often recommended.

STORAGE

There are several ways to store your spring water: in a small reservoir; in a cistern-type, underground storage; in a metal or redwood tank. The least expensive method is tank storage.

Both redwood and metal tanks cost about the same—approximately $80 for a 500-gallon tank. Metal tanks must be shaded so that the sun doesn't heat the water. They are easier to install than the redwood tank as long as a truck can be used to haul them right up to the storage site. Steel tanks need periodic painting inside and out. Galvanized tanks require no such periodic treatment.

Redwood tanks swell and shrink. However, they'll usually outlast the metal tanks.

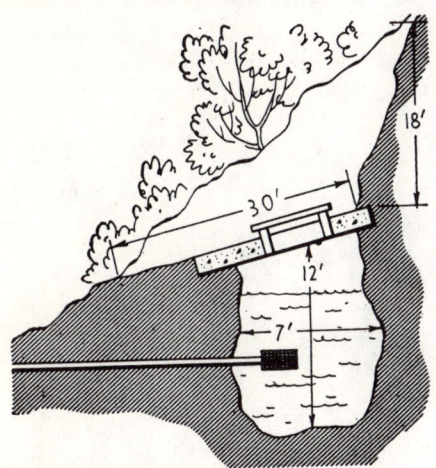

Hillside spring developed by digging broad collection trench, covering it with a roof to protect it from surface contamination. Spring flows about 3 gallons a minute, wet years and dry; fills 25,000-gallon reservoir

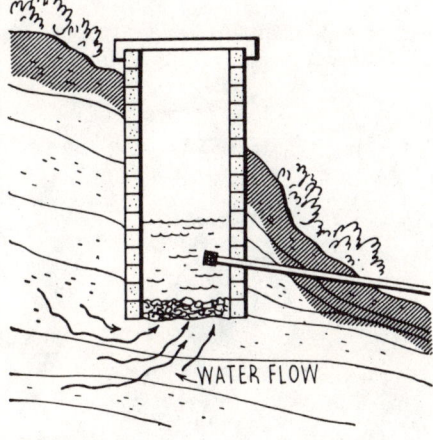

This spring was once tapped by screened well point. When flow weakened, this hole was dug. It's 6 feet deep, 2 feet in diameter. Walls are of brick; gravel is at the bottom. Spring flow is 600 gallons daily

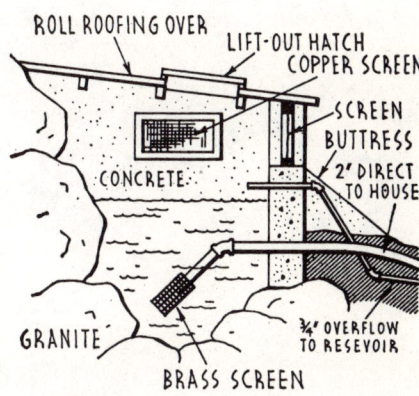

Spring opening was simply boxed in with walls of concrete and roofed over to protect natural collection basin. Spring flows about 14 gallons an hour in dry years, as much as 83 gallons an hour in wet years

Septic tank and filter systems

THE CONVENTIONAL septic tank and drainage field has solved sewage disposal satisfactorily on country homes for years. But one insistent weakness of the system, especially in areas of clay soil, has been the failure of leaching fields to dispose of water from the tank.

Septic tanks settle solids and pass out a liquid which carries a heavy load of dissolved solids and bacteria in suspension. The job of the leaching field is to percolate away the liquid, and to convert the solid material into a soluble form by oxidizing action.

With the usual system, percolation is successful enough in sandy soil, but it happens too fast to permit thorough oxidation. In heavier soils, real trouble sets in.

(1) Whole system laid out; grades figured before digging. Optical level, carpenter's level and sights, or line level on cord used

(2) Cleat for baffle, and outlet hole. Sideboards, beveled, loosely nailed to uprights. Uprights left long to suspend form in place

(3) Planks nailed together temporarily to support edges of excavation and forms, with cross pieces nailed to the form uprights

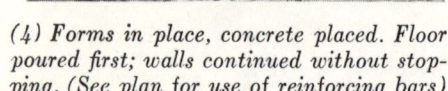
(4) Forms in place, concrete placed. Floor poured first; walls continued without stopping. (See plan for use of reinforcing bars)

(5) Forms removed after concrete sets. View of outlet end and soil pipe to distributing box. Latter is cast of concrete like tank

(6) Cover slabs cast in parts, given "shiplap" fit. Center section must be cast so it can be raised without removing other parts

(7) 1¼" coat of concrete put in cover forms; 3 reinforcing rods, ⅜", set in. Handles are old horseshoes, etc. Fill forms, then level off

(8) Section of trench filter system showing stake set to grade of 4-inch fall to 100 feet. Filter rock put to top of stakes—12 inches

(9) Trench filter section (see sketch). Flat tile pieces over ends of runs prevent access by rodents. Roofing paper strips over joints

The solids in the liquid settle at the sides and bottom of the drain ditches, clogging them and excluding air. With no air, a perfect environment for anaerobic bacteria is created. These bacteria work only where air is excluded—they are the ones that make slimes and give off the rotten egg smell of hydrogen sulphide.

Up to now the answer to this predicament has always been "extend your drainage ditches." Elaborate tables have been worked out to give you an ideal drain ditch length — based on the percolation rate of your own particular soil. But even extending your drain line does not always work. And when you have a small lot, extension may be inconvenient or impossible. To Mr. Fred Horne, of Robles Del Rio, California, the obvious solution to this leaching problem was simply to supply air to all the soil in the leaching field. Mr. Horne is a supplier of septic tank chemicals and has done considerable research on the subject.

He found that one material — pumice — when mixed with soil, would permanently aerate the leaching field, and promote a considerable amount of water movement laterally as well as downward.

The septic tank itself remains unchanged. But, instead of a network of pipes in ditches to carry the runoff from the tank, you dig a square or rectangular field, 15 to 18 inches deep. Refill this shallow excavation with a mixture of pumice (half-inch screened) and excavated soil. If you have a power cultivator that churns deep, you don't have to excavate—just mix in the pumice from the surface. The mix runs from 30 to 60 per cent pumice, the balance soil. Thirty per cent is for very sandy soil. Heavier soils call for a larger proportion of pumice. You lay the drain tiles in this mixture, just below the surface.

Basically, it's the pumice that makes this system effective. Pumice is a natural gray or white rock, ejected by volcanoes, and frothed by gases, giving it a spongelike character. The openings are sealed at one end, making many dead-end pores within each particle. The dead ends prevent water from completely saturating the particles, so air is not excluded.

When you have 40 per cent pumice in a soil mix, 18 inches deep, you have a large amount of air present even at an 18-inch depth, at all times. This air, locked underground, gives the beneficial air-loving aerobic bacteria a chance to function, and thwarts the anaerobic bacteria. The result is efficient sewage disposal, without smells, filming, or sliming.

Although the cellular openings in the pumice particle retain air, they also absorb a certain amount of water. This absorption makes it possible for water in the soil to travel sidewise and even upward, by capillary action. With pumice in the drain field, you are more likely to get even distribution of the liquid waste.

Such even distribution, along with effective oxidation should result in quick and continuous purification of the liquid from your tank.

BEFORE YOU BUILD

A number of informative bulletins are available from agricultural colleges and extension services on septic tank building. Check one of them before starting construction. In addition, most county health departments issue specifications for construction of septic tank systems.

Be sure to check with the various government agencies concerned, including the county health department, the FHA, and the State Department of Public Health. Also, note whether or not the specifications are for minimum requirements. If you add more baths, or extra equipment, the capacity requirements change.

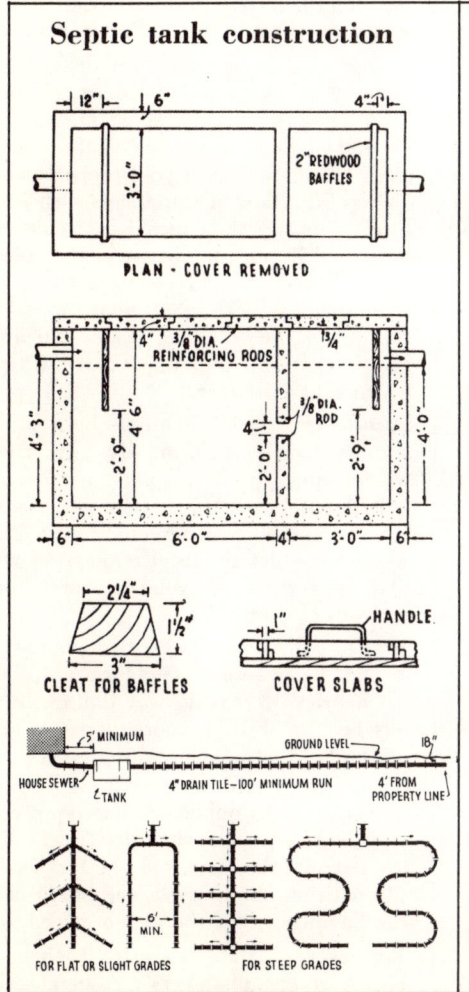

Septic tank construction

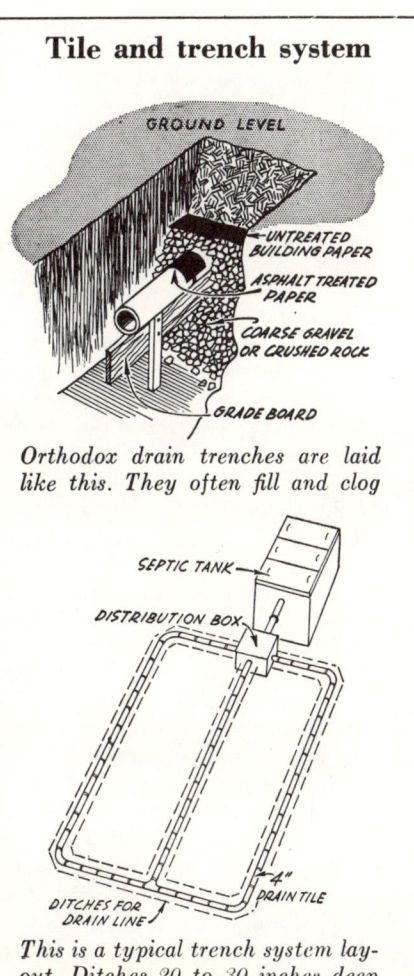

Tile and trench system

Orthodox drain trenches are laid like this. They often fill and clog

This is a typical trench system layout. Ditches 20 to 30 inches deep

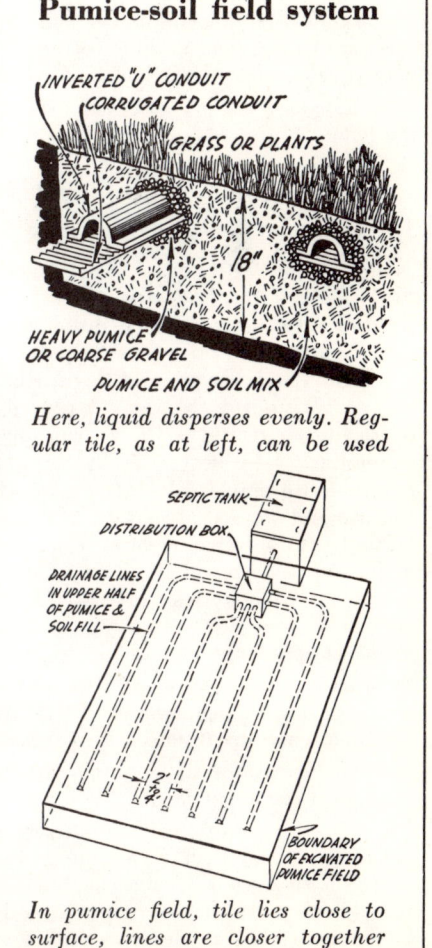

Pumice-soil field system

Here, liquid disperses evenly. Regular tile, as at left, can be used

In pumice field, tile lies close to surface, lines are closer together

Fire precautions

In case of fire, what could you do to stop it? Preparedness, of course, is vital wherever you live, but in the country, lack of it sometimes can spell disaster.

In incorporated areas, you have adequate water supplies; you're usually near enough to neighbors that you can count on their help; and you can usually count on the help of a well equipped fire department.

In the country the water supply is often inadequate for fighting fires. Fields of grass and areas covered with brush or timber may add extra fire hazards. Your nearest neighbor may be a mile away. Fire departments, if any, are apt to be even farther away and may be dependent on volunteer help.

One country-living family we discussed fire safety with reported: "Every fire we've had out here has burned the house to the ground."

Fire protection, even in the country, doesn't have to be that inadequate.

If you do live in unincorporated country, these are things you can do to better prepare yourself and your neighbors for fire:
1. Eliminate the chief cause of fires in the home.
2. Set up some local protection.
3. Establish an adequate water supply.
4. Work out a family plan for coping with a fire emergency.

ELIMINATE THE CAUSE OF FIRES

According to the National Board of Fire Underwriters, carelessness with matches and cigarettes is the greatest single cause of fires. Misuse of electricity (primarily overloading circuits) is the second chief cause.

Solutions are simple: take extra care with the use and storage of matches; be particularly careful that children can't get at them, and keep and use generous-sized ash trays for cigarettes. Have an electrician check your electrical circuits and the loads that you impose on them.

Another frequent cause of fires is the improper use of incinerators. There are common sense precautions in that regard:

Buy an incinerator that is approved by your local fire department.

Place the incinerator in the center of a clearing, with at least 10 feet of cleared space on all sides of it. Burn material in it only when lids or doors are properly closed and when a mesh screen covers the flue.

GRASS FIRES

Grass fires cause much of the annual fire damage in outlying areas, and they frequently occur on the property of absentee owners. Check to see whether your county has ordinances calculated to eliminate this type of hazard, and work with other year-around neighbors to see that action is taken to enforce those ordinances. Obey local ordinances yourself.

The most important step you can take to protect your home is to isolate (and insulate) it as much as possible from native grass and chaparral that feed fire.

Just as the fire department spends about nine months of the year cutting and clearing fire breaks in our Southern California hills, any home owner living in a potentially hazardous area should keep clearing his own fire-resistant break between his house and the brush and grass. This break doesn't necessarily have to be skinned to the bare ground; lawn, ivy, and other low-growing ground covers such as cistus, though they are not fire-*proof*, are fire-resistant.

The break between brush or grass and house should be a minimum of 30 feet in width, though a wider break is advisable.

Fire resistant plants?

For several years, forestry and flood control experts have been trying to determine whether certain plants are more fire-resistant than others. But so far they have found no truly fire-resistant plant.

They do know that certain species of cistus (rockrose) do not burn readily and are excellent growers in areas where drought conditions prevail. (The two species you can buy locally are *C. laurifolius* and *C. purpureus.*) Other recommended ground covers, where regular watering is not a problem, include small-leafed ice plants and ivy (if you don't let a woody "mat" build up under the top green cover).

Native plants, on the other hand, are generally highly volatile. Fire departments recommend against heavy screen plantings of taller growing woody plants.

If you control-burn grasslands on your own property, remember that burning grass creates its own draft and will burn uphill. Therefore, if you burn off your own hillside, start at the top. Don't start at all unless the area is small enough that you can keep the fire under control at all times. Don't burn trash in open heaps during the dry season without a permit.

Provide room for fire-fighting equipment to get near your house and maneuver around it. If the fire department can't get safely onto your property to fight the fire as it passes, it must wait until the main blast of flames has passed, and this may be too late.

Fire fighters also recommend that you have your street address and name clearly visible at the road. A local chief and his men may know exactly how to get to any house in their district, but when thousands of acres are on fire, other firefighters and equipment are called in from great distances. They can't be expected to know where you live unless your address is clearly marked at the road.

WAYS TO GET LOCAL PROTECTION

First of all, find out whether your property is under the jurisdiction of any organized fire fighting facility: a country fire department, a volunteer fire department, a special fire district, a state forestry service, or the United States Forest Service.

If you belong to a county fire district, or some other separate fire district, get acquainted with your fire department. Call the station and ask the fire chief or some other official to inspect your property and discuss fire protection problems with you. Fire chiefs say their own jobs would be simplified if everyone living in the country would do this. It enables them to learn the exact location of your property, the quickest way to get there, and any special problems they might have in trying to fight a fire there.

Forest service fire fighters—both state and Federal—are primarily concerned with keeping fire from spreading to valuable public lands. However, if you are on or next to a state or national forest, it is wise to contact the local ranger—so you may know what help you can expect from them in case of a fire.

If no organized facility exists in your area, it may be possible to organize a special fire district. Here is the way that can usually be done: Fifty or more taxpayers and **residents of an unincorporated area petition county board of supervisors.** The supervisors hold a public hearing so protests may be aired. Then they decide whether the new fire district should be formed. If the petition is approved, the board fixes the boundaries for the new organization.

Residents of the area elect their own board of commissioners to operate the new service. Funds to pay for organizing and operating the fire district are raised through taxation on the property within the area.

Sometimes a small district can contract with a nearby city or county department for fire protection. Or, if the district operates its own department, expenses can often be minimized by organizing a volunteer group of fire fighters.

Another means of obtaining fire protection is by petitioning for annexation to an adjoining district that has a fire department. Generally, 51 per cent of the owners of the property which adjoins the existing district are required to be represented on the petition.

THE PROBLEM OF WATER SUPPLY

As a rule, water mains in unincorporated areas are seldom adequate for fire fighting. Firemen consider any main smaller than 4 inches in diameter to be merely a supplementary supply. Many country places have only their own water system—a well or springs—which is almost always inadequate in an emergency. Your local fire chief or county fire warden can tell you what auxiliary water supplies you should have for adequate fire protection.

If you set up an additional supply in a tank or pond, be sure that it is accessible—a fire truck should be able to get within 20 feet of it.

Some areas within a fire district have their own private water supply that serves a comparatively few homes. We know of one group of families, served by a small private water company, that improved their fire protection by installing fire hydrants and mapping out a cooperative plan to follow in case of fire.

The property of this group is under the jurisdiction of a fire district, but district funds were insufficient to give them the amount of protection they wanted. The water pressure in the area is low, and the water mains are only 2 inches in diameter. They conferred with fire district officials and a representative of the water company, who suggested they buy and install 2 used hydrants.

Now, if a fire breaks out, a signal warns the group. The 11 families involved will turn off their water to increase the pressure, and the fire department will then be able to use the line as a supplementary source.

A wise precaution in unincorporated areas—if you have sufficient water for it—is to install a sprinkling system on top of your house. Use the same type that you would in your lawn. Run the pipe along the top of the roof, with branches out to any gables. But don't install more sprinklers than the water pressure will service. Discuss this with your water company.

Your own fire hose

ART HUPY

If fire breaks out you want the greatest volume of water you can possibly get as fast as you can get it. In the city this is furnished by fire hydrants and fire department hoses. But in the country, beyond the easy reach of fire departments, you have to arrange for such an emergency water supply.

This is a serious enough piece of business that you should not undertake laying it out on your own. Hire or consult an architect or a plumber or talk to a fireman about where you should tap your water line for your fire hose connection, what size fittings and pipe to use, and where to locate the hose.

Fire hose units like the one pictured here are available to home owners as well as to institutions. Complete units (hose, steel hose rack, couplings, valve, and nozzle) sell for around $50 for a 50-foot hose, $60 for a 75-foot hose, and $70 for a 100-foot hose. Those are standard lengths. In addition, you can buy cabinets to fit the hose and rack for $40 and up.

There are about half a dozen manufac-

Fire hose, *hose rack, and valve fit neatly in built-in cabinet; handy, yet unimposing*

turers of these rigs, three of them on the West Coast. To shop for sizes and types, go to a plumbing supply house. They will have all the catalogs.

A FAMILY PLAN

It is a good idea to keep certain information posted right at your telephone: the telephone number of the fire department; and clear, easy-to-follow directions on how to reach your house.

Every person in the family should know the location of garden hoses, ladder, and bucket.

A garden hose, with pressure type nozzle, should be attached at all times to a faucet in front and in back of your house. Both hoses should be long enough to reach any part of the house—inside and out—and the top of the roof. Your ladder should be easy to get, easy to handle, and long enough to reach the roof.

It is a pretty good idea to have two or three fire extinguishers in your country place. Hang one on the garage wall, keep one on the wall of the stable or barn, and store another one in a convenient spot inside the house.

There are several types of extinguishers, some that use water, some that expel carbon dioxide, and others that use chemicals. Some kinds are dangerous to use on electrical fires; others sometimes develop toxic gases. Consult your local fire authorities about what to use both in and out of the house before you buy an extinguisher.

Have an occasional family conference to rehearse what you should do in case of a fire. Remember that a spray on a starting fire is better than stream of water. Direct water toward the bottom of a wall fire.

BEFORE EVACUATING A HOUSE...

If and when fire does come, it will help if you have already talked with your fire and sheriff's departments about your particular house situation. Here are precautions you may take to help safeguard your property before you evacuate:

• Turn off gas at meter, shut off electricity at fuse box or circuit breaker.

• Move any inflammable patio furniture away from the house, out in the open. Sparks falling on a canvas awning, which, in turn, collapsed onto a patio full of canvas and wood patio furniture, caused total loss of one Malibu house.

• Don't wait until the last minute to evacuate. Heat and lack of oxygen can quickly contribute to a vapor lock in your car. The results could leave you stranded, and possibly block fire-fighting equipment on a narrow road or driveway.

Close all doors and windows any time you leave your house during the fire season. This won't keep your house from burning in the event of a brush fire, but it will help keep the fire *outside* the house until fire-fighting equipment can get there to extinguish an exterior blaze.

Fanned by strong winds, sparks have been known to be forced inside a house through cracks even at closed doors and windows. But closing doors and windows (some fire chiefs even recommend locking doors as a precaution against their blowing open) will prevent drafts that might fan a small blaze into a holocaust in minutes.

Tips on closing a cabin

Ideas on storing bedding and food so that cabin-site pests can't get at them

CLOSING THE CABIN for a week, or for the winter, is always a tricky problem. It pays to make an inventory list of everything you intend to leave in the cabin. This way, when you are getting your gear packed, you won't have to wonder whether a certain item is in the attic upstairs or already in the cabin.

If your cabin is used only on weekends, you generally feel the necessity of leaving a certain amount of food on hand. Even if you are closing your cabin for the whole winter, it is nice to be able to leave some of the staple items on hand. However, remember that unless all foods are tightly sealed, you're going to have rodent or mildew trouble, or both. One obvious solution in such cases is the use of tin cans, in which every item a mouse or rat would like is sealed. This would handle the mildew problem, too.

Leaving liquids on hand can cause lots of trouble if your cabin is in cold country. Liquids are likely to freeze solid in cold weather, expanding and bursting their containers. Exceptions to this are liquids containing alcohol, such as vanilla. Another tip to those whose cabins are in a cold zone is to be sure to drain all the pipes of as much water as possible. First, turn off the water at the source. In most cases, close by the water turn-off valve, there is a plug which can be removed allowing all the residual water to drain away. Be sure to remove all the U-shaped traps under sinks and basins and empty them, as they collect water which will not drain away by itself. After you have removed as much water as possible, put coarse rock salt down all drains to lower the freezing point and help to keep remaining water from bursting the pipes.

BEDDING STORAGE

Some of the common solutions for the storage of bedding and the like are:

- Tying everything in a bundle and supporting it from the rafters.
- Lining one bunk with metal and closing up everything in it.
- Using rodent-proof boxes which serve as storage units even while the cabin is in use. For example, here are two boxes hinged so that when open they are a piece of furniture, but when closed are rodent-proof.

Piled one over the other, they will make a very usable storage wall. Or, you also can use deep boxes for a wardrobe. These

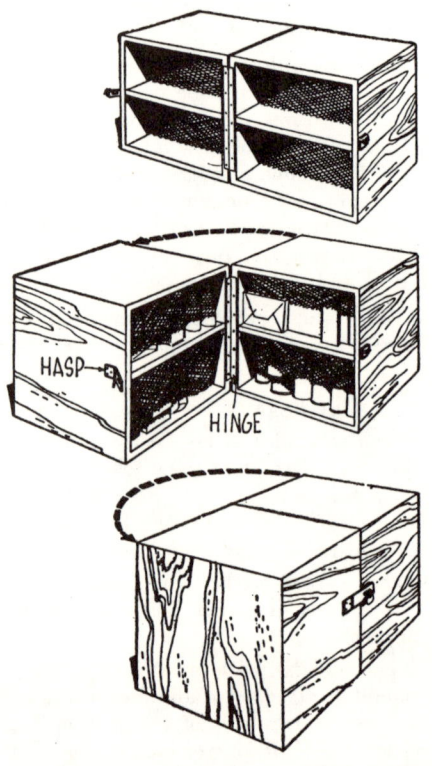

not only give safe over-winter storage, but provide a workable wardrobe for bunkrooms, sleeping porches, and many other accessories.

BOX FOR BEDS

One *Sunset* family found that they can leave their bedding on their beds in between visits to their cabin by setting their beds in built-in units that look like this:

The beds are located in an alcove. Each bed is set on a wooden frame so that it is a few inches higher than the height of a normal bed. Underneath each double bed is a trundle bed. The trundle beds are low and lightweight so that they may easily be rolled to any spot in the cabin.

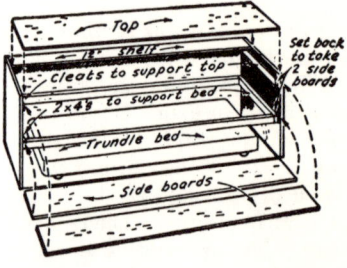

There's a shelf above each double bed and narrow cleats along the head board and foot board of each. The shelves and the cleats provide support for the tops that cover the beds when the cabin is closed up. The shelves are used for books and magazines when the beds are open for sleeping.

The tops of the beds are made of three-quarter-inch plywood and are in one piece. The front and foot of the beds are made of one-inch pine. When closed tightly against mice and dust, the beds look like two large packing boxes. To prepare the double beds, the plywood top and the upper half of the front board are removed. If the trundle beds are to be used, the lower front piece is lifted out, and the bed is pulled out. Front pieces are locked on with regular barrel type bolts.

METAL-LINED STORAGE

Some of the best solutions we've seen for rodent-proof storage have been with tin, zinc, or aluminum lined cupboards or cabinets. Sometimes, it is easier to line completely a large pantry than it is to line separate cabinets or shelves.

Here's how you can use aluminum, for instance, to rodent-proof a bedding storage box:

The most difficult part of lining the cupboard will be fitting the metal to corners. Best solution is to make a paper pattern. Fold a piece of shelf paper into one of the bottom corners of the cupboard, crease with your hands, make the necessary cuts with scissors so that the paper fits the corner without wrinkling. Lap the paper up the side only about an inch from the bottom. The resulting pattern for our box looked like this:

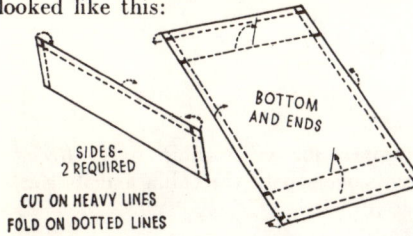

Buy enough 2-S-soft aluminum, .020 thickness, to line the cupboard. It comes in sheets measuring 24 by 72 inches. If 2-S-soft is not available, ask for 3-S-soft, or utility sheet. You usually can get them from a sheet metal shop, or a lumber yard, or one of the mail order houses.

Trace your pattern on the aluminum. Make cuts with a pair of tin snips. Bend as follows:

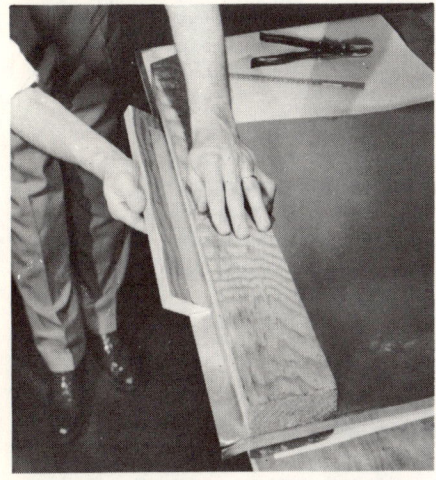

Lay the aluminum along the edge of a bench, table, or other sharp-edged object. Make bends with a small piece of wood, working it into a rounded bend. Rounded bends are easier to clean than sharp corners. If you prefer a sharp corner, you can hammer it into shape with a wooden mallet after you get it rounded. Another method of bending is to sandwich the sheet of aluminum between two two by fours, then bend it up or down with a piece of wood. If you have C-clamps to hold the two by fours, they will help.

When all bends have been made, place the piece in the corner. Trim off loose ends, de-burr all sharp edges with a metal file. If sides or other joining pieces require folding, another pattern should be made.

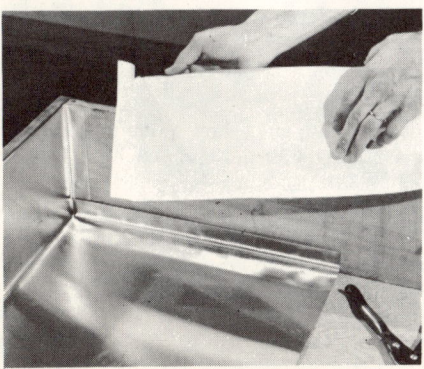

If the bottom bend on the first piece is rounded instead of sharply squared, it is a good idea to keep the pattern about a quarter of an inch above the rounded bend. To get a perfect fit, shape the paper to the corner and then cut it off along the crease. A perfectly squared edge wouldn't give a tight fit because of the double thickness of aluminum at the bottom.

Trace the pattern for the side piece on the sheet of aluminum. Cut the piece from the sheet like this:

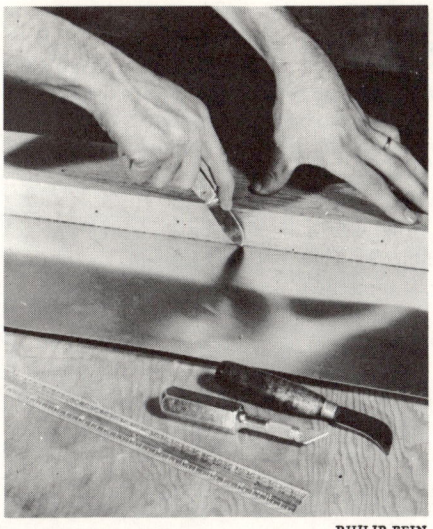

PHILIP FEIN

Tin snips are okay for little cuts into aluminum, but the easiest way to cut a large piece from a sheet is by using the method shown above. Lay any straight-edged object along the line to be cut. Scribe along the straight edge with a sharp pocket knife, hobby knife, or linoleum cutter. Repeat the cut two or three times. Bend back and forth until the sheet breaks at the cut mark. The best way to hold the sheet in place while bending is to sandwich it between two two by fours, held together with C-clamps. Flatten out any irregularities along the edge with a wooden mallet, file off burred edges with a metal file. Bend the top to fit over the edge of the box.

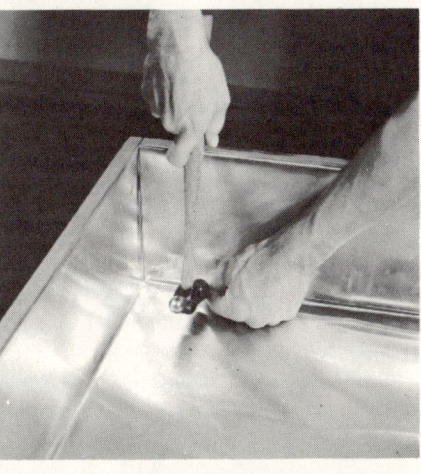

Place the side piece in position and secure all aluminum to the walls and floor of the cupboard with nails. Use half-inch galvanized or aluminum nails. Flat-headed, cadmium-plated screws work well also. Place a tack, or screw, every four inches. For appearance's sake, you can clean the aluminum with a mild detergent to remove grease or finger marks. Follow with a heavy coat of paste wax or clear lacquer.

This method of making patterns of paper and tracing them on the aluminum can be repeated wherever bends in the metal are required—for shelves, closets, drawers, or cupboards. If solid sheets of metal are not available, or if it would be impractical to move metal sheets into your cabin or permanent camp site, you can use flattened tin cans and tin can lids or pieces cut from five-gallon oil cans for lining your storage boxes. Heavy duty window screen is usually effective, also.

There are a number of other things of a less permanent nature you can do. You can build a cupboard with legs and set the legs in buckets of water, or put a strip of tin around each leg, similar to the rat guards used on a ship's line. You can hang some things from wires stretched between trees, but be sure the wire doesn't pass near low-hanging limbs and be sure it's far enough off the ground so that bears can't get at it.

One point to remember is that you should not underestimate the ability of an animal to work through almost any material.

It is not only important that you seal your storage room with some sort of material, but that you give no opportunity whatsoever to a rodent to work on it. For example: although any non-wooden wall will exclude rats, they still can gain entry from underneath. All a rat needs is a toe hold within 10 inches (rat height) of a free gnawing edge, to make a hole and gain entry. Rats usually enter buildings from under the studding, because they can get a toe hold on foundations there.

CLOSE ALL ENTRANCES

Just before leaving, check all doors and windows to be sure they are shut. Close the dampers in stoves and fireplaces. If there are no dampers, it is a good idea to stuff paper in the flue as this keeps warmth in as well as animals out. However, when you open the cabin again, don't forget to remove any paper from flues before you start a fire.

To close off the part of the chimney above the damper, make a fairly tight cover, shaped like a shallow box, that will fit on top of the chimney. It can be made of wood, wood lined with metal, or just plain metal. It can be lashed down with wire or rope. To cover a stovepipe, a coffee can is good. It fits very tightly on top of the standard stovepipe and cannot blow off. The object of this is well known to anyone who has left a cabin chimney open for several months, because it seems to have a great attraction for birds and rodents of all kinds—not to mention the fact that snow and rain get in and rust the flue lining if it is made of metal.

Financing and insurance

In cold dollars and cents, financing and insuring a cabin offer no rugged barriers to cabin ownership. But banks and insurance companies look at cabins and residential dwellings in two separate lights. It is wise to know the rules.

BANK FINANCING

Although banks do not reckon vacation property the equal of full-time dwellings as an investment, they will often finance a cabin or beach house.

As a general rule, you will have more success at getting a loan through banks in the immediate locale of your building site than you will if you try to finance a distant retreat with a bank where you live.

The local banker is much more familiar with current conditions and values; and, of course, any bank is more likely to loan money on a project that is close enough to permit easy and inexpensive inspection and supervision.

You will probably have to make a substantial down payment—about 50 per cent. Chances are that interest rates will be the same or slightly higher than you would pay on a permanent residence. The average term for such loans is about 10 years.

If you are unable to get a loan on the construction, you may want to borrow money on other collateral.

Banks usually require that you have a firm title to the land on which you propose to build.

Policies and practices of financing vacation construction vary so widely from bank to bank and area to area that you would probably do well to learn the name of the local bank or banks near your property and inquire directly about financing policies. If you are unfamiliar with the area, you can get bank names and addresses from the chamber of commerce.

INSURANCE

Once you have invested heavily of your time and money in a vacation place, it's a good bet that you will want to do everything you can to give it protection from all the calamities of nature and man that might befall it.

It is a good idea to consult an insurance company *before* you start to build. One of their men who is trained in fire engineering can give you valuable and up-to-date advice; experienced underwriters also can give you an accurate picture of what to expect insurance-wise from the cabin you have in mind.

If possible, go to the same representative who handles insurance for your house and/or your car. If you are a good risk, his company's records will show it, and chances are they will take you on. Walking in "cold" on an insurance company which knows nothing about you might result in a turn-down. This is understandable when you consider the many inherent dangers of cabin insurance. Snow collapse, falling trees, faulty wiring, unoccupancy most of the year, no building codes to follow in many areas, unapproved flues—these are only a few of the many hazards which cabins can fall prey to.

1. *Fire insurance.* The basic threat to a cabin or beach house is fire—so the basic insurance policy is fire insurance. All insurance of this type automatically covers lightning.

Rates are generally low, though they differ widely from place to place. They are determined by a grading schedule of the National Board of Fire Underwriters which works with an elaborate system of points of deficiency, depending upon the extent of variance from standards formulated from a study of conditions over almost half a century. In incorporated areas each town is assigned a single rate. If the area is unprotected by an organized fire department, a county rate applies—and is generally higher than town rates. Factors which affect these basic rates include: availability and amount of water supply, fire department manpower, size and capacity of equipment manned by the department, fire alarms, police, building laws, fire prevention, structural conditions, and general geography. Structure of the individual house also affects the fire insurance rate. Both roof and wall construction are taken into consideration. Frame wall construction rates are higher than rates for masonry walls. Many companies refuse to sell fire insurance for cabins which do not have continuous masonry foundations.

2. *Extended Coverage Endorsement.* This supplementary coverage may be added to the basic fire insurance at small extra cost. It adds protection against damage from explosions, riots, civil commotion, aircraft, vehicles, and smoke; also, windstorm and hail on a $50 deductible basis. If you wish, you can waive the deductible provision for windstorm and hail, but you will have to pay a larger premium.

3. *Special Form and Broad Form.* If you wish, you may extend your policy to cover —on a $50 deductible basis—vandalism and malicious mischief, water damage from plumbing and heating systems, glass breakage, falling trees, collapse, ice, snow, and freezing. *Special Form* provides this insurance for your cabin only; *Broad Form* covers both the cabin and its contents.

ENDORSEMENT OR SEPARATE POLICY

Cabin or beach house *fire insurance*—and its two extensions—can be written as endorsements to the fire insurance policy which you carry on your regular dwelling. Or some of the coverages may be written as a separate policy.

OTHER COVERAGE

Earthquake insurance is available at rather high cost for full coverage. In California, there is a mandatory 5 per cent deductible clause. Rates vary only according to the relative susceptibility of the locale to earthquakes.

Theft policies can be written either as *a specific endorsement* on your basic fire policy, or as *a separate policy*. If you carry a homeowners' policy on your regular dwelling, it will cover your cabin also, for theft up to $1,000 if the policy is for $10,000 (your cabin must be in actual use at the time).

If you want or need *complete* coverage of personal property, you may wish to investigate the *personal property floater* which can be written to protect all contents of a cabin from practically all hazards including "unknown" risks. Cost of this policy is high.

PERSONAL LIABILITY COVERAGE

If you have a personal liability policy on your home, you can have it endorsed to cover a "secondary" residence for about one-third of the original cost. Liability coverage is particularly desirable if your cabin or beach house is in a fairly heavily used region where the possibility of injury to non-family members on your property may be high.

HOW MUCH DOES IT COST?

The cost for fire insurance and extended coverage is comparatively low when you consider the various factors involved. Premiums do vary considerably. A cabin at a remote mountain lake will probably cost considerably more to insure than a similar structure in a densely populated beach colony which has organized fire protection.

As an example of how premiums vary, here are costs for fire and extended coverage for a $5,000 cabin in three widely separated areas of California (assuming, in general, unprotected districts): mountain cabin in Tuolumne County, $63.55; beach cabin at Laguna Beach, $52.65; desert cabin in Riverside County, $36.45. (All rates are for 1959.)